P9-CMA-267

# Patchwork & Appliqué

**Books by Pauline Chatterton**

*Crochet: Fashion and Furnishings*

*The Art of Crochet*

*Patchwork and Appliqué*

Patchwork & Appliqué
PAULINE CHATTERTON

The Dial Press
New York

Library of Congress Cataloging in Publication Data

Chatterton, Pauline.
Patchwork and appliqué.

1. Patchwork. 2. Appliqué. I. Title.
TT835.C44 1977 746.4 76-47513
ISBN 0-8037-6854-0
ISBN 0-8037-6859-1 pbk.

Published by
The Dial Press
1 Dag Hammarskjold Plaza
New York, New York 10017


*Manufactured in the United States of America*

*First printing*

# Acknowledgments

*I would like to thank the following people and organizations for their help in my work on this book:*

Peter Maurer for taking the photographs, Museum of Contemporary Crafts in New York, Columbia-Minerva for supplying the yarn, Mrs. Ida Upham for typing the manuscript, Dorothy Kapstein, Harlee Hayman-Chaffey, Joan and Richard Chatterton, Mr. C. W. Packham, Mrs. Alice Beal, and all the artists who willingly contributed their work.

My special thanks go to Mrs. Betty J. Alfers and the Stearns and Foster Company for their interest and help, and to my editor, who has made working on this book such a pleasant and worthwhile experience.

# Contents

# 11

# Introduction

Patchwork and appliqué are very close relatives. Although one can point to the obvious differences—patchwork being the sewing together of different pieces of material to form a continuous fabric, and appliqué, the sewing of different shapes of contrasting fabric onto a ground fabric, often with the intention of creating a pictorial effect—there are no clearly defined boundaries. Any traditional patchwork shape can be "applied" to a ground fabric, thus creating a type of work that falls between the two categories. Generally speaking, appliqué tends to the more pictorial and fantastic, whereas patchwork remains dominated by traditional geometric shapes and patterns. However, one must bear in mind that the two crafts grew and developed side by side, and the differences between them eventually became indistinct.

The earliest remnant of applied work is an Egyptian piece dating back to about 1000 B.C. Patchwork and appliqué made their way into southern Europe during the time of the Crusades. Apparently the Saracens' custom of using magnificently patched and appliquéd banners did not go unnoticed by their Christian foes. Velvet and leather patchwork were fairly commonplace in Morocco during this period; its practice was eventually to spread throughout the Mediterranean area.

In northern Europe, patchwork and appliqué for some unknown reason had a poor reception, England and Holland being the only countries where they thrived. It is interesting to note that it is primarily from these two countries that the first settlers came to the United States. They brought with them the arts of patchwork and appliqué—skills that were to prove particularly suited to an inhospitable environment, devoid of luxury of any sort, and, all too often, comfort as well.

The early American pioneer families were faced with the practical difficulties of making hard-to-obtain items, such as fabric, last as long as possible. Even though fabrics imported from Europe might be available in the more fashionable ports along the eastern seaboard, it was unlikely that such luxuries would very often reach the frontier towns, where even the bare necessities of life were often hard enough to come by.

However, with tremendous ingenuity, the pioneer woman made a virtue of necessity and produced the first "crazywork" patchwork quilts. The pieces would be cut from such things as worn-out household linens or clothing. Any scrap of fabric could be used, regardless of shape. The best pieces would be cut into patches to form the top layer of the quilt, an old, often unsightly blanket would form the next layer down, and at the bottom would come another layer of patched fabrics, not as good as the pieces used on top. As with crazy paving, one had to have patience to fit all the pieces together with a minimum of waste. They were usually sewn together with strong thread. Quilting stitches were used, not primarily for decoration as they are now, but for the purely practical purpose of keeping the three layers of the quilt together. In this way, a thrifty housewife could turn an ugly old blanket and the worn-out linens and clothing of her family into a warm and serviceable quilt which would give many years of hard wear.

But as soon as the bare necessities of life are provided for, the human spirit seeks self-expression in the surrounding environment, and it was not long before the women of those pioneering families demanded more of their craft than mere warmth and utility. They wanted to enhance the livability of their often severely bare homes with the work of their own hands. Their quilts began to express their urge to decorate their homes and to put their own mark on an environment that at times must have appeared only too impersonal and forbidding in its grandeur. The almost fussy detailing in early American quilts and in the primitive painting of the period expresses the same urge to impose a human handprint and order on the larger-than-life landscapes of frontier America. A bride was not sent out into the wilderness of her new life without the comfort of a superb marriage quilt made for her by the matrons of the community. The quilt was as much an expression of the real human support from all the women in the community as it was a practical and useful gift.

Patchwork quilts are an integral part of the social history of early America. The names given to the designs themselves tell us a story about how those women lived and what their preoccupations were. See what pictures these names conjure up in your mind: "Log Cabin," "Barn Raising," "Bay Leaf," "Wild Goose Chase," "Basket of Scraps," "Cup and Saucer," "Streak o' Lightning," "Grandma's Dream," "Old Maid's Ramble," "Birds in the Air," "Road to California," "Schoolhouse," "Flower Baskets," "Star of Bethlehem," "Rising Sun," and "Rainbow."

In America, the quilt continued to be an extremely practical provider of warmth on cold winter nights, no matter how beautiful it might be. In Europe, although patchwork was still motivated by the same desire to make maximum use of a scanty supply of fabrics, decoration soon superseded utility; in England, for instance, quilting for warmth became quite dissociated from patchwork sometime before 1850. Finer fabrics, such as silks, were being used. This difference in bedcovering principles can be seen even in the present day. Where quilting abounds in contemporary American mass-produced comforters, the typical English counterpane is still, more often than not, made of the flimsiest taffeta or other impractical fabric. I particularly like the use of the word *comforter* for modern American bedcovers. It seems to spring directly from the tradition of the bridal quilt. I am certain that these gifts from the community of women in pioneer towns were indeed a constant source of comfort to a young woman faced with the harsh realities of life in remote places. The quilt would be a constant reminder of the support she could expect from the other women in her community in times of adversity.

Interestingly, the differences in the American way of life produced a striking departure from the European roots of design. The pioneer wife was expected to travel around in a wagon and make her quilts as best she could. Not for her the intricacies of the complex patterns laid out on carpeted floors by her European counterparts. She could not handle an entire quilt over her knees in the back of a wagon. She needed a basic design that could be worked in small sections, which were later sewn together to produce a pattern when the family had settled in some new place. This requirement accounts for the alternating and repetitive motifs so characteristic of American quilts.

As far as the historical and social background of patchwork and appliqué is concerned, I have mentioned only fabric work. The first four chapters will provide the groundwork for creating designs in this medium.

However, contemporary interest in patchwork, not as a result of necessity but in pursuit of an interesting design concept, extends the possibilities of the craft into a number of different fields. I have chosen to explore the twin crafts of patchwork and appliqué insofar as they can be used in knitting, crochet, and Bargello. Projects are provided in all these sections, but I do hope the reader will be tempted to translate a particular patchwork favorite into a new medium, thus giving a degree of originality to a traditional theme.

# Patchwork & Appliqué

Those with no previous knowledge of patchwork will find the basic techniques explained in this chapter. Those who have already tried their hand at the craft can pick up helpful hints and suggestions for creative work of their own design.

### Suitable Fabrics

Patchwork can be made in almost any firm fabric, but by far the best for the beginner is a good quality, closely woven cotton. This fabric has good body to it and will not fray excessively. It is also relatively cheap, should mistakes be made in cutting patches.

It is a good idea to start collecting pieces of fabric for patchwork. Because few of us have the time to do a lot of sewing, the kind of basket of fabric scraps the early pioneer women had is a rarity. However, I am not one of those

purists who believe that modern patchwork is some terrible perversion of the honorable purpose of the original craft of making maximum use of worn-out clothing and household linen. We can still make use of what might otherwise go to waste by searching out small pieces of fabric from the remnant counter of our local fabric store. There is still the sense of putting to good use pieces of fabric that have been set aside because they are too small for a dress or blouse.

If you are just beginning to take an interest in patchwork, I strongly recommend a visit to the remnant counters of stores in your area. Keep an eye out for small ends of good cotton, which you will be able to buy at bargain prices, thus satisfying even the thriftiest and most puritanical critics of contemporary patchwork! If, like me, you have none of those scruples anyway, and are able to buy a piece of fabric for the sheer pleasure of it and for the beauty it will add to your design, then be really daring and buy pieces by the yard! After all, you are merely making use of the material to transform it into something uniquely personal, just as you do when you buy yarn to make a sweater. I think it would be quite a difficult, and certainly very lengthy, process for the modern quilter to build up a sufficiently varied collection using remnants alone. However, if you do have old clothes in suitable fabrics, these too can be cut up and used. Once you begin working regularly in patchwork, you will, quite naturally, accumulate a collection of your own scrap materials, left over from previous projects. Then, indeed, you can work these into future designs, not wasting a single piece.

A very good approach to the problem of collecting is to start by choosing a color theme. I have three personal favorites:

—Red, white, and blue
—Black, red, and white
—Oranges, reds, yellows, and white

Within these three categories I look for dots, checks, floral patterns, and some good pieces of plain color to coordinate the design. Choose whatever color combination appeals to you, or is suitable to the decor in the room where you intend to display the finished piece. Here are a few more color-theme suggestions:

—Naturals—all the beiges, coffees, golds, and browns—a very popular combination for home decoration.
—Blues and greens.

—Black and white—one of the most stunning combinations—and the simplicity of the color theme can coordinate a very large number of juxtaposed prints and patterns.

Looking for remnants will be much easier and a lot more fun if you start out with a color theme in mind.

Of course, if you simply buy up all the suitable remnants of cotton you see, and end up with a very curious and jumbled assortment of patterns and colors, it is still possible to create a design, with hardly any attention paid to a color or design theme. The double bedspread shown in Fig. 1-1 is a good example of this. The only unifying elements in this design are the rosette motif and the patches of plain cream fabric separating them, which are shown in Fig. 1-2. The random design is visually pulled together by the addition of a border made entirely from fabric of the same pattern. Other than this the design is about as random as one can get, and illustrates how well one can coordinate the most unlikely-looking pieces of fabric into a successful design.

One more word about fabrics before we move on. I would not suggest that any beginner stray from the safe haven of cotton. However, if you have already had some experience of working in cotton, you can begin to look for other interesting fabrics. It is definitely a mistake to mix fabrics of different weights and qualities in the same project though, so you will need to keep all your materials carefully sorted to avoid the temptation of using different kinds together. When considering an interesting remnant, examine the cut edges of the fabric. If they are badly frayed, the fabric will certainly not be suitable for patchwork. You will have a

Fig. 1-1 *Double bedspread with rosette motif*

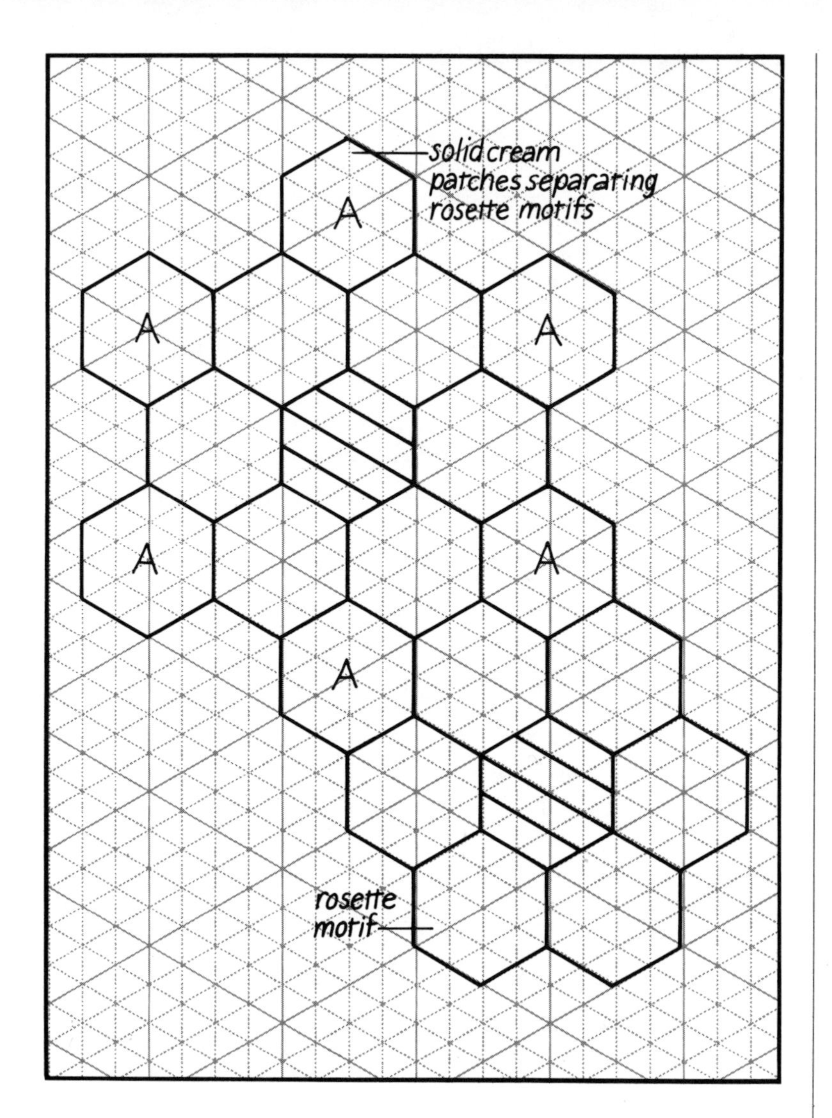


terrible time working with it, and it is simply not worth all the extra effort involved when there is such a wonderful supply of highly suitable, nonfraying fabrics to choose from.

One must be particularly careful when looking at upholstery fabrics. They tend to fray much more than dressmaking fabrics, simply because they are not made to withstand the same kind of wear and tear. And though silks and velvets have traditionally been used for patchwork, I doubt if these are economical enough in present times, except for small items such as cushions.

## Tools

In addition to suitable fabrics, you will also need a pair of sharp embroidery scissors for clipping and removing tacking threads, a pair of old or cheap scissors for cutting paper, and a pair of larger dressmaking scissors for cutting fabric pieces. Actually, I prefer pinking shears when cutting out patches; the pinking eliminates practically all fraying. But pinking shears can be rather heavy and awkward if you are not

Fig. 1-2 *Detail from double bedspread*

accustomed to using them, and once dull, they are almost impossible to sharpen, whereas a good pair of dressmaking scissors will be a lifetime possession. So as long as your scissors are sharp, use the kind you prefer.

You will also need a selection of fine but very strong sewing thread, fine sewing needles and pins, and a tape measure.

The items just listed are those used in most handsewing. However, patchwork requires some rather more specialized materials in addition, namely templates and backing papers. It is a good idea to start saving old Christmas and birthday cards, which are exactly the correct weight for those items and are readily available in most households.

## Templates

*Template* is the word given to the basic patchwork shape which is to be used as a guide for cutting all the other pieces. Two sizes of templates are needed: a larger, from which the fabric pieces are cut, and a smaller, from which the backing papers are cut. One backing paper is needed for each patch. The fabric piece (cut from the larger template) is folded over one of the backing papers (cut from the smaller template) and sewn—right through the paper—thus achieving the perfect size and shape of each patch. Use of the backing papers provides an easy method of achieving the neat edges and accurate angles that are so crucial to patchwork.

The templates shown in Figs. 1-3 to 1-8 are of the smaller size—that used for cutting backing papers—and therefore indicate the size of the *finished* patch. When making use of the template patterns given, place a piece of tracing paper over the shape you want, and trace the outline very carefully. Transfer the shape onto a piece of stiff paper or a card and cut it out very precisely. You now have a template for the size of the finished patches. Cut all the paper backings from this original piece, drawing around the outline of the template onto the paper or card and then cutting each piece out.

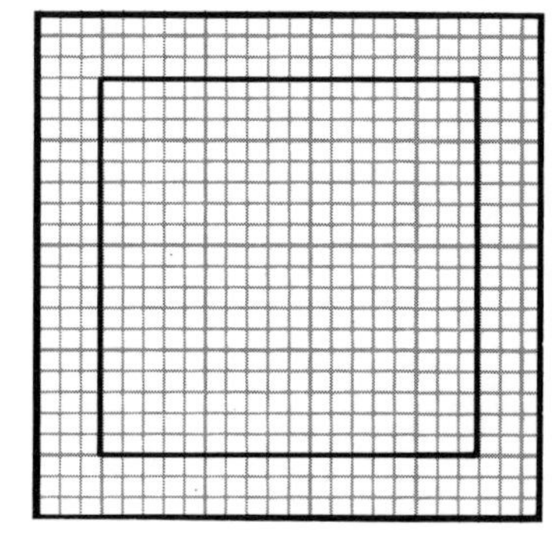

Fig. 1-3 *Square with sides of 1½ inches*

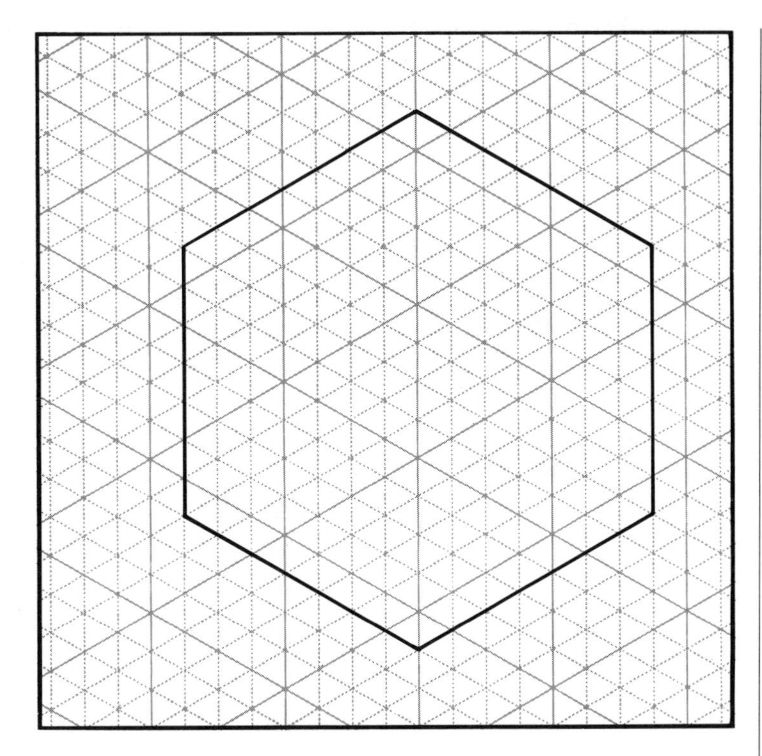

Fig. 1-4 *Hexagon with sides of 1½ inches*

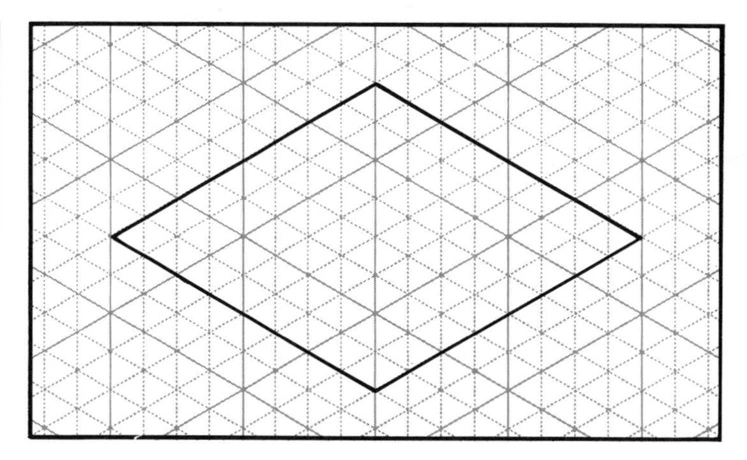

Fig. 1-5 *Diamond with sides of 1¾ inches*

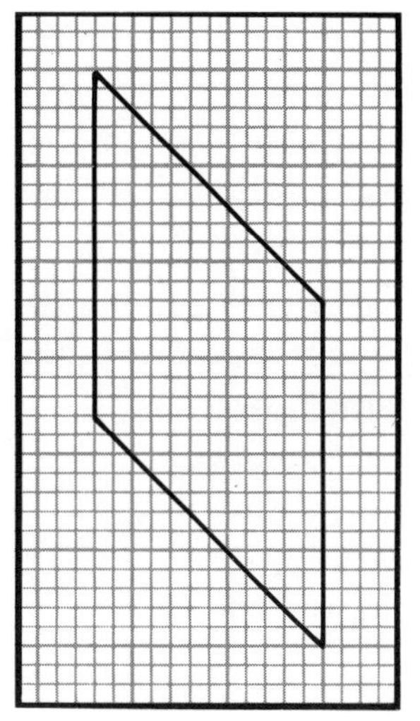

Fig. 1-6 *Long diamond with sides of 1½ inches*

Fig. 1-7 *Triangle with sides of 1½ inches*

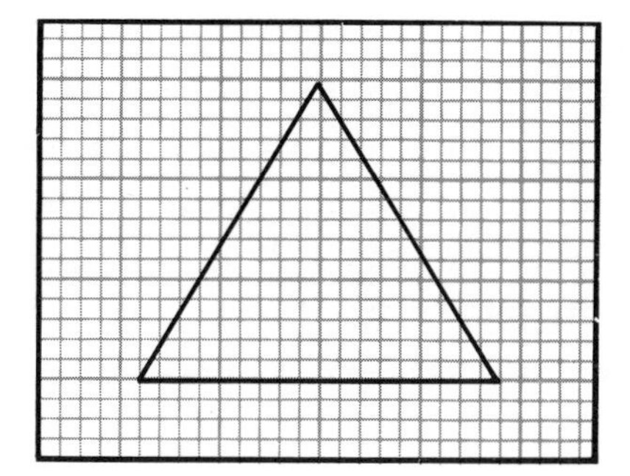

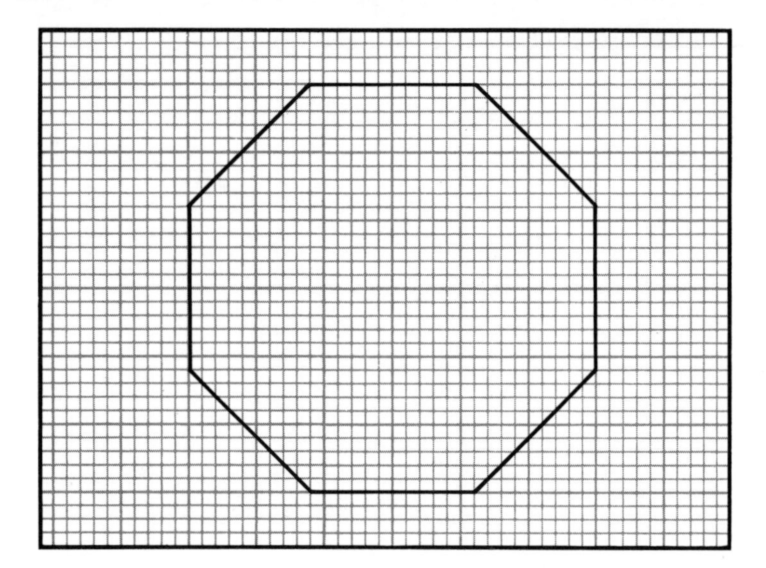

Fig. 1-8 *Octagon with 1-inch sides*

To cut the fabric you will need the larger template, which should be exactly a quarter of an inch bigger all around than the first to give yourself a seam allowance to turn under when you make the patches. You should use a piece of stiff card for this template also. It is relatively simple to make this second, larger template if you use graph paper. As you transfer the shape to the graph paper, place the base line of the patch on one of the heavy lines. In this way it will be easy to draw a second shape larger than the first, by noting how many squares you have to quarter of an inch, and drawing in a line that number of squares outside the original shape. The same procedure can be used for making larger or smaller any of the templates given here.

There are many excellent template sets available on the market also, which provide the smaller and larger shapes for each patch. The larger template in such kits usually has the great advantage of being made in clear plastic, so that you can see exactly which part of the fabric will appear on the finished patch. This is very important if you want to get a precise motif or part of the fabric pattern in a particular patch. With the aid of these "window" templates, you will be able to make the fullest possible use of the printed fabrics in your design. I highly recommend these kits for anyone who is planning to do a number of patchwork projects.

For those who want to make their own templates, six different shapes are provided in Figs. 1-3 to 1-8.

## Cutting and Sewing

Using the window, or the larger size of the two templates, cut out the number of pieces required of each fabric. Use the smaller template to cut out the same number of pieces of backing papers.

Place the backing paper onto the wrong side of the fabric piece, exactly ¼ inch in from the edge of the fabric (Fig. 1-9).

Fold over the ¼-inch seam allowance as shown in Fig. 1-10.

Tack through the paper around the entire patch, turning corners as shown in Fig. 1-11.

Sew one stitch in each corner to secure the turnings (Fig. 1-12).

Place two patches with right sides together and sew with small oversewing stitches along the edges to be joined (Fig. 1-13). (Any one

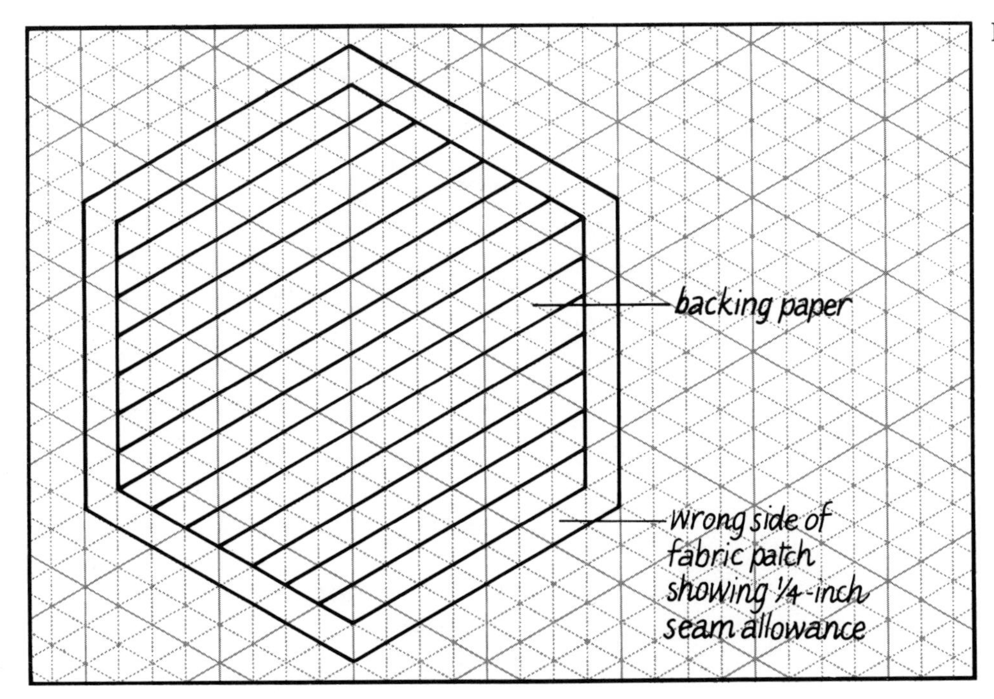


Fig. 1-9 *Sewing the patches—Step 1*

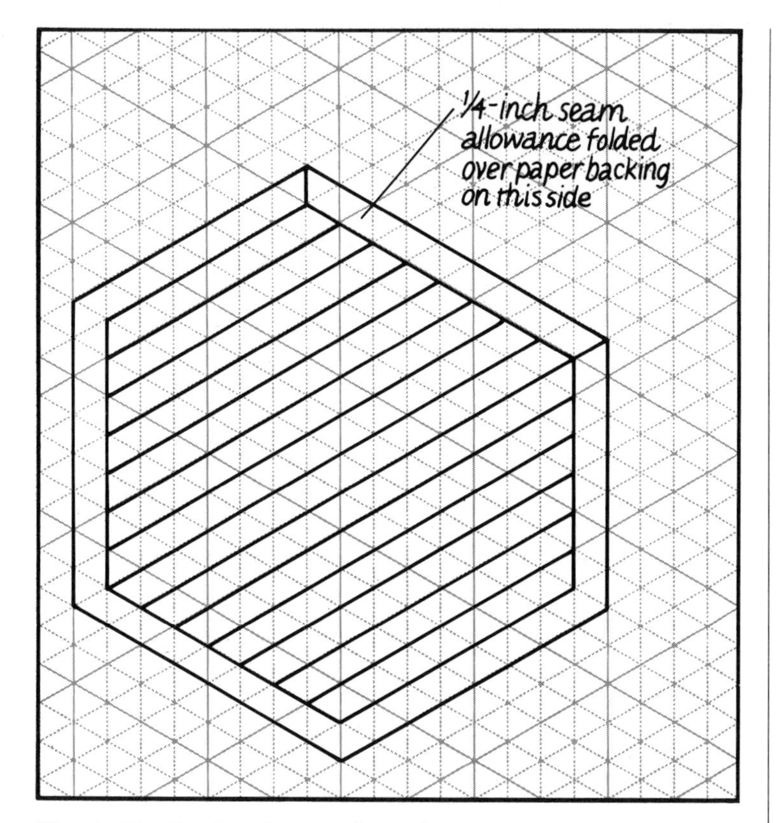


Fig. 1-10 *Sewing the patches—Step 2*

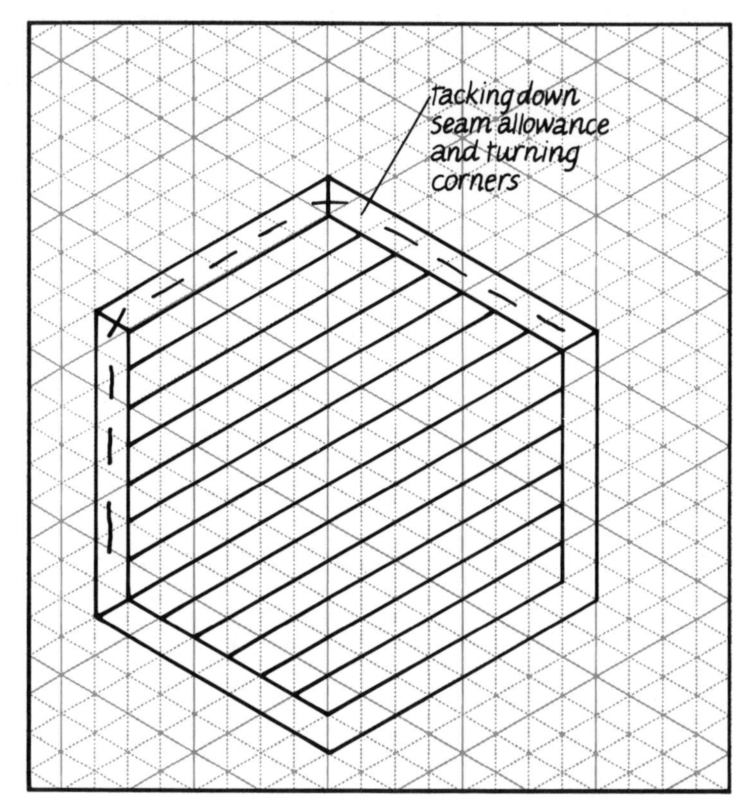


Fig. 1-11 *Sewing the patches—Step 3*

patch will, of course, be joined to any other along only one of its edges.)

When all the sewing is complete, clip the tacking threads, and remove both them and the backing papers.

## Finishing Patchwork

Press your finished patchwork thoroughly with a hot iron over a damp cloth.

You will need to use a backing fabric, unless

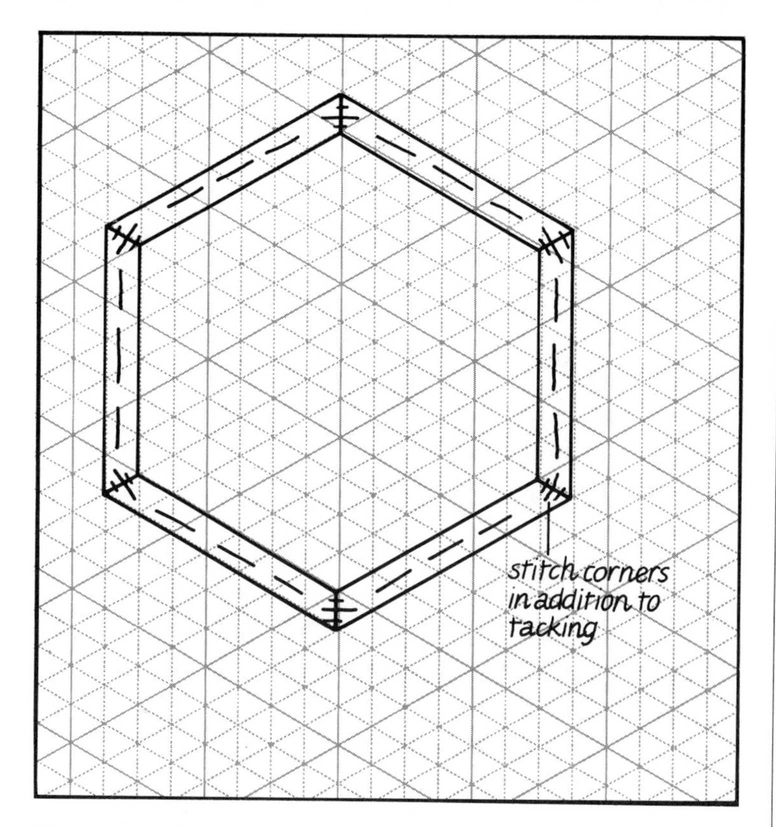


Fig. 1-12 *Sewing the patches—Step 4*

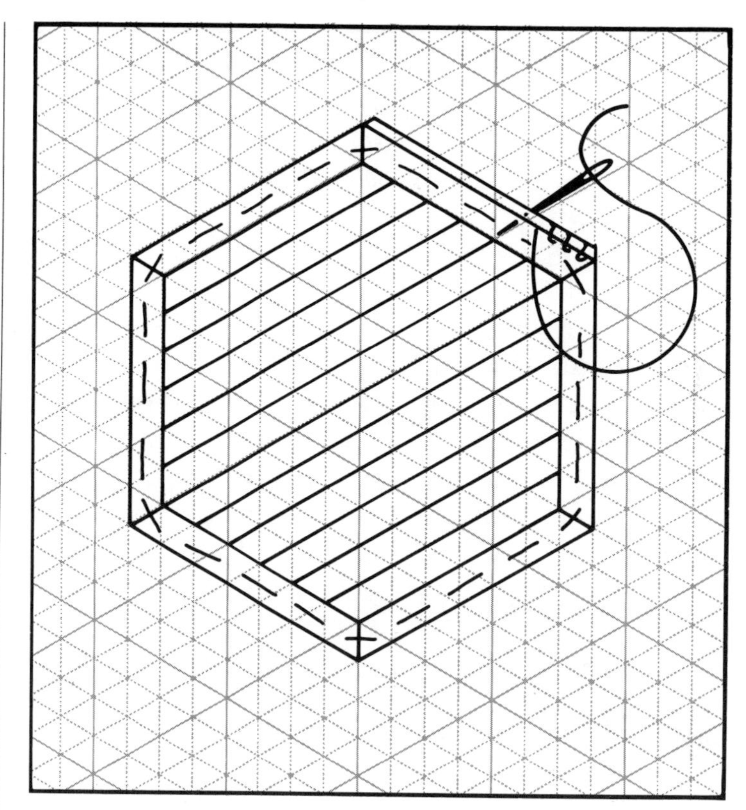

Fig. 1-13 *Sewing two patches together*

you are going to make something like a cushion, where all the patchwork seams will be on the inside anyway. Choose a firm fabric for backing, of the same quality and weight as the patchwork itself. You will need a piece of fabric that is ½ inch larger in each direction than the finished area of your patchwork design. Turn under ½ inch of seam allowance all around the patchwork and backing. Place the two with wrong sides together and tack in place. Machine stitch around entire edge. If you have a large area of patchwork, you will need to attach it to the backing with a basting stitch or two at regular intervals across the back. This will prevent the backing fabric from slipping away from the patchwork and causing bulges.

### Quilting

Various household patchwork items can be made even more attractive by adding a layer of polyester quilting fabric between the patchwork and the backing, and then sewing in patterns across the patches and through all three layers of fabric. The good quiltings on the market are fully washable, light, and easy to work with. If you are planning to quilt large areas, you will definitely need a quilting frame to keep the layers from shifting away from each other during work and causing distortions. Smaller areas can be basted into place. Use a contrasting color thread for this, so that you can easily distinguish your basting from the quilting stitches. Baste from the center out, like the spokes of a wheel. The most commonly used stitches for quilting are running, back, and chain stitch.

When the quilting is completed, you will need to bind the edges of the work with fabric cut on the bias. You can choose one of the colors used in the patchwork design, or a complete contrast. Lay the right side of the binding on the right side of the work and stitch, taking care not to pull too tight. Roll the binding over to the wrong side of the quilt, turn under ¼ inch of raw edge, and hem stitch into position.

### Planning Your Own Project

Use graph paper to plan your design exactly before you start. Work to scale, so that you can easily calculate the yardages for each color. Cut out some fabric patches in the materials you are going to use. Try arranging them in different patterns, and note down your final choice of design on the graph, with each patch color-coded. Count up the number of patches required in each color and note that down. Now calculate how much fabric you will require in each color, and before beginning make certain you will have enough. It will be a very simple process to follow your graphed design. You can make it even easier for yourself by coloring in the patches with magic markers. You will be able to calculate how much backing fabric and quilting you will require by measuring the finished patchwork.

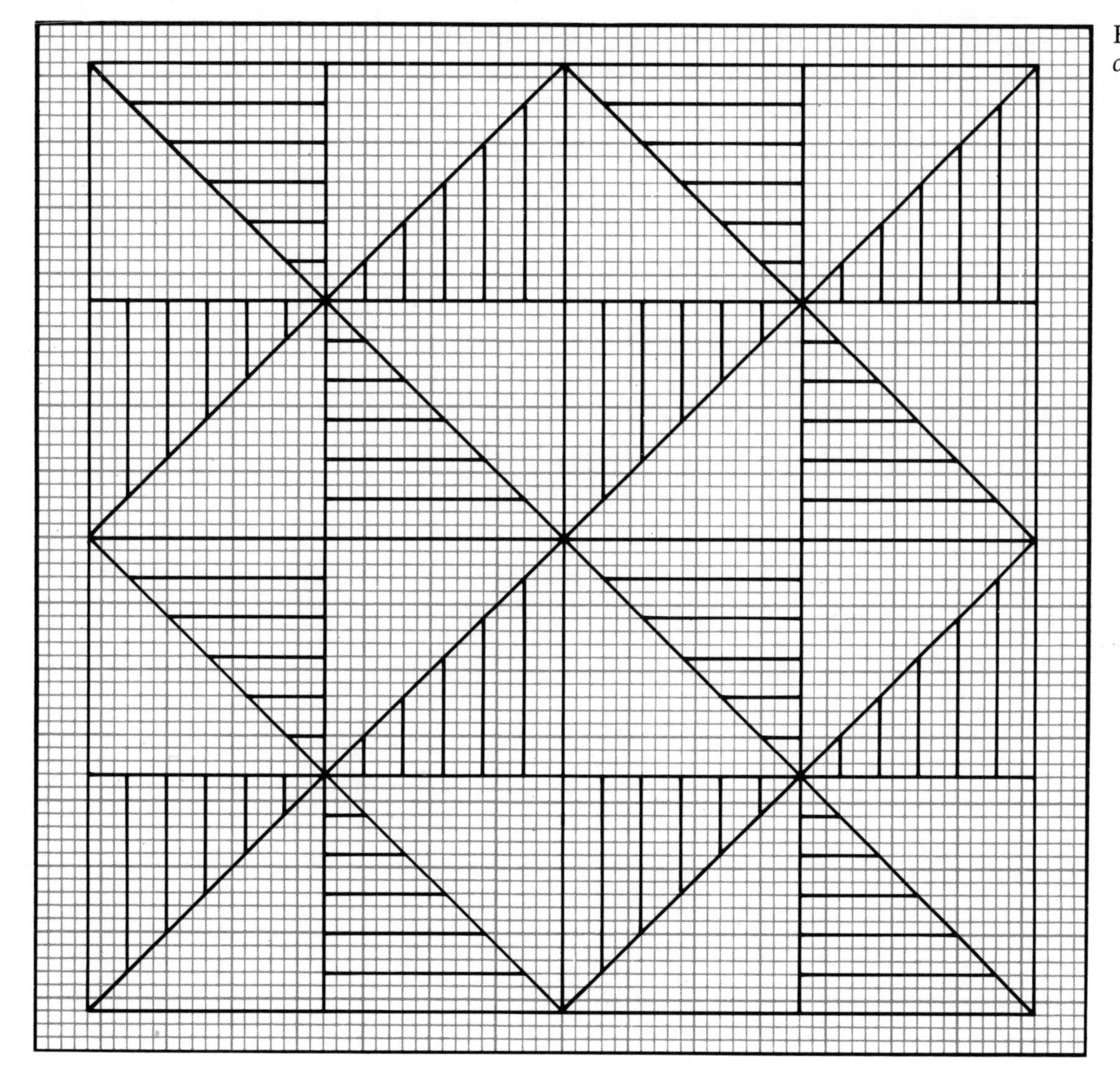

Fig. 1-14 *Pattern based on triangles*

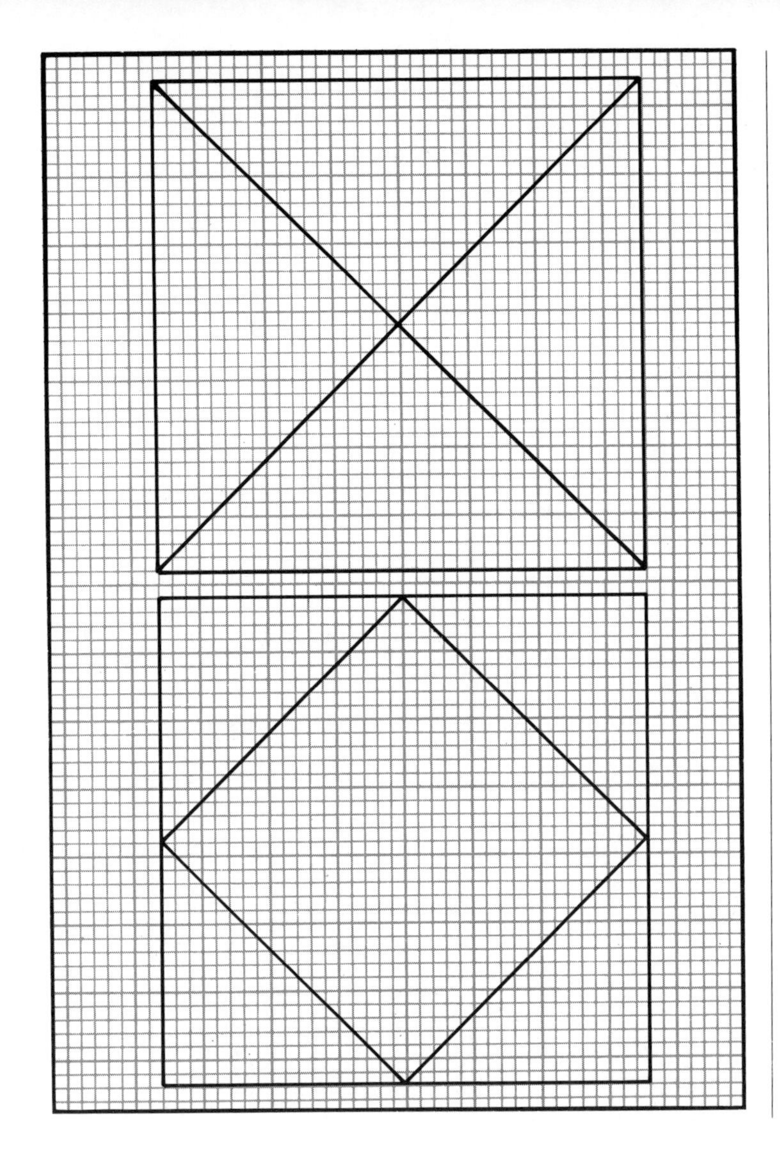

If you want to make an item in crazy patchwork, decide on the dimensions. Choose a piece of stiff paper larger than your finished item will be. Draw in the frame or boundary lines of the item you want to make, for example, a 16-inch square for a cushion. Draw in the random lines of a crazy-quilt pattern you particularly like, or create your own. Use tracing paper to make an exact copy of the drawing. Number all the pieces on the original drawing and copy the same numbers onto the tracing. With a sharp paper cutter, cut out each numbered piece on the stiff paper or light card. Pin these pieces with the numbers showing onto the back of the chosen fabrics, and cut the same shape in fabric, but ¼ inch larger all round. Fold the fabric over the card, just as you would for any of the more regular-shaped patches. Follow the numbering on the tracing to ensure that your pieces will all fit together as you sew. This is a delightful project to try out for yourself if you already have some experience in patchwork. Try adding embroidery stitches to the surface of your crazy patchwork—especially along seams—to emphasize the irregular shapes.

Fig. 1-15 *Patches based on squares and triangles*

Figs. 1-14 and 1-15, it is hoped, will prove useful to those who want to use basic patchwork patterns in their own style.

Figs. 1-16, 1-17, and 1-18 show three fine examples of the work of Michiko Sato, whose beautiful compositions can surely provide an inspiration for all.

Fig. 1-16 *Quilt in orange, brown, and purple by Michiko Sato*

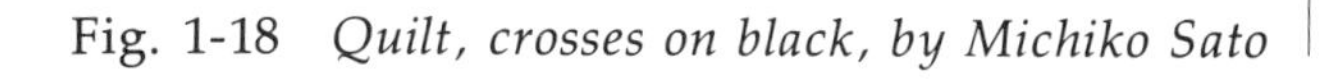

Fig. 1-18 *Quilt, crosses on black, by Michiko Sato*

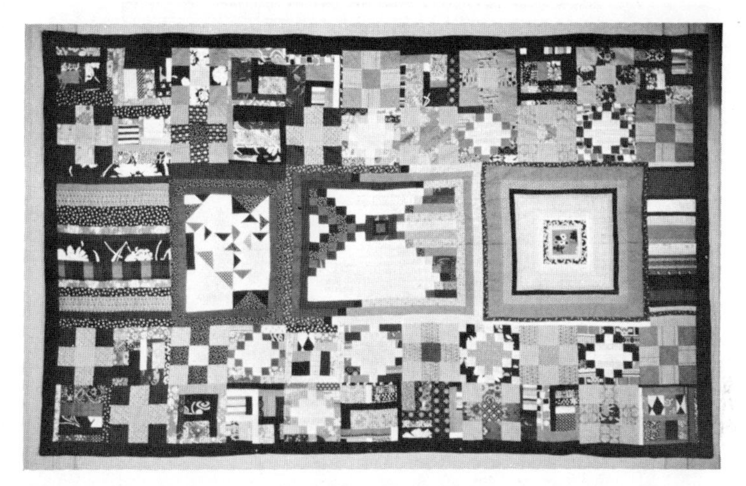

Fig. 1-17 *"My Crazy Quilt," by Michiko Sato*

# 2 Patchwork Projects

## Guide to the Projects

1. Very simple, small projects that are made in squares are marked*, and are suitable for beginners.
2. All yardages given include a 1/4-inch seam allowance around the entire outer edge of each patch.
3. Measurements given for *patches* are for the *finished* size. When cutting the fabric, add 1/4 inch for seam allowance on all sides.
4. Colors are not given for the designs, but the pattern layouts are letter-keyed so that you can choose your own color scheme. The yardages for each symbol—A, B, C, and so on—are given in the instructions.
5. The designs can be altered by changing the arrangement of colors, or by enlarging or diminishing the size of the patches. Remember, however, that if you do alter the size of the patches, the yardages given in the in-

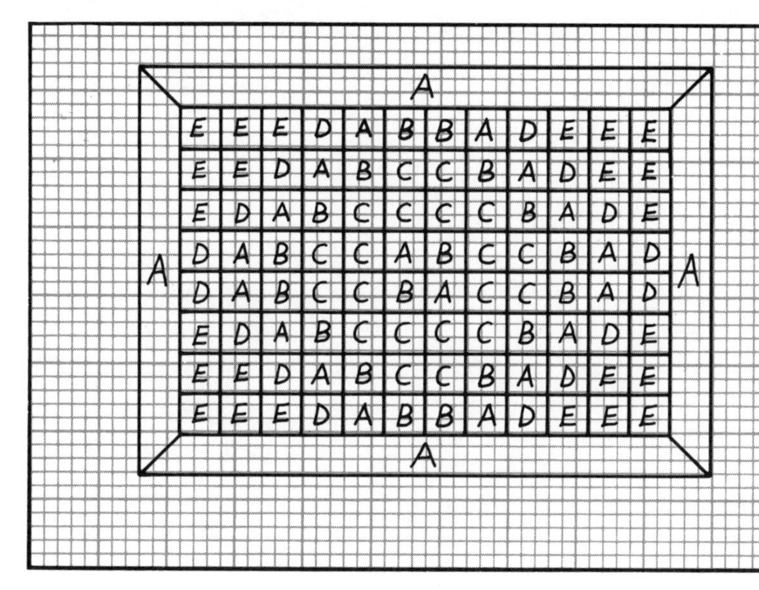


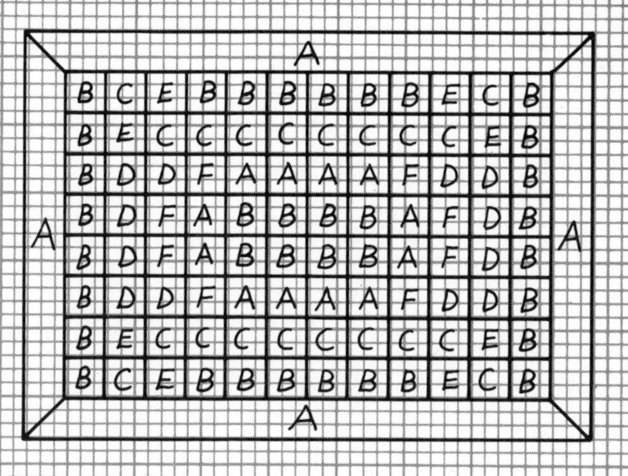


1 square = 1½" x 1½"

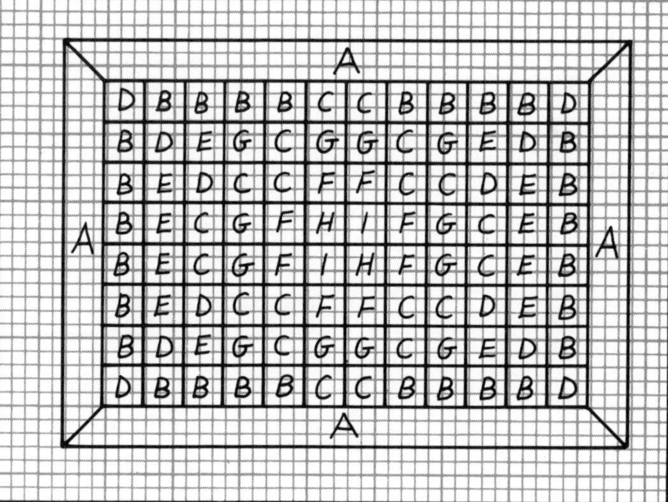


Fig. 2-1 *Three patterns for place mats*

structions will no longer apply, but you should find it very simple to calculate the new amounts of fabric that you will require.

## The Projects

### **Place Mats*** (Fig. 2-1)

Fig. 2-1 shows the layout of three place-mat designs. To make six, simply double the quantities given, and work two mats in each pattern.

Finished Size: Approx. 21″ × 15″

You Need: 36″-wide fabric for a set of three mats:

40″ × 36″ in A (which is used both for all the borders and for backing each mat)

| | |
|---|---|
| 10″ × 36″ in B | 2″ × 36″ in F |
| 8″ × 36″ in C | 2″ × 36″ in G |
| 6″ × 36″ in D | 2″ × 4″ in H |
| 6″ × 36″ in E | 2″ × 4″ in I |

Method

Cut the following 1½-inch squares (finished sizes are given throughout):

| | |
|---|---|
| 30 in A | 16 in F |
| 82 in B | 12 in G |
| 60 in C | 2 in H |
| 40 in D | 2 in I |
| 44 in E | |

Assemble the squares as shown in Fig. 2-1.

Borders and Backing

Cut the following finished-size pieces in A:

3 pieces 21″ × 15″

6 pieces 21″ × 1½″

6 pieces 1½″ × 15″

Sew the border strips together as shown in Fig. 2-1, and miter each corner. Attach the patchwork to the border, and join to the 21″ × 15″ backing.

Fig. 2-2 *Square cushion*

**Square Cushion*** (I) (Fig. 2-2)

The layout for this cushion is shown in Fig. 2-3.

Finished Size: Approx. 16½″ × 16½″

You Need: 36″-wide fabric

17″ × 36″ in A (which is used to make a plain back for the cushion)

4″ × 36″ in B

4″ × 36″ in C

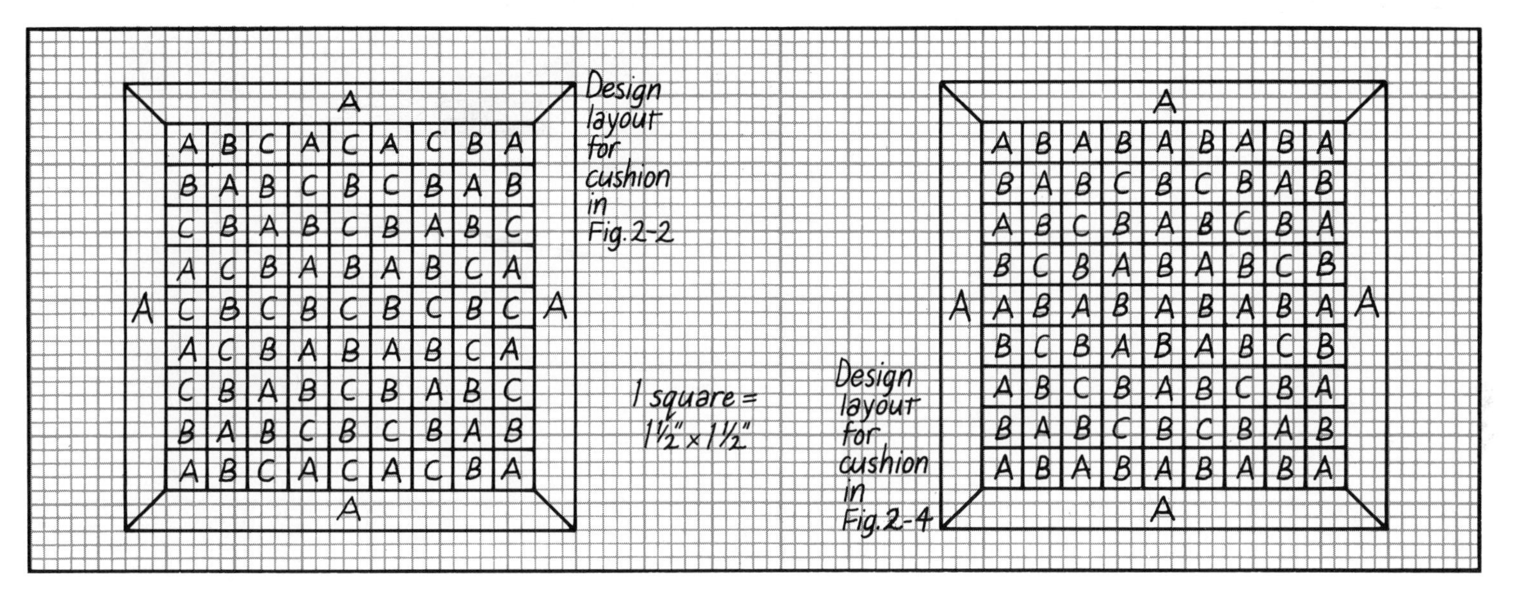


Fig. 2-3 *Two patterns for cushion covers*

METHOD

Cut the following 1½-inch finished-size squares:

24 in A
32 in B
25 in C

Assemble the patches as shown in Fig. 2-3.

BORDERS AND BACKING

Cut the following border strips in A:

4 pieces 16½" × 1½"

Miter the corners and join to patchwork as shown in Fig. 2-3.

Cut a 16½-inch square for backing and make up the cushion cover.

**Square Cushion*** (II) (Fig. 2-4)

The layout for this cushion is shown in Fig. 2-3.

FINISHED SIZE: Approx. 16½" × 16½"

YOU NEED: 36"-wide fabric

17" × 36" in A (which is used to make a plain back for the cushion)

6″ × 36″ in B
2″ × 36″ in C

METHOD

Cut the following 1½-inch finished-size squares:
29 in A
40 in B
12 in C
Assemble the patches as shown in Fig. 2-3.

BORDERS AND BACKING

Follow instructions under this heading in Project II to complete the cushion.

**Square Cushion*** (III) (Fig. 2-5)

The layout for this cushion is shown in Fig. 2-6.

FINISHED SIZE: Approx. 18″ × 18″
YOU NEED: 36″-wide fabric
18½″ × 36″ in A (for backing and borders)
4″ × 36″ in B
6″ × 36″ in C
4″ × 36″ in D

METHOD

Cut the following 1½-inch finished-size squares:
24 in B
44 in C
32 in D
Assemble the patches as shown in Fig. 2-6.

Fig. 2-4 *Square cushion*

BORDERS AND BACKING

Cut the following finished-size pieces in A:
4 pieces 1½″ × 18″
1 piece 18″ × 18″
Follow instructions under this heading in Project II to complete the cushion.

**Square Cushion*** (IV) (Fig. 2-7)

The layout for this cushion can be seen in Fig. 2-6.

FINISHED SIZE: Approx. 18″ × 18″
YOU NEED: 36″-wide fabric
18½″ × 36″ in A (for backing and borders)
6″ × 36″ in B
10″ × 36″ in C

METHOD

Cut the following 1½-inch finished-size squares:
44 in B
56 in G
Assemble the patches as shown in Fig. 2-6.

BORDERS AND BACKING

Work as for Project IV.

**Patchwork Picture or Cushion** (I) (Fig. 2-8)

The layout for this design can be seen in Fig. 2-9.

FINISHED SIZE: Approx. 24″ × 24″
YOU NEED: 36″-wide fabric
6″ × 36″ in A    4″ × 36″ in C
8″ × 36″ in B    5″ × 36″ in D
If you want to make a plain cushion backing in one of the colors, you will need a square of fabric measuring 24½″ × 24½″.

Fig. 2-5 *Square cushions*

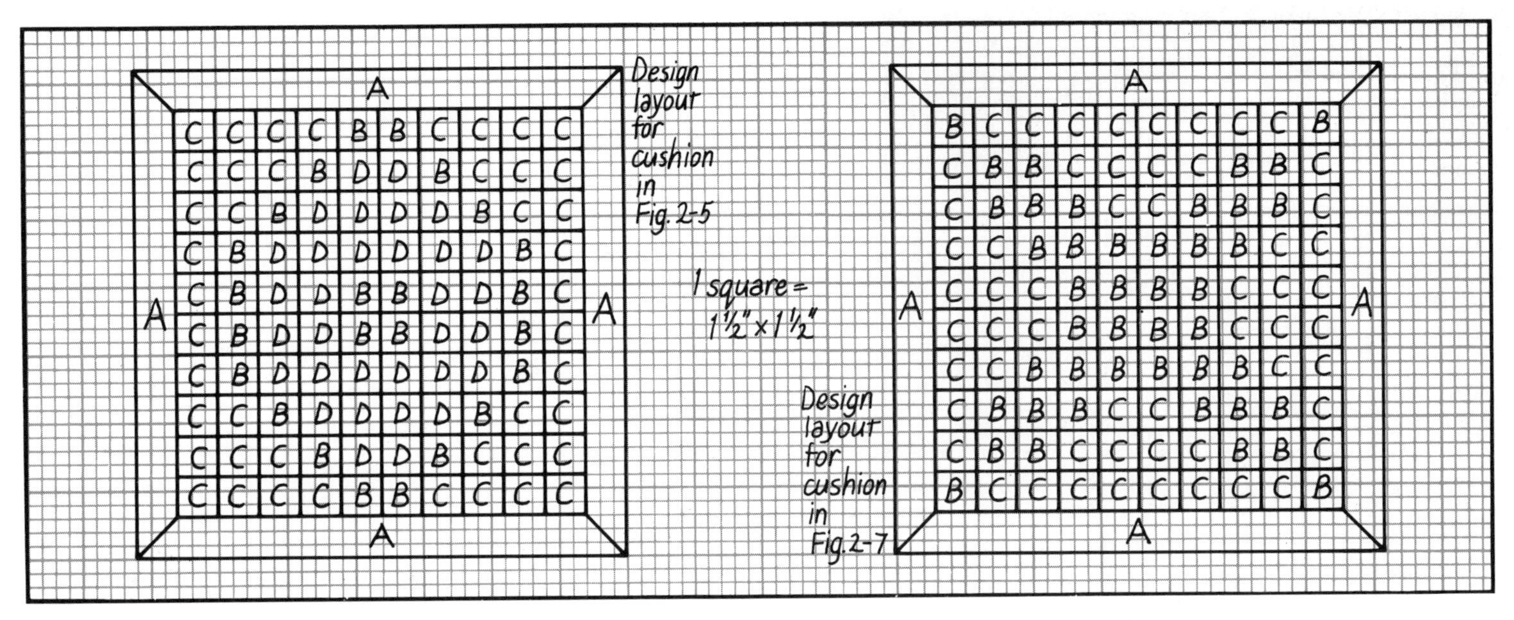


Fig. 2-6 *Two patterns for cushion covers*

Fig. 2-7 *Square cushions*

Fig. 2-8 *Patchwork picture or cushion*

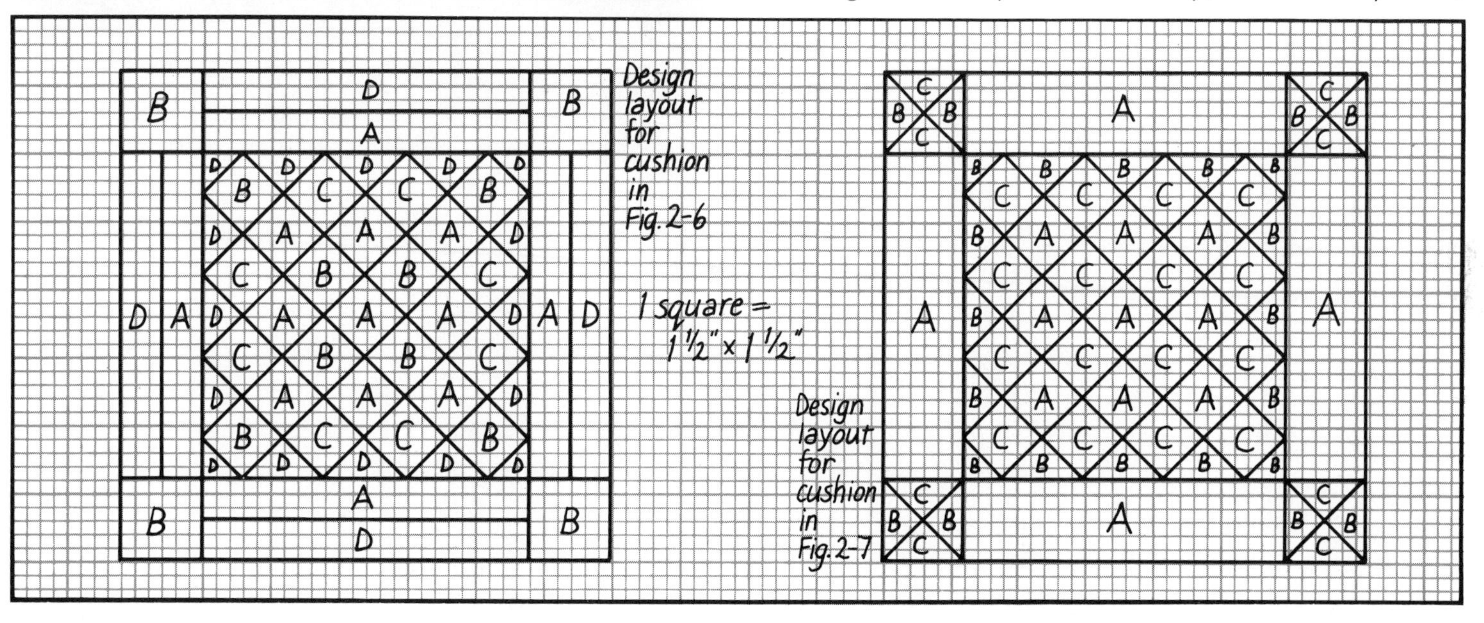


Fig. 2-9 *Two patterns suitable for cushions or pictures*

Method

Cut the following finished-size patches:

*2" × 16" rectangles:*

4 in A
4 in D

*4" × 4" squares:*

4 in B

*3" × 3" squares:*

9 in A
8 in B
8 in C

*Isosceles triangles with 4-inch base:*

12 in D

*Right-angle triangles with 2-inch sides:*

4 in D

Assemble the patches as shown in Fig. 2-9. The finished patchwork can either be made into a cushion or mounted on a board and hung on the wall.

**Patchwork Picture or Cushion** (II) (Fig. 2-10)

The layout for this design can be seen in Fig. 2-9.

Finished Size: Approx. 24" × 24"
You Need: 36"-wide fabric

13" × 36" in A
14" × 36" in B
9" × 36" in C

Fig. 2-10 *Patchwork picture or cushion*

Method

Cut the following finished-size patches:

*4" × 16" rectangles:*

4 in A

*3" × 3" squares:*

9 in A
16 in C

*Isosceles triangles with 4-inch base:*

20 in B
8 in C

*Right-angle triangles with 2-inch sides:*

4 in B

Assemble the patches as shown in Fig. 2-9. The completed patchwork may either be made into a cushion or mounted on a board to hang.

### Wall Hanging or Tablecloth in Squares (Fig. 2-11)

The layout for this design may be seen in Fig. 2-12. The finished piece may either be used as a tablecloth or mounted on a bar and hung on the wall.

FINISHED SIZE: Approx. 60″ × 60″
YOU NEED: 36″-wide fabric

40″ × 36″ in A (including borders)
20″ × 36″ in B
28″ × 36″ in C
28″ × 36″ in D
40″ × 36″ in E
15″ × 36″ in F
A piece of backing fabric measuring 61″ × 61″ (A seam allowance of ½-inch is given for each side.)

METHOD

Cut the following 2-inch finished-size squares:

104 in A    144 in D
104 in B    216 in E
144 in C    72 in F

Assemble the patches as shown in Fig. 2-12.

BORDER AND BACKING

Cut 4 strips measuring 2″×60″ (finished size) in A. You will have to join pieces of fabric together to make the 60-inch strip. Attach the border strips to the finished patchwork, and miter the corners. Back the entire finished piece with the square of backing

Fig. 2-11 *Wallhanging or tablecloth in squares*

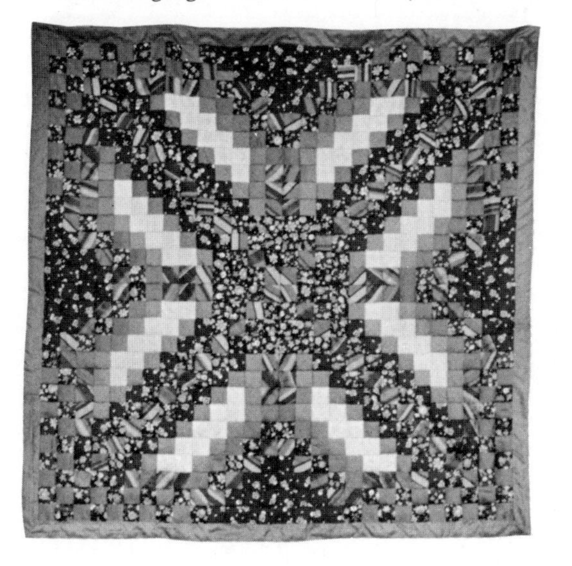

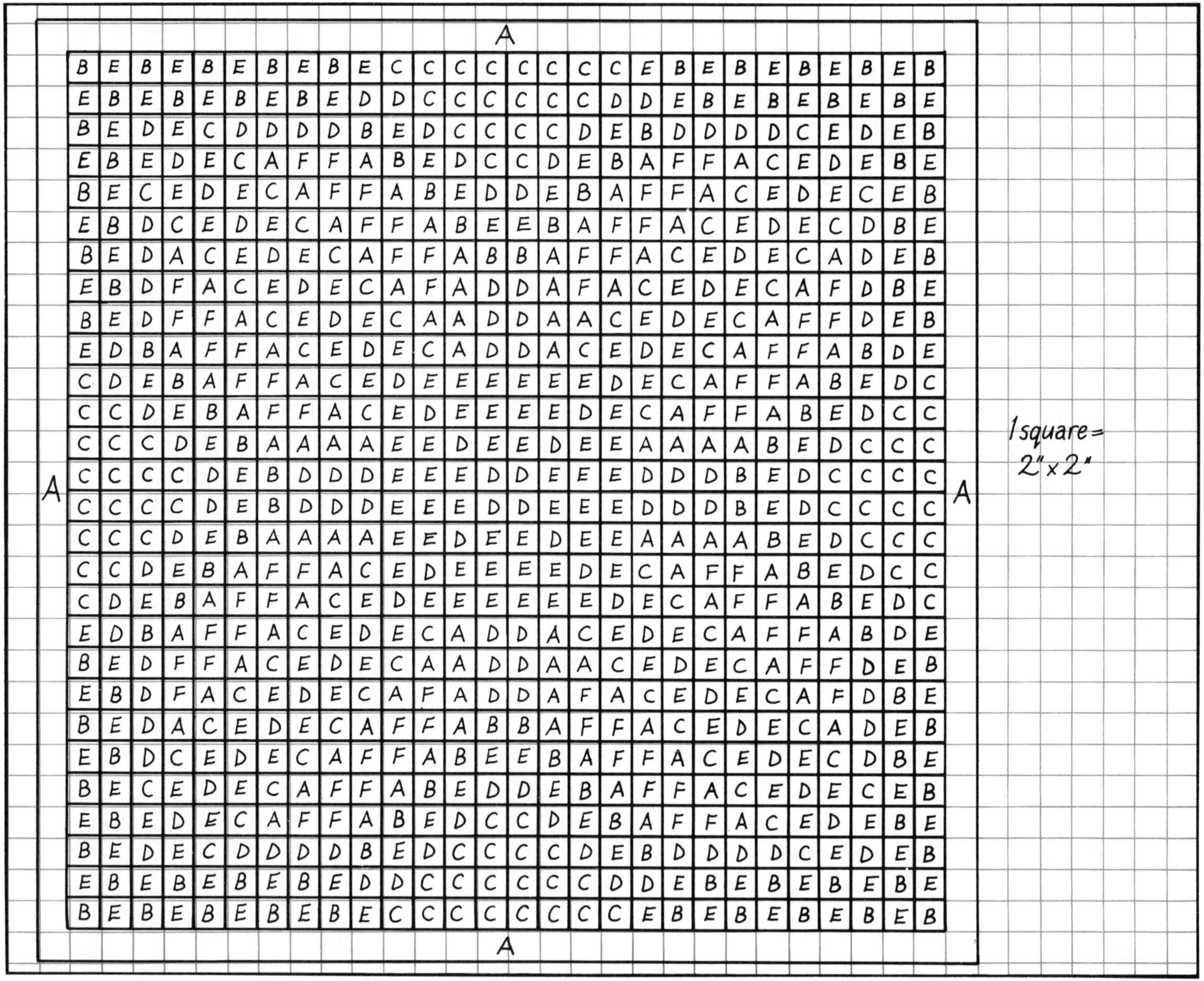

A

| | | | | | | | | | | | | | | | | | | | | | | | | | | | |
|---|---|---|---|---|---|---|---|---|---|---|---|---|---|---|---|---|---|---|---|---|---|---|---|---|---|---|---|
| B | E | B | E | B | E | B | E | B | E | C | C | C | C | C | C | C | C | E | B | E | B | E | B | E | B | E | B |
| E | B | E | B | E | B | E | B | E | D | D | C | C | C | C | C | C | D | D | E | B | E | B | E | B | E | B | E |
| B | E | D | E | C | D | D | D | D | B | E | D | C | C | C | C | D | E | B | D | D | D | D | C | E | D | E | B |
| E | B | E | D | E | C | A | F | F | A | B | E | D | C | C | D | E | B | A | F | F | A | C | E | D | E | B | E |
| B | E | C | E | D | E | C | A | F | F | A | B | E | D | D | E | B | A | F | F | A | C | E | D | E | C | E | B |
| E | B | D | C | E | D | E | C | A | F | F | A | B | E | E | B | A | F | F | A | C | E | D | E | C | D | B | E |
| B | E | D | A | C | E | D | E | C | A | F | F | A | B | B | A | F | F | A | C | E | D | E | C | A | D | E | B |
| E | B | D | F | A | C | E | D | E | C | A | F | A | D | D | A | F | A | C | E | D | E | C | A | F | D | B | E |
| B | E | D | F | F | A | C | E | D | E | C | A | A | D | D | A | A | C | E | D | E | C | A | F | F | D | E | B |
| E | D | B | A | F | F | A | C | E | D | E | C | A | D | D | A | C | E | D | E | C | A | F | F | A | B | D | E |
| C | D | E | B | A | F | F | A | C | E | D | E | E | E | E | E | E | D | E | C | A | F | F | A | B | E | D | C |
| C | C | D | E | B | A | F | F | A | C | E | D | E | E | E | E | D | E | C | A | F | F | A | B | E | D | C | C |
| C | C | C | D | E | B | A | A | A | A | E | E | D | E | E | D | E | E | A | A | A | A | B | E | D | C | C | C |
| C | C | C | C | D | E | B | D | D | D | E | E | E | D | D | E | E | E | D | D | D | B | E | D | C | C | C | C |
| C | C | C | C | D | E | B | D | D | D | E | E | E | D | D | E | E | E | D | D | D | B | E | D | C | C | C | C |
| C | C | C | D | E | B | A | A | A | A | E | E | D | E | E | D | E | E | A | A | A | A | B | E | D | C | C | C |
| C | C | D | E | B | A | F | F | A | C | E | D | E | E | E | E | D | E | C | A | F | F | A | B | E | D | C | C |
| C | D | E | B | A | F | F | A | C | E | D | E | E | E | E | E | E | D | E | C | A | F | F | A | B | E | D | C |
| E | D | B | A | F | F | A | C | E | D | E | C | A | D | D | A | C | E | D | E | C | A | F | F | A | B | D | E |
| B | E | D | F | F | A | C | E | D | E | C | A | A | D | D | A | A | C | E | D | E | C | A | F | F | D | E | B |
| E | B | D | F | A | C | E | D | E | C | A | F | A | D | D | A | F | A | C | E | D | E | C | A | F | D | B | E |
| B | E | D | A | C | E | D | E | C | A | F | F | A | B | B | A | F | F | A | C | E | D | E | C | A | D | E | B |
| E | B | D | C | E | D | E | C | A | F | F | A | B | E | E | B | A | F | F | A | C | E | D | E | C | D | B | E |
| B | E | C | E | D | E | C | A | F | F | A | B | E | D | D | E | B | A | F | F | A | C | E | D | E | C | E | B |
| E | B | E | D | E | C | A | F | F | A | B | E | D | C | C | D | E | B | A | F | F | A | C | E | D | E | B | E |
| B | E | D | E | C | D | D | D | D | B | E | D | C | C | C | C | D | E | B | D | D | D | D | C | E | D | E | B |
| E | B | E | B | E | B | E | B | E | D | D | C | C | C | C | C | C | D | D | E | B | E | B | E | B | E | B | E |
| B | E | B | E | B | E | B | E | B | E | C | C | C | C | C | C | C | C | E | B | E | B | E | B | E | B | E | B |

A

1 square = 2" x 2"

fabric. You will probably have to make joins in the backing to create a large enough square. Make sure the seams on the backing fabric are pressed flat before the patchwork is joined to it. You will certainly want to secure the backing to the fabric with a few small stitches, evenly spaced, on the reverse of the work. This is particularly important if you want to use the finished piece as a tablecloth, as the stitching will help to prevent the patchwork and the backing from separating and slipping.

**Patchwork and Appliquéd Tablecloth or Hanging** (Fig. 2-13)

The center of each square in this design is applied onto the patch before sewing the main pieces together.

FINISHED SIZE: Approx. 66″ × 58″
YOU NEED: 36″-wide fabric

| | |
|---|---|
| 50″ × 36″ in A | 26″ × 36″ in C |
| 60″ × 36″ in B | 15″ × 36″ in D |

A piece of backing fabric measuring 67″ × 59″

METHOD

Cut the following finished-size patches:

*Squares 12″ × 12″:*
16 in B
*Rectangles 4″ × 12″:*
14 in A
6 in C

Fig. 2-12 (Facing page) *Wallhanging or tablecloth*

Fig. 2-13 *Patchwork and appliquéd tablecloth or wallhanging*

*Squares 2″ × 2″:*
*64 in C*
*80 in D*
*Strips 4″ × 66″:*
5 in A

Assemble the 16 appliquéd sections as shown in Fig. 2-14. Pin and tack each appliqué to the center of a 12-inch square in B, turning under the seam allowance and hemstitching into position (see Fig. 2-13). Now assemble the patches as shown in Fig. 2-14. Follow the backing instructions given for Project VIII.

Basic layout before applying patchwork decoration to each square

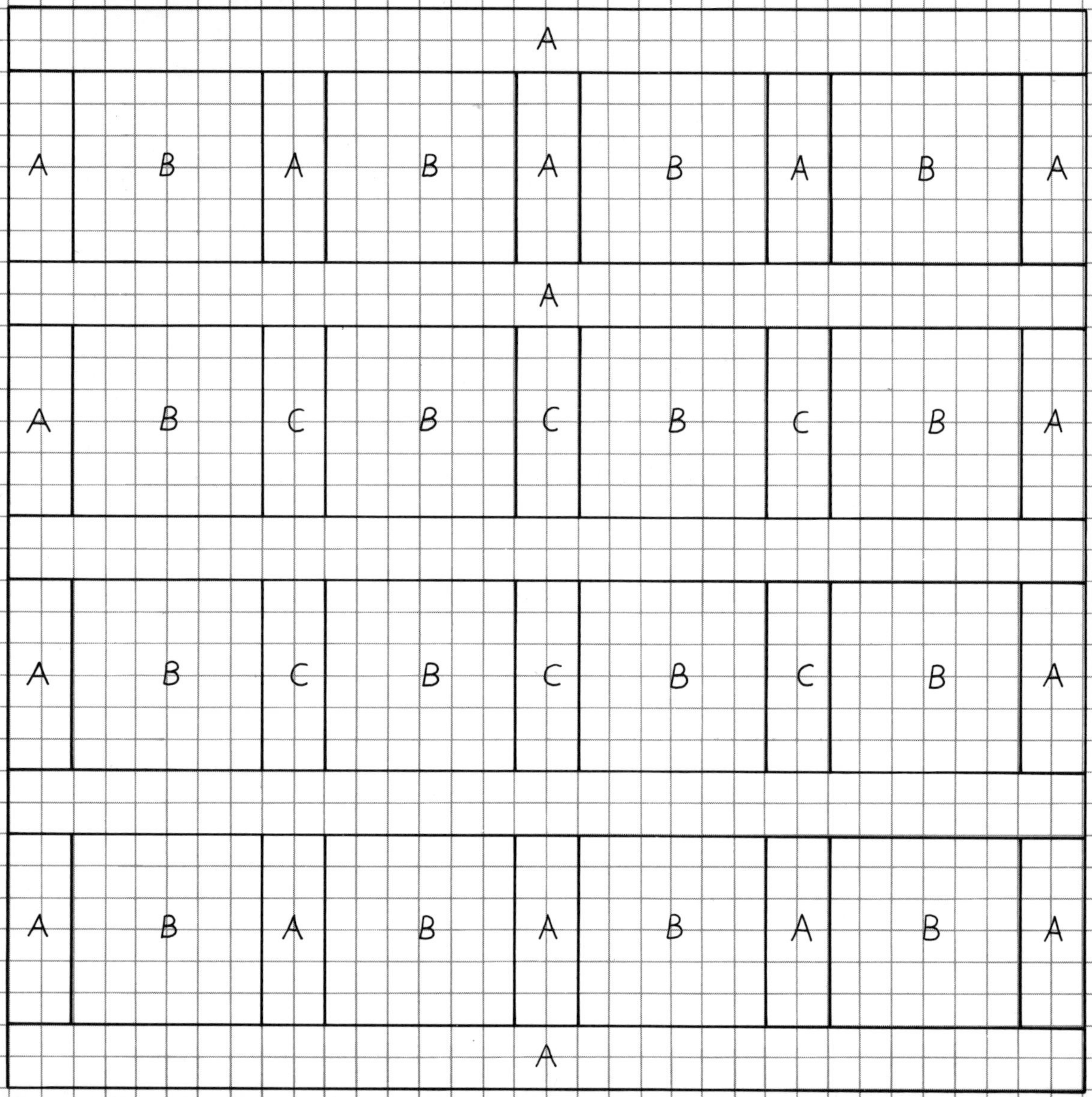

A

A B A B A B A B A

A

A B C B C B C B A

A B C B C B C B A

A B A B A B A B A

A

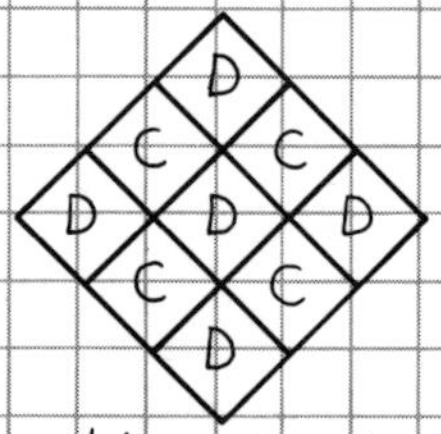

D

C C

D D D

C C

D

This patchwork section is applied to each square (make 16)

1 square = 2" x 2"

### **Tablecloth in Squares on the Diagonal** (Fig. 2-15)

The simple device of working basic squares in a diagonal pattern gives a totally different look to the finished patchwork.

Finished Size: Approx. 56″ × 56″

You Need: 36″-wide fabric

| | |
|---|---|
| 30″ × 36″ in A | 16″ × 36″ in F |
| 38″ × 36″ in B | 8″ × 36″ in G |
| 30″ × 36″ in C | 6″ × 36″ in H |
| 14″ × 36″ in D | 6″ × 36″ in I |
| 14″ × 36″ in E | |

A piece of backing fabric measuring 56″ × 56″

Method

Fig. 2-16 shows one quarter of the finished patchwork design. Start with the center patch in Shade D and work out from that to the edges. Cut the following finished-size 2-inch patches:

| | |
|---|---|
| 116 in A | 134 in F |
| 190 in B | 66 in G |
| 128 in C | 54 in H |
| 115 in D | 48 in I |
| 128 in E | |

Borders and Backing

After sewing the squares together as described above, cut the following border strips:

1½″ × 56″ (finished size): 4 in A

1½″ × 54½″ (finished size): 4 in B

3″ × 53″ (finished size): 4 in C

Join the strips together as shown in Fig. 2-16, mitering the corners to create a "frame" in which to place the patchwork. Turn under the seam allowance around the edges of all squares at the edge of the work, and apply the patchwork to the border strips. Machine or hand stitch into position. Attach the backing fabric as described for Project VIII.

Fig. 2-15 *Tablecloth in squares on the diagonal*

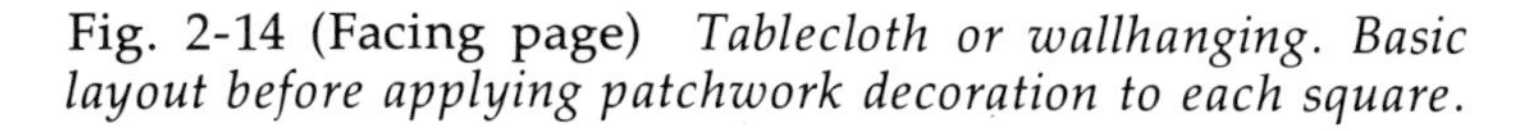

Fig. 2-14 (Facing page) *Tablecloth or wallhanging. Basic layout before applying patchwork decoration to each square.*

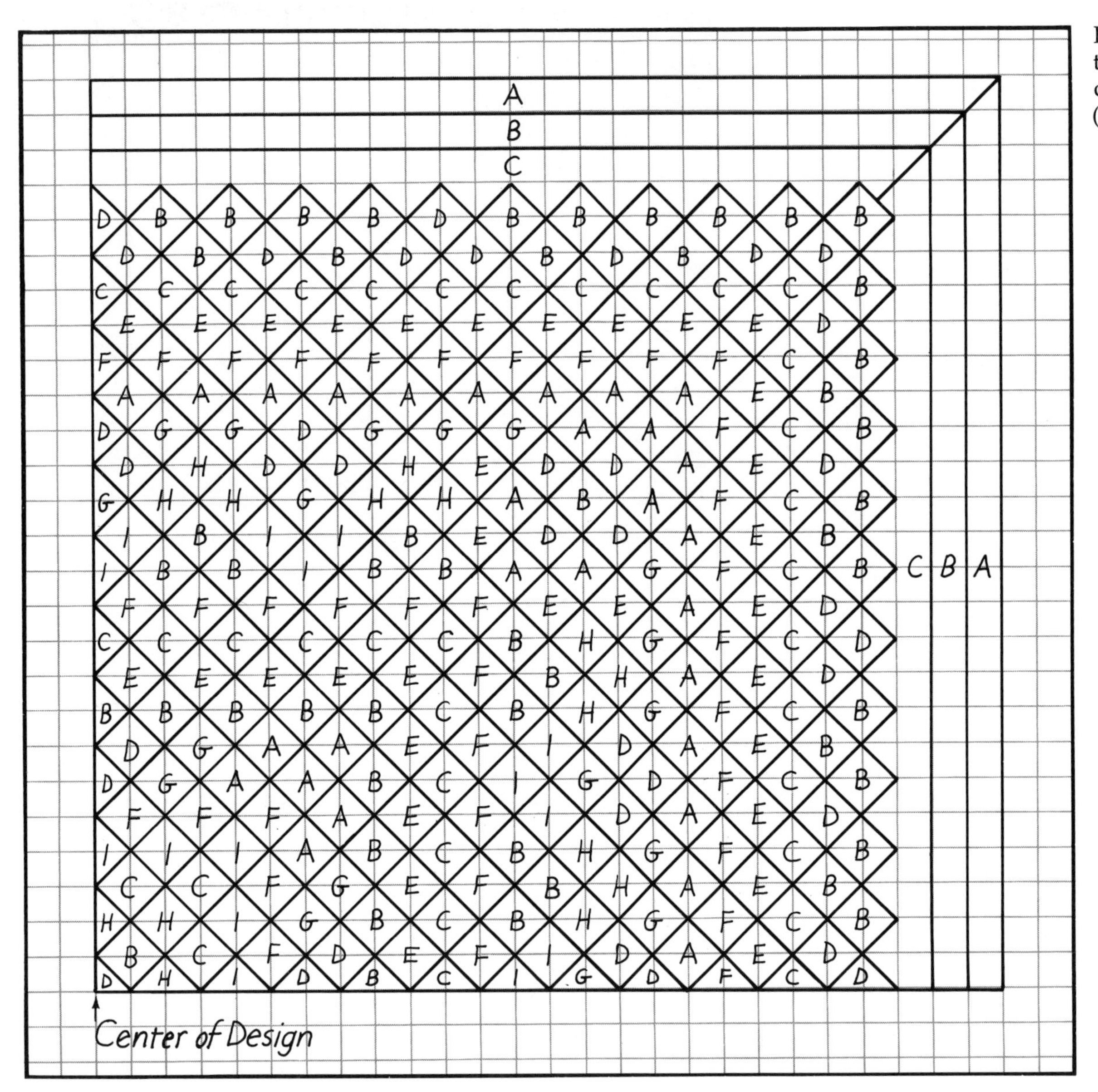


Fig. 2-16 Layout for tablecloth in squares on the diagonal. (*Not to scale.*)

**Table Center in Hexagons** (Fig. 2-17)

This design uses the hexagon with sides of 1½ inches shown in Chapter 1 (Fig. 1-4).

YOU NEED: 36″-wide fabric

4″ × 36″ in each of Shades A, B, C, D, and E
About ½ yard of backing fabric

METHOD

Shade E is indicated by diagonal lines on the layout (Fig 2-18). Cut the following hexagons:

| | |
|---|---|
| 12 in A | 12 in D |
| 12 in B | 7 in E |
| 12 in C | |

Assemble the patches as shown in Fig. 2-18. Place the finished patchwork onto the backing fabric and trace the outline in pencil. Cut out the shape drawn on the backing. Turn under the seam allowances, and join backing to patchwork.

**Tablecloth in Hexagons** (Fig. 2-19)

This design is worked in hexagons with sides of 1½ inches, as shown in Fig. 1-4 in Chapter 1.

FINISHED SIZE: Approx. 44″ × 49″
YOU NEED: 36″-wide fabric

50″ × 36″ in A
48″ × 36″ in B
8″ × 36″ in C, D, E, and F

Fig. 2-17 *Table center in hexagons*

METHOD

Cut the following 1½-inch hexagons:

| | |
|---|---|
| 108 in A | 18 in D |
| 159 in B | 20 in E |
| 19 in C | 19 in F |

Assemble the patches as shown in Figs. 2-20 and 2-21.

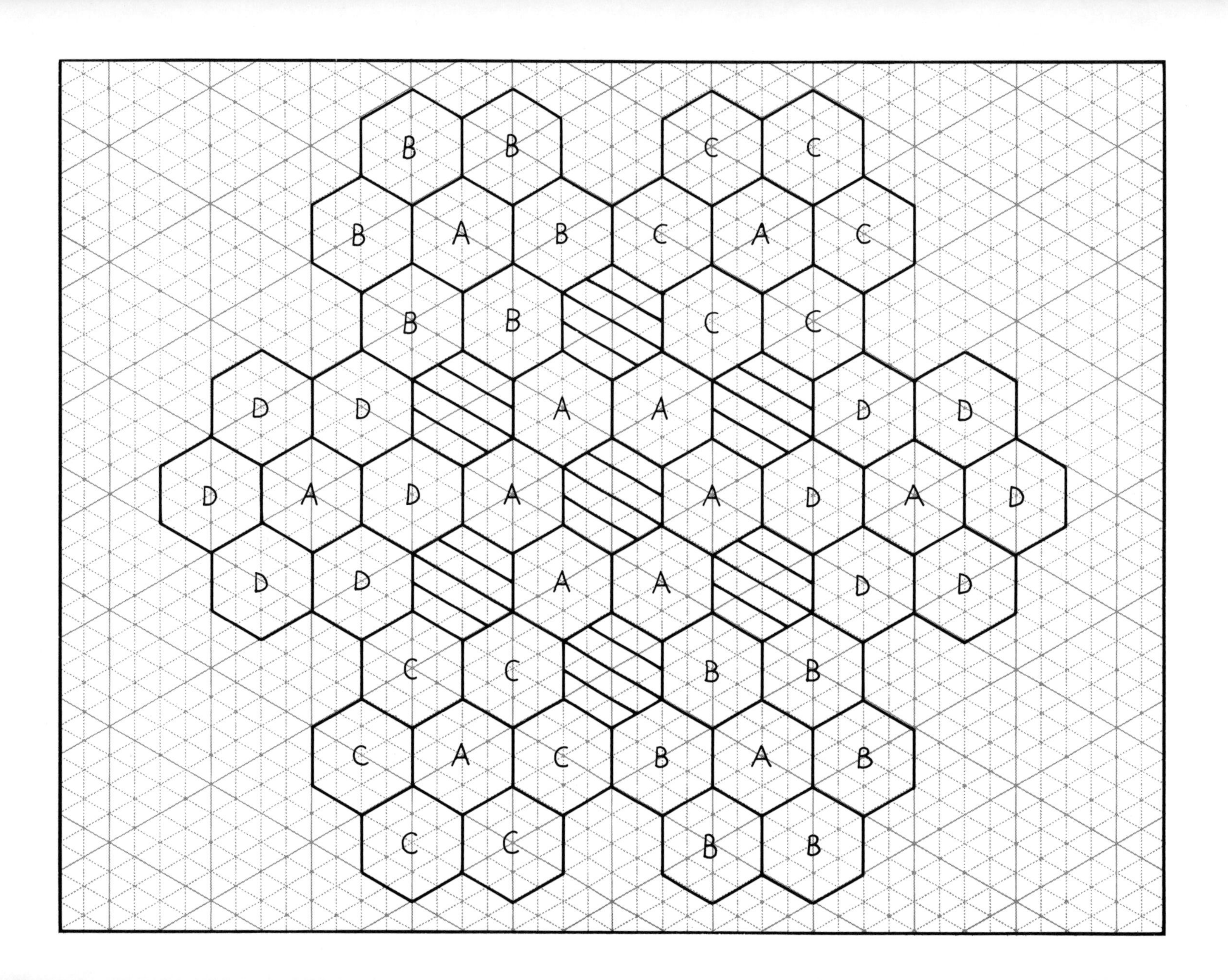

B B C C
B A B C A C
B B C C
D D A A D D
D A D A A D A D
D D A A D D
C C B B
C A C B A B
C C B B

Fig. 2-19 *Tablecloth in hexagons*

Fig. 2-18 (Facing page) *Layout for table center in hexagons*

BORDER AND BACKING

Cut the following finished-size border strips in A:

3″ × 44″ (2 pieces)

3″ × 49″ (2 pieces)

Join the strips together to form a "frame" for the patchwork, mitering the corners. Apply the patchwork to the border strips and to the backing as described in Project X.

If desired, three additional patches may be applied in each corner using Shade C. Refer to Fig. 2-19 for the position of these additional patches.

The tablecloth worked in hexagons shown in Fig. 2-22 and the quilt shown in Fig. 2-23, also in hexagonal patches, are examples of how patchwork may be used to add color to the home, and how well patchwork in different media can be blended together to create your own individual decorative style.

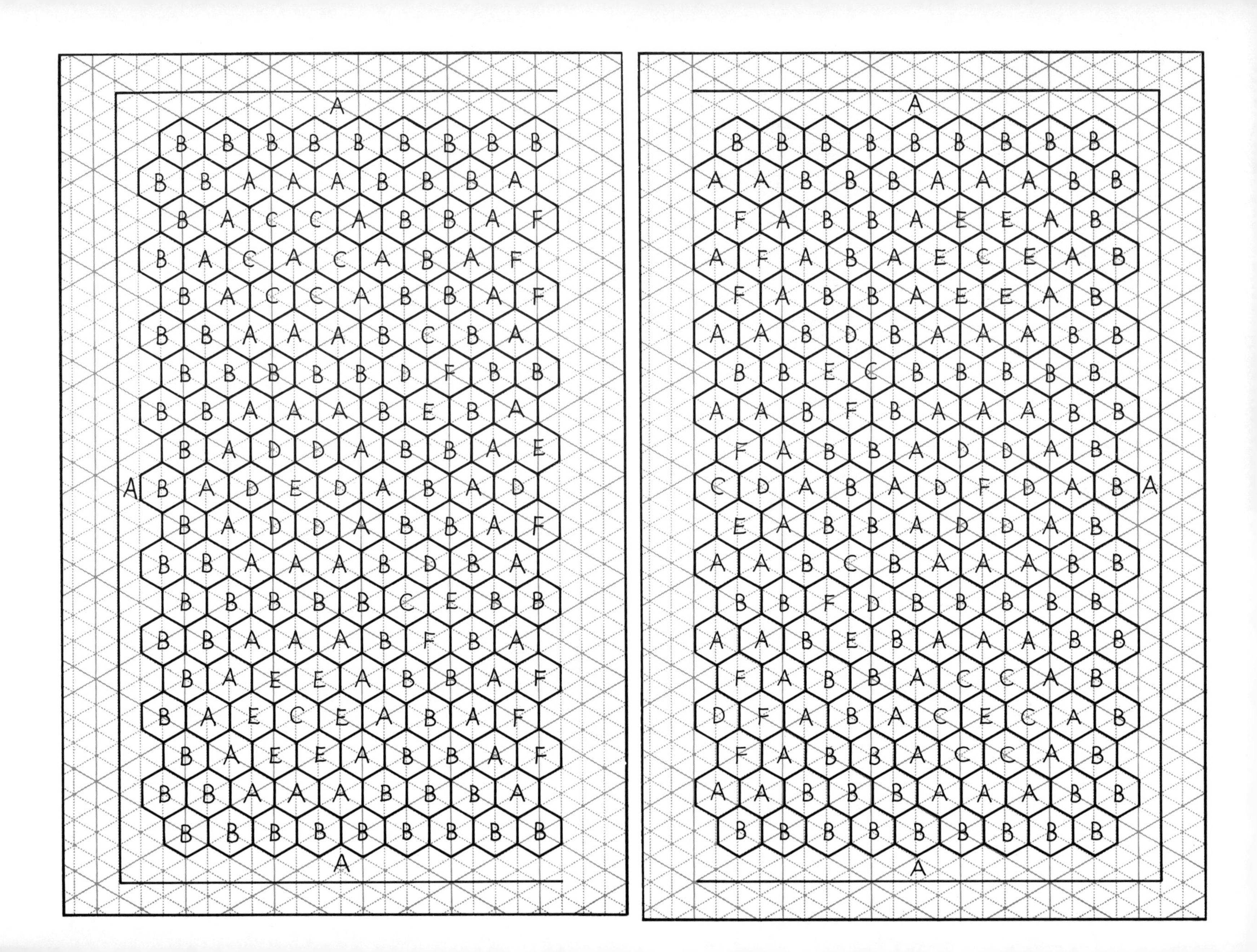
A
B B B B B B B B B
B B A A A B B B A
B A C C A B B A F
B A C A C A B A F
B A C C A B B A F
B B A A A B C B A
B B B B B D F B B
B B A A A B E B A
B A D D A B B A E
A B A D E D A B A D
B A D D A B B A F
B B A A A B D B A
B B B B B C E B B
B B A A A B F B A
B A E E A B B A F
B A E C E A B A F
B A E E A B B A F
B B A A A B B B A
B B B B B B B B B
A
A
B B B B B B B B B
A A B B B A A A B B
F A B B A E E A B
A F A B A E C E A B
F A B B A E E A B
A A B D B A A A B B
B B E C B B B B B
A A B F B A A A B B
F A B B A D D A B
C D A B A D F D A B A
E A B B A D D A B
A A B C B A A A B B
B B F D B B B B B
A A B E B A A A B B
F A B B A C C A B
D F A B A C E C A B
F A B B A C C A B
A A B B B A A A B B
B B B B B B B B B
A

Fig. 2-22 *Tablecloth in hexagons*

Fig. 2-23 *Quilt in hexagons*

Fig. 2-20 (Facing page, left) *Layout for tablecloth in hexagons—left side*

Fig. 2-21 (Facing page, right) *Layout for tablecloth in hexagons—right side*

# 3 Appliqué

Appliqué is more difficult than most craft subjects to describe and give instructions for in a book. In its most intricate and creative forms it can rival painting in visual effect. My approach to appliqué, therefore, is somewhat different from the treatment given to patchwork in the first two chapters. The reader will not find explicit work patterns given for appliqué. Apart from the obvious technical difficulties of providing patterns within the limitations of a book, I feel that appliqué is, more than with any other craft, an expression of an individual urge to create. Therefore, the basic techniques, providing a sound background in the craft are discussed in this chapter; Chapter 4 will, I hope, encourage creative exploration.

**Fabrics**

Those fabrics suitable for patchwork, described in Chapter 1, are also the best ones for appliqué. However, there is one fabric that is especially good for appliqué and not generally used for patchwork, and that is felt. The beauty of using felt for appliqué lies in the fact that it is never necessary to turn under raw edges. One has far greater freedom in the shapes used.

If working with felt, apply the pieces to the background fabric with small hemming stitches. Always bring the needle up through the background fabric close to the applied piece to be sewn. Then take the needle down through the appliqué to the back of the work. Bringing the needle up through the appliqué near the cut edge of the felt could lead to holes or stretching. Apart from this precaution felt is a carefree fabric to use, and one I would recommend to beginners to the exclusion of all others.

## Tools

You will need the same basic tools for appliqué as were listed in Chapter 1 for patchwork. You may also find a small tool called a seam-ripper useful for turning under seam allowances. You can use the longer of the two prongs of this tool for tucking under the edges of fabric when the appliqué is pinned in place.

## Planning a Design

Decide what size you want your finished piece to be, then take a sheet of paper large enough on which to draw the entire design. If you are working an exceptionally large piece, tape several sheets of paper together, placing the tape at the back so as not to interrupt the flow of the drawing.

Begin to draw in your outlines using a soft pencil which can easily be erased whenever corrections become necessary. When you are quite sure that your outline is to your satisfaction, go over the entire drawing with a fine-pointed felt pen. Make a tracing of the picture. Again, if you are working with an exceptionally large piece, you can tape pieces of tracing paper together.

Now that you have the drawing completed, decide on which fabrics you are going to use, and note the colors both on the drawing and on the tracing. Cut out all the shapes on the drawing paper. These form the templates from which you will now proceed to cut out the fabric. You can see exactly where each piece belongs on the background fabric by referring to the tracing for guidance.

## Cutting the Pieces

When you cut out the appliqué shapes in any fabric except felt, allow for a turn-under of ¼ inch all around if you are using the hand-stitching method. If you are going to use machine stitching or are working in felt, you can cut the appliqués to the exact size shown by the paper templates.

Whichever method of sewing you are going to use, remember to keep all the fabrics in approximately the same weight and quality in any given piece. Also, it is always best to keep the grain of the fabric on an appliqué running in the same direction as the grain on the background. It may be easy enough to see the direction of threads on the background fabric, since the selvages will probably still be intact. However, it is not always so easy to see which way the grain is running with the tiny scraps of fabric you may have collected for your appliqué work. One simple answer to this is to pull out a thread from near the edge of the scrap. You will now be able to see which way the threads are running, and can pin your template onto the fabric accordingly. This may seem unnecessary labor for anyone eager to get on with the sewing, but the resulting appliqué will be much flatter if a little extra care is taken at this point. This technique is especially important when you are making anything that is to hang free. You might be able to skip the process if you are working a cushion or any object that is to be stuffed or quilted.

Pin each appliqué in position ready for sewing.

## Sewing the Appliqués

### *Hand Sewing*

When hand sewing is used for a fabric with a raw edge which can fray, that is, anything other than felt, you will have to make a ¼-inch turn-under allowance on each piece. When it comes to turning under this edge on appliqué shapes, you are faced with two recurring problems: the convex and concave shapes.

With a convex shape, as shown in Fig. 3-1, you have too much material to turn under. If your shape has a point, as shown in Fig. 3-1, you can use this as a starting place for turning under. Fold under the allowance on the left-hand side of the point (Fig. 3-2). Press the fabric hard between the first finger and thumb to score the fabric along the turn-under allowance. It is very easy to do this with a good, crisp cotton fabric. Now turn under the other side as shown in Fig. 3-3. Work other points in the

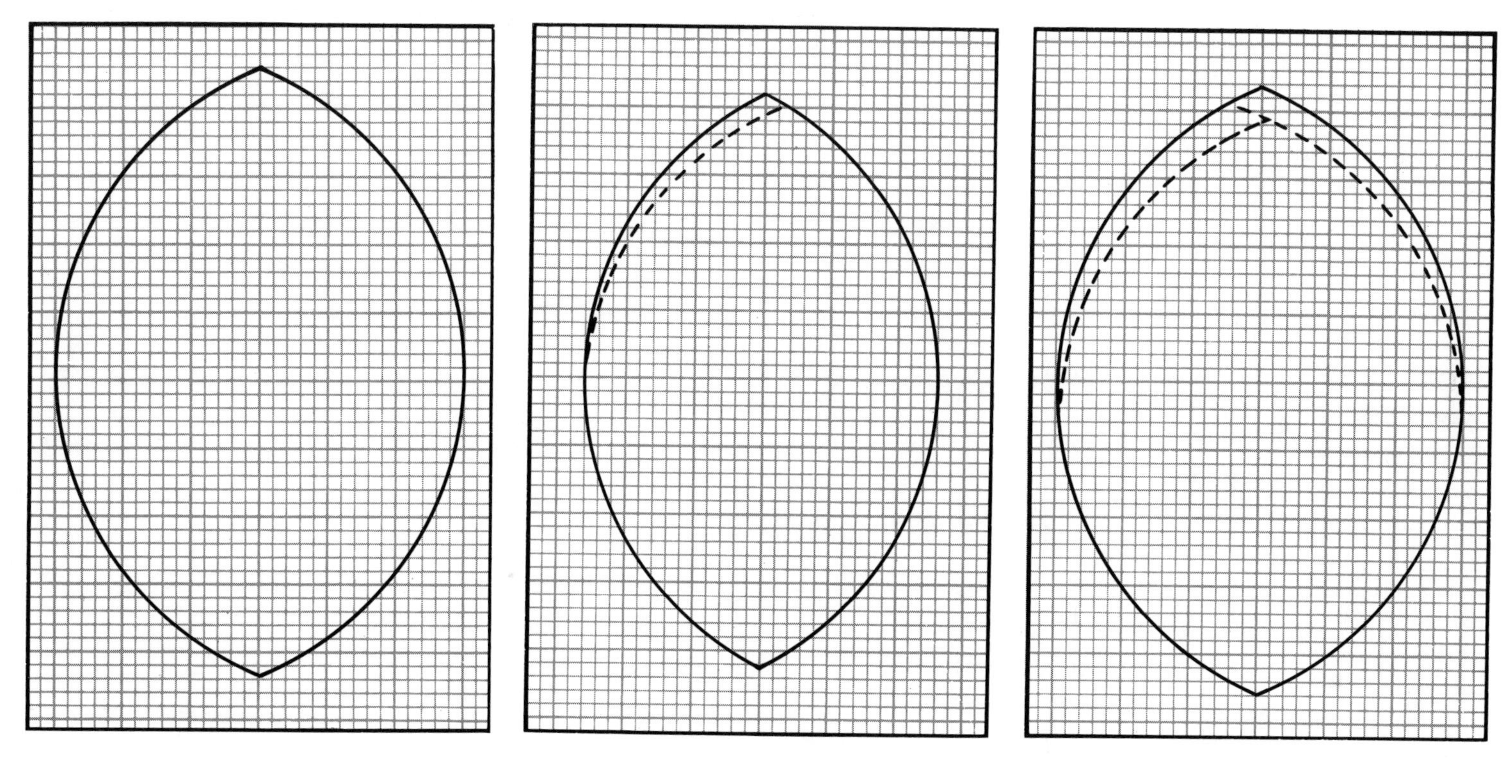

Fig. 3-1 *Convex shape*

Fig. 3-2 *Folding under the allowance—Step 1*

Fig. 3-3 *Folding under the allowance—Step 2*

same manner, blending in the allowance along the sides.

With a complete circle (Fig. 3-4), you may have to make tiny notches in the turn-under allowance. To do this, cut away tiny V-shaped pieces of fabric at short intervals to allow the fabric to lie flat when it is turned. Simply clipping the fabric, not in V shapes, is used on the concave curves of appliqué pieces. Fig. 3-5 shows how small cuts are made to allow the fabric to expand, rather than contract, when it is turned, in much the same way a collar is clipped when attached to a dress or blouse in dressmaking. Whenever you are cutting into the turn-under allowance, use a pair of sharp-pointed embroidery scissors, and never cut too deep into the piece. One should stop the cut or notch just before the score line of the turn-under allowance is reached.

Embroidery stitches can be used to sew appliqués in place—a favorite for this purpose being the buttonhole stitch, which gives a neat, firm edge. You can, of course, sew the pieces onto the ground fabric using almost invisible hemming stitches in a thread that matches the appliqué. If, on the other hand, you choose to apply with embroidery stitches, do pick a color to contrast with the particular piece you are sewing. It always seems a shame to let beautiful hand embroidery go unnoticed. Surface stitching on top of appliqués can be particularly useful where large shapes are used. Without it, they have a tendency to hang away from the ground fabric, and may look much better when secured with a few embroidery stitches, if you can work these into your completed design.

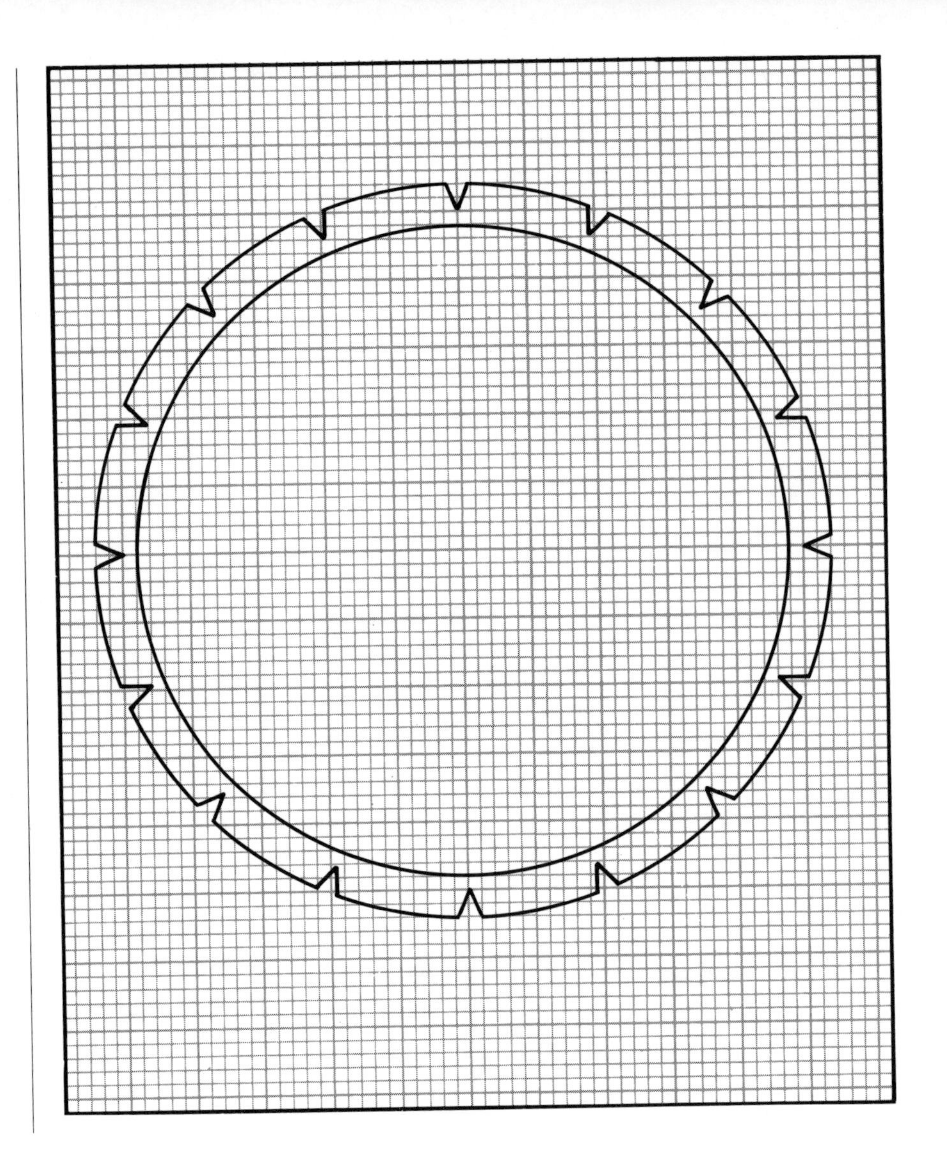

Fig. 3-4 *Circular shape*

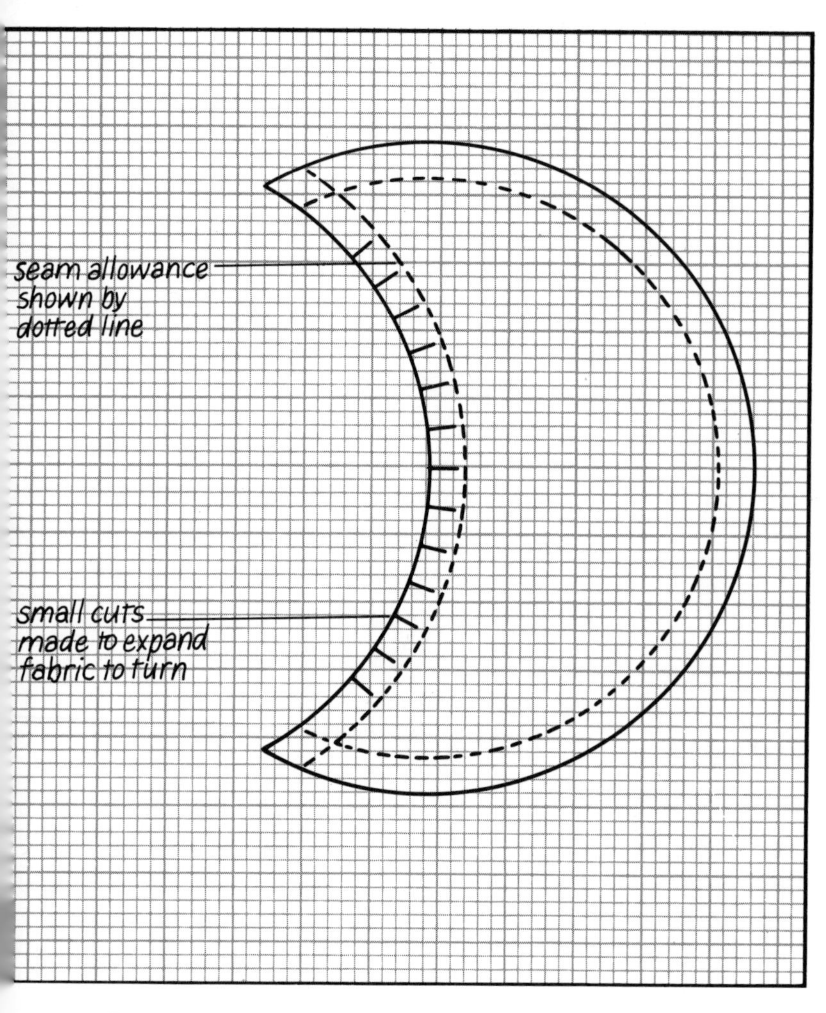


Fig. 3-5 *Cutting the fabric for turning*

*Machine Sewing*

Using a zig-zag machine is by far the easiest way to make appliqué. Your pieces of fabric can be cut to exactly the same size as the smaller template papers from your original sketch. You will have none of the bother of turning under a small seam on awkward shapes. As with felt, you will have much greater freedom in the shapes you use. All you need is a sewing machine that will do a short zig-zag stitch. Set the machine on zig-zag, and make your stitch length as short as possible to condense the stitches and create a firmer edge.

You can attach your appliqués in either a matching or a contrasting color thread, but since there is no doubt that machine work is not as attractive as hand embroidery, you may prefer not to draw too much attention to the stitching, away from the design itself. Always try out your zig-zag stitch on a piece of waste fabric first, to check that it is exactly what you want. Machine, like hand, embroidery can be effectively used on the surface of appliqués.

Appliqué, more than any other craft, is suitable for individual experimentation. Once you have mastered the basic techniques, you can do anything. I would suggest you start with something small, such as a cushion or table napkin. Perhaps you could try cutting out bold letter shapes, and monogram clothes or household items. Let your own imagination work.

Or if you still feel you would like to start out with a concrete paper pattern in front of you, a large range of beautiful appliqué designs is available on the market. For a matter of a few cents you will receive a clear instruction sheet with the applied shapes drawn to their finished size. One thing beginners often find irritating about books on appliqué is that since they have to fit on a standard book page, most of the patterns are of necessity scaled-down drawings. By the time you have labored over enlarging the drawing, you find you would have been better off creating something simpler for yourself. The advantage of the purchased patterns is that they are printed on the paper in the right size. Then, if you really feel horrified at the thought of drawing anything for yourself but want to exercise some degree of creativity, these patterns can be very successfully mixed together. In any case, someone afraid of drawing will certainly find in them a rich supply of geometric and floral shapes.

# 4 Inspiration for Appliqué

This chapter is not intended to give step-by-step instructions for specific projects, but to show the reader examples of some excellent appliqué work which use both folk themes and contemporary-art design styles, and which may prove inspirational.

**Folk Themes**

South America has an exceptionally rich supply of traditional applied work. Often the wall hangings echo themes to be seen in Aztec or Mayan sculpture and pottery design. The figures are bold and simple, often bordered with bias strips of fabric, which serve to accentuate different sections of the design, rather like the leaded joins in a stained-glass window.

Fig. 4-1 is a very finely worked example of a symbolic figure applied in dazzling colors to a black background. Because of the simple shapes

Fig. 4-1 *Bolivian appliquéd wallhanging. Collection of Mrs. Harlee Hayman-Chaffey.*

Fig. 4-2 *Bolivian appliquéd wallhanging. Collection of Mrs. Harlee Hayman-Chaffey.*

Fig. 4-3 *Bolivian appliquéd wallhanging. Collection of Mrs. Harlee Hayman-Chaffey.*

used, it would not be difficult to work this design, or something similar, for oneself. Figs. 4-2 and 4-3 show other examples in the same genre. All three are from Bolivia, and are worked in hand-woven cloth.

Figs. 4-4 and 4-5 both come from Colombia. Fig. 4-4 is very similar in feeling to the Bolivian pieces. The main frog shape is cut out in velvet and applied to a background of hand-loomed wool, which is about the same weight as the

Fig. 4-4 *Velvet frog appliqué on wool, originally from Colombia. Collection of Dorothy Kapstein.*

Fig. 4-5 *Embroidered appliqué showing everyday life in a Colombian village. Collection of Dorothy Kapstein*

velvet. The details are then applied on top of the velvet, the stitching helping very cleverly to keep the large panel from sagging, while at the same time completing the overall design. Here necessity is beautifully integrated with creative design. This, too, would be a very simple project to copy.

Fig. 4-6 *Stylized Dahomean bird in cotton. Collection of Dorothy Kapstein.*

Fig. 4-5 is anything but simple! The entire panel is a riot of detail, all taken from everyday life in a Colombian village. Embroidery stitches are added to give extra dimension to the work, especially on the human faces.

Fig. 4-6 is included as a representative example of the exquisitely clear-cut type of work to be seen in Africa. This magnificent stylized bird comes from Dahomey, and is worked entirely in finely woven cotton in the most brilliant colors.

## Contemporary Artists Working in Appliqué

For a completely different and more contemporary feeling, we turn to the work of three artists currently creating in the field of appliqué.

Michiko Sato, some of whose patchwork designs we have already seen in Chapter 1, also creates exquisite appliqué. Fig. 4-7, "Flower Variation No. 2," and Fig. 4-8, "Circles Black and White," form an interesting contrast to the complexity of her patchwork design. Here the shapes are lyrically curvilinear; the design, bold and uncluttered.

Sas Colby makes interesting use of printed and plain fabrics to create her designs. She says her work "Who Put All Those Things in Your Head?" (Fig. 4-9) is a silk banner with its title taken from a Beatles song. The nude figure had been transferred to fabric by a photo process done by the 3M Company. The figure has been padded and stitched to add dimension.

"Silk Bib" (Fig. 4-10) is a body ornament, not necessarily intended for wearing. It combines photo transfers with appliqué and a padded, machine-drawn figure, with the words "straight arrow." Mirrors are appliquéd in the Indian manner, and star sequins add luster. It is lined and bound in printed satin.

Fig. 4-7 *Michiko Sato, "Flower Variation No. 2"*

Fig. 4-8 *Michiko Sato, "Circles Black and White"*

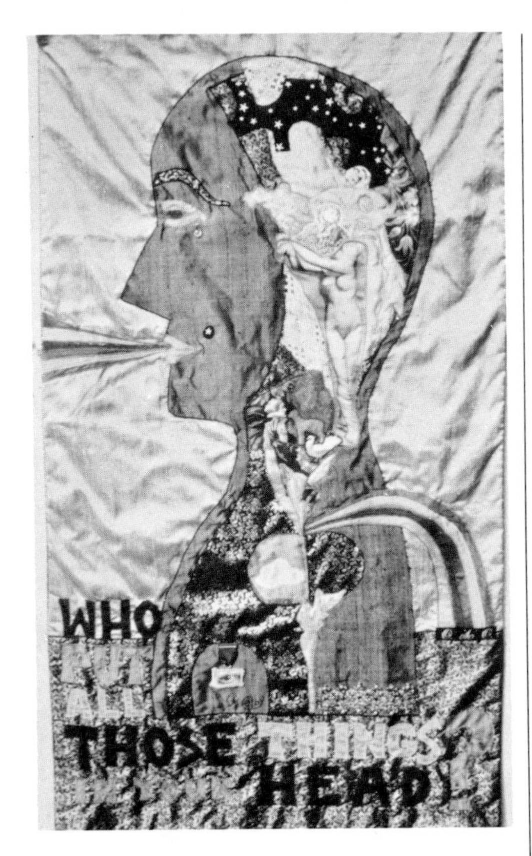


Fig. 4-9 *Sas Colby,*
*"Who Put All Those Things in*
*Your Head?"*

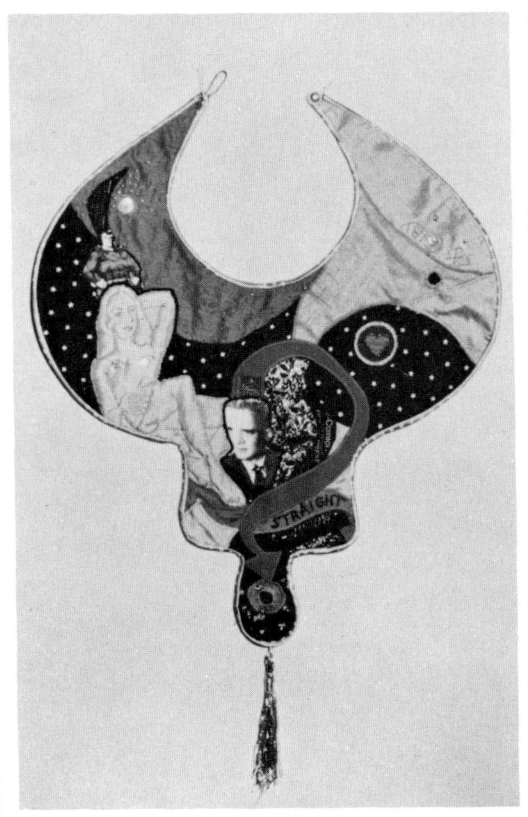


Fig. 4-10 *Sas Colby,*
*"Silk Bib with Mirror Appliqué*
*and Sequins"*

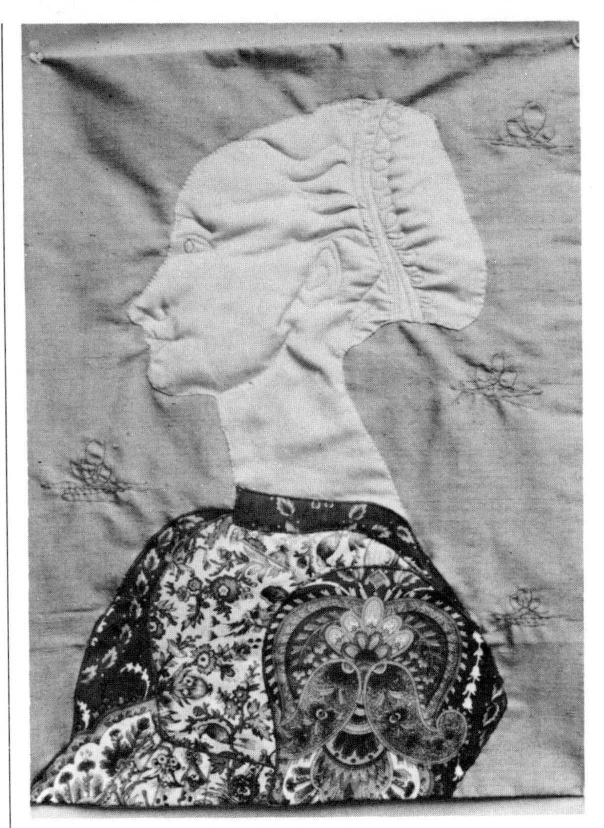

Fig. 4-11 *Sas Colby, "Venetian Lady"*

Fig. 4-12 *Patricia Malarcher, "Mylar Appliqué on Linen"*

Fig. 4-13 *Patricia Malarcher, detail of work in Fig. 4-12.*

"Venetian Lady" (Fig. 4-11) is a fabric interpretation of a painting by Domenico Veneziano. The head is padded silk; the dress is of printed cottons. It is a page from a one-of-a-kind fabric book, called "Silky Book."

Patricia Malarcher works in mylar applied to linen. In this way she is able to create three-dimensional effects, as in Fig. 4-12. A detail of the same piece is shown in Fig. 4-13. You might be able to achieve a similar effect by using heavyweight felt, and then stuffing the shapes with dacron. Of course you would not be able to achieve the reflective play of light created by the mylar.

Figs. 4-14 and 4-15 show further examples of Patricia Malarcher's work.

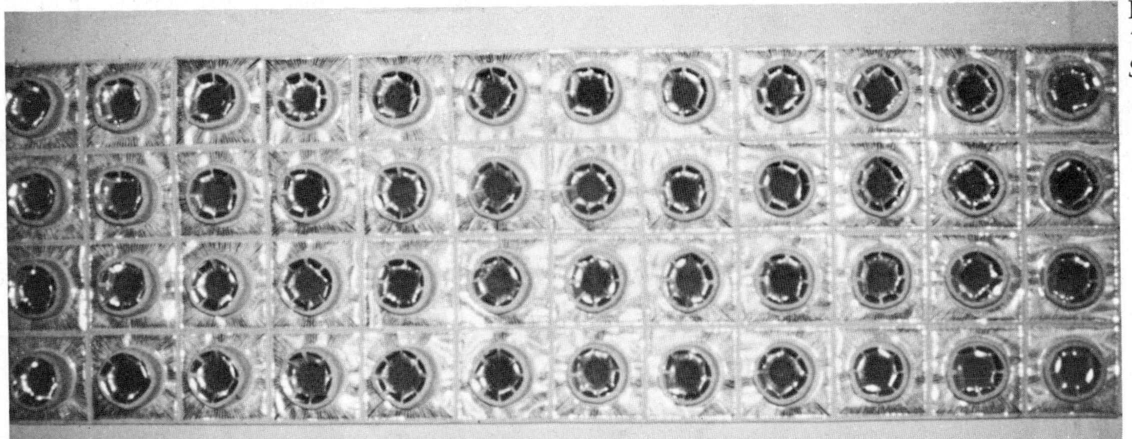

Fig. 4-14 *Patricia Malarcher, "Mylar Appliqué and Stitching on Linen"*

Fig. 4-15 *Patricia Malarcher, "Mylar Appliqué with Topstitching and Embroidery on Linen"*

Patchwork Bag in Bargello by Angela Reuben

This series of color plates includes some of the projects for which detailed instructions are given elsewhere in the book; as well as a selection of the work of artists using patchwork or appliqué as their medium. These latter may inspire more adventurous readers to experiment freely with their own creative projects.

All items in this section were designed by the author except where otherwise credited.

Quilt in crosses by Michiko Sato

Quilt in hexagons, with patchwork pillows

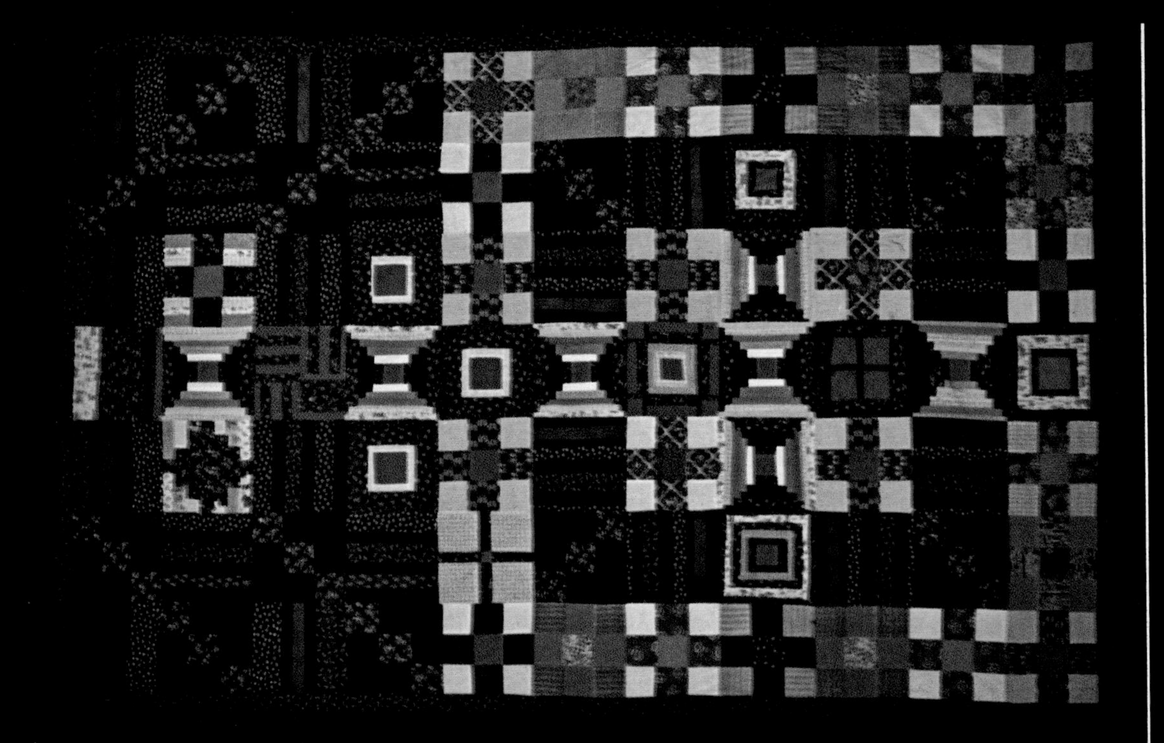

Left: "My Crazy Quilt," by Michiko Sato

Below: Cushion in squares

Far right:
Tablecloth in hexagons

Right:
Quilt by Michiko Sato

"Log Cabin," pillow or wallhanging in Gobelin

"Variations in Blue and Green," rug in Gobelin

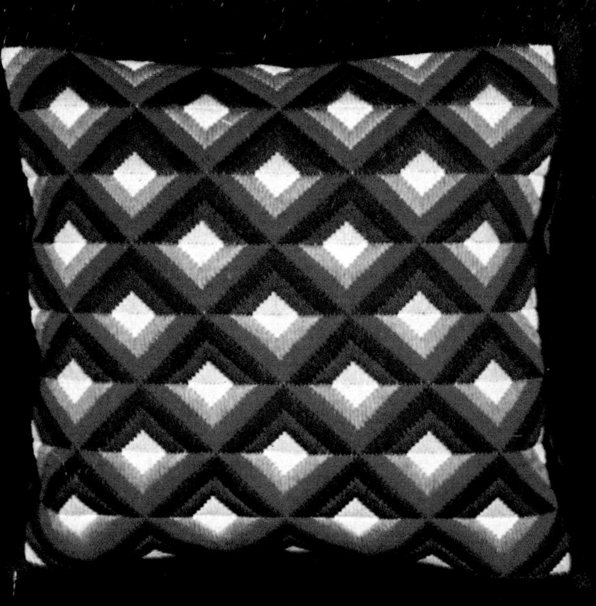

"Checkers," pillow in Bargello

"Kaleidoscope," pillow or wallhanging in Gobelin

Tablecloth or wallhanging in patchwork and appliqué

Top left: "Patio," pillow in Gobelin

Left: "Waves," pillow in Bargello

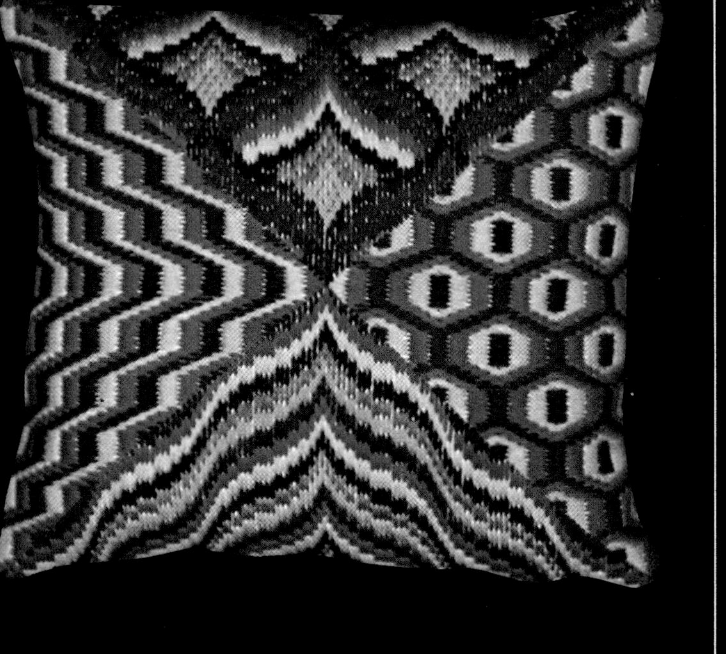

Above: Tablecloth in hexagons

Top left: "Autumn Leaves," pillow in Bargello

Bottom left: Multi-patched, crocheted afghan

Tablecloth or wallhanging in squares

"Flower Variation #2," appliqué by Michiko Sato

**Bolivian appliquéd wallhanging**
**(Courtesy Mrs. Harlee Hayman-Chaffey)**

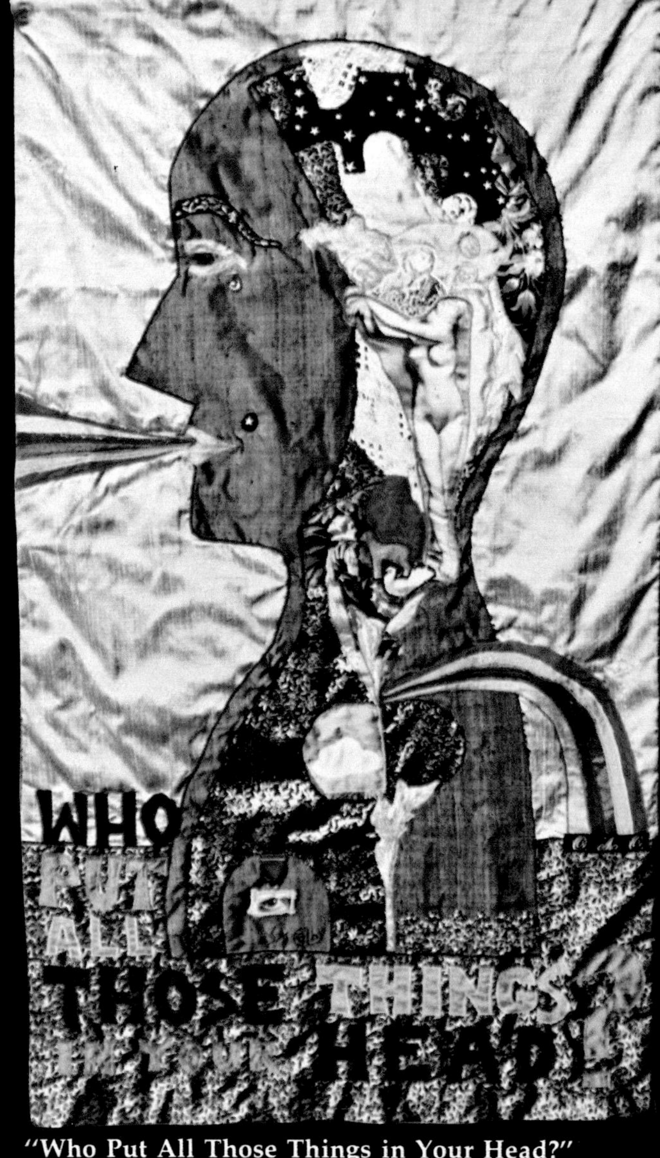


**"Who Put All Those Things in Your Head?"**
**appliqué by Sas Colby**

# 5 Patchwork Crochet

## Planning a Patchwork Crochet Project

Begin by deciding what you want to make and what purpose it will be expected to serve. For example, if you choose to make an afghan, ask yourself if you want it to be primarily useful, that is, warm, or whether you are going to place it in a specific room setting mainly for decoration. If you want warmth, choose one of the closely knit patches—those worked predominantly in single crochet would be ideal—and, of course, even warm afghans can be made decorative by using attractive design features. However, if decorativeness is uppermost in your requirements, you can choose from among the open-work and lacy patterns. These more open patterns can also be combined with solid ones to good effect.

Having decided what you want to make and what you want it for, give careful consideration to the yarn you will use. There are many different weights of yarn ranging from fine fingering to rug qualities. Make sure you choose something suitable for your project. Bear in mind that pure wool generally has more body than acrylics, and is less likely to fluff up. Acrylics, however, are extremely hard wearing, and will survive any amount of washing and tumbling dry.

Now that you have chosen the style of the patches as well as the yarn you would like to use, select a suitable hook for your yarn weight, and try out the crochet pattern for the patches with the yarn. You will be able to spot any potential problems at this stage and be able to alter yarn, patch, or hook until you are perfectly satisfied.

At this point determine for yourself the exact size of the patches and you are ready to draw a rough outline of your design on a piece of graph paper. Work on the sketch until you have all the details of the design exactly as you want them.

You can make a rough estimate of the amount of yarn required by seeing how much of a skein you used to make your practice patch or patches. If you want to be more accurate, weigh a finished patch on the kitchen scales and from that weight calculate how much yarn to buy. If you are using several colors in one project, you can buy yarn as you work. This is one place where changes in dye lot are unlikely to show since colors are alternated frequently. All patchwork and appliqué projects, in whatever medium, are a wonderful way of using up old scraps. Just remember, when crocheting never mix yarns of different weights in the same project.

## Instructions for Crocheting the Patches

This section provides instructions for a selection of crocheted patches which the reader can use to create original designs. At the end of the chapter you will find helpful information about the joining of the patches. However, for those who prefer to work with detailed instructions, Chapter 6 consists entirely of such projects, using some of the patches which now follow.

### Abbreviations Used in Instructions

| | | | | | |
|---|---|---|---|---|---|
| ch | = | chain | sp | = | space |
| st | = | stitch | sl | = | slip |
| sc | = | single crochet | inc | = | increase |
| dc | = | double crochet | dec | = | decrease |
| hdc | = | half double crochet | beg | = | beginning |
| tr | = | triple crochet | yo | = | yarn over |
| dtr | = | double triple crochet | cl | = | cluster |

Fig. 5-1 *Square patch #A1*

*A 3-dc cluster* is made like this: (yo, draw up a loop in st, yo and through 2 loops) 3 times, yo and through all 4 loops on hook. Clusters can be made with more or fewer dcs, or with longer stitches such as the tr and dtr. The same method is followed for these stitches also. Leave the last loop of each stitch on your hook until the final stitch has been worked, then yo and draw through all the remaining loops.

*A puff st* is made like this: (yo, draw up a ½-inch loop in st) 4 times, yo and through all 9 loops on hook.

Other stitch instructions will be given as they arise in working the patches.

**A. Squares**

#A1 (Fig. 5-1)
Ch 16.
*Row 1:* Starting in 2nd ch from hook, work 1 sc in each ch across, ch 1, turn. (15 sts.)
*Row 2:* 1 sc in each sc across, ch 1, turn. Repeat Row 2 until 18 rows have been worked, fasten off.

#A2 (Fig. 5-2)
Ch 2.
*Row 1:* Working in 2nd ch from hook, make 4 sc in this ch, join with a sl st to first sc to form a ring.

Fig. 5-2 *Square patches #A2, #A3, and #A4*

*Row 2:* Ch 1, 2 sc in each sc around, sl st in top of first sc (8 sc).

*Row 3:* Ch 1,* 1 sc in next sc, 3 sc in next sc for a corner, repeat from* around, sl st in top of first sc.

*Row 4:* Ch 1, 1 sc in each of next 2 sc,* 3 sc in next sc for a corner, 1 sc in each of next 3 sc, repeat from * around, working 1 sc in remaining sc at end of last repeat, sl st in top of first sc.

*Row 5:* Ch 1, 1 sc in each of next 3 sc,* 3 sc in next sc for a corner, 1 sc in each of next 5 sc, repeat from* around, working 1 sc in each of remaining 2 sc at end of last repeat, sl st in top of first sc.

*Row 6:* Ch 1, 1 sc in each of next 4 sc,* 3 sc in next sc for a corner, 1 sc in each of next 7 sc, repeat from* around, working 1 sc in each of remaining 3 sc at end of last repeat, sl st in top of first sc and fasten off.

Fig. 5-3 *Square patch #A5*

#A3 (Fig. 5-2)
Work exactly as for #A2 to end of Row 4, break off A (first color) and join B (contrasting color).

*Row 5:* As Row 5 of #A2, but worked in contrasting color, break off B, join C (second contrasting color).

*Row 6:* As Row 6 of #A2, worked in second contrasting color, fasten off.

#A4 (Fig. 5-2)
Work exactly as for #A2, but change colors as follows:

*Rows 1–3:* Color A
*Rows 4 and 5:* Color B
*Row 6:* Color A

#A5 (Fig. 5-3)
Worked in 2 colors. With color A, ch 5, join with sl st to form a ring.

*Row 1:* Ch 3 to count as 1 dc, 7 more dc in ring, break off A, join B, sl st in top of ch 3.

*Row 2:* * Ch 10, 1 tr in 5th ch from hook, 1 tr in each of next 2 ch, 1 dc in each of next 2 ch, 1 hdc in last ch, sl st in next dc on ring, repeat from* around: 8 petals, sl st in base of first petal, fasten off. Join A to a ch-4 sp at top of a petal.

*Row 3:* 1 sc, ch 3 and 1 sc in same ch-4 sp,* ch 3; 1 sc, ch 2 and 1 sc in ch-4 sp of next petal; ch 3, 1 sc, ch 3 and 1 sc in ch-4 sp of next petal, repeat from * around, end last repeat with ch 3, sl st in first sc.

*Row 4:* Sl st in ch-3 sp, ch 3; 3 dc, ch 3 and 4 dc in same ch-3 sp,* ch 1, 3 dc in next sp, ch 1, 3 dc in next ch-2 sp, ch 1, 3 dc in next sp, ch 1; 4 dc, ch 3 and 4 dc in next sp for *a corner,* repeat from* around, end last repeat with ch 1, sl st in top of ch-3. Break off A, join B to corner sp.

*Row 5:* Ch 3; 3 dc, ch 3 and 4 dc in same sp, work 3 dc and ch 1 in each sp on sides and 4 dc, ch 3 and 4 dc in each corner sp, end sl st in top of ch-3. Break off B, join A to a corner sp.

*Row 6:* Work 1 more row the same with color A, fasten off.

Fig. 5-4 *Square patch #A6*

#A6 (Fig. 5-4)
Worked in 2 colors. With Color A, ch 10.

*Row 1:* In 10th ch from hook, work (1 sc, ch 9) 6 times, 1 sc in same ch, ch 4, 1 dtr in same ch.

*Row 2:* Ch 4, 5 tr in dtr,* 6 tr in 5th st of next ch-9 sp, repeat from* 6 times more, break off A, join B with sl st in top of ch-4.

*Row 3:* Ch 4, 5-tr cluster over next 5 tr,* ch 8, 6-tr cluster over next 6 tr, repeat from* 6 times more, ch 8, break off B, join A with sl st in top of ch-4.

*Row 4:* Ch 1, 1 sc in same place as sl st,* ch 10, 1 sc in top of next cluster, ch 8, 1 sc in top of next cluster, repeat from* 3 times more, end last repeat with sl st in first sc, fasten off.

### B. Rectangles

#B1 (NOT ILLUSTRATED)

Ch 20.

*Row 1:* Starting in 2nd ch from hook, work 1 sc in each ch across, ch 1, turn (19 sts).

*Row 2:* 1 sc in each sc across, ch 1, turn. Repeat Row 2 until 39 rows have been worked, fasten off.

#B2 (FIG. 5-5)

Ch 20.

*Row 1:* As row 1 of #B1.

*Row 2:* 1 sc in first sc,* 1 puff st in next sc, 1 sc in next sc, repeat from* across, ch 1, turn. (The puff appears at the BACK of the work.)

*Row 3 (and each alternate row):* 1 sc in each st across, ch 1, turn.

*Row 4:* 1 sc in first sc, 1 puff st in next sc, 1 sc in each of next 15 sc, 1 puff st in next sc, 1 sc in last sc, ch 1, turn.

Fig. 5-5 *Rectangular patches #B2 and #B3*

*Row 6:* 1 sc in first sc, 1 puff st in next sc, 1 sc in each of next 3 sc, (1 puff st in next sc, 1 sc in next sc) 5 times, 1 sc in each of next 2 sc, 1 puff st in next sc, 1 sc in last sc, ch 1, turn.

*Row 8 (and all even-numbered rows up to and including Row 28):* 1 sc in first sc, 1 puff st in next sc, 1 sc in each of next 3 sc, 1 puff st in next sc, 1 sc in each of next 7 sc, 1 puff st in next sc, 1 sc in each of next 3 sc, 1 puff st in next sc, 1 sc in last sc, ch 1, turn.

*Row 30:* As Row 6.

*Row 32:* As Row 4.

*Row 34:* As Row 2.

*Row 35:* As Row 3, fasten off.

#B3 (Fig. 5-5)

Work as #B2 to end of Row 5.

*Row 6:* 1 sc in first sc, 1 puff st in next sc, (1 sc in each of next 7 sc, 1 puff st in next sc) twice, 1 sc in last sc, ch 1, turn.

*Row 8:* 1 sc in first sc, 1 puff st in next sc, 1 sc in each of next 6 sc, 1 puff st in next sc, 1 sc in next sc, 1 puff st in next sc, 1 sc in each of next 6 sc, 1 puff st in next sc, 1 sc in last sc, ch 1, turn.

*Row 10:* 1 sc in first sc, 1 puff st in next sc, 1 sc in each of next 5 sc, (1 puff st in next sc, 1 sc in next sc) 3 times, 1 sc in each of next 4 sc, 1 puff st in next sc, 1 sc in last sc, ch 1, turn.

*Row 12:* 1 sc in first sc, 1 puff st in next sc, 1 sc in each of next 4 sc, (1 puff st in next sc, 1 sc in next sc) 4 times, 1 sc in each of next 3 sc, 1 puff st in next sc, 1 sc in last sc, ch 1, turn.

*Row 14:* As Row 10.

*Row 16:* As Row 8.

*Row 18:* As Row 6.

Repeat from Row 7 to Row 18 once more.

Repeat Row 3.

Repeat Row 2.

Repeat Row 3, fasten off.

#B4 (Fig. 5-6)

Worked in 2 colors.

With A—ch 28, join with sl st to form a ring, careful not to twist chain.

*Row 1:* Ch 3, 2 dc in same place as sl st, ch 3, 3 dc in next ch, (ch 1, skip 1 ch, 1 dc in each of next 3 ch) twice, ch 1, skip 1 ch,* 3 dc in next ch, ch 3, 3 dc in next ch for a *corner,** ch 1, skip 1 ch, repeat from* to* once, (ch 1, skip 1 ch, 1 dc in each of next 3 ch) twice, ch 1, skip 1 ch, repeat from* to* once, ch 1, sl st in top of ch-3. Break off A, join B to a ch-3 sp.

*Row 2:* Ch 3; 2 dc, ch 3 and 3 dc in same ch-3 sp,* (ch 1, 3 dc in next ch-1 sp for a *group*) 3 times, ch 1; 3 dc, ch 3 and 3 dc in next ch-3 sp for a *corner*, repeat from* around, end last repeat with ch 1, sl st in top of ch-3. Break off B, join A to a ch-3 sp.

*Row 3:* Repeat Row 2 having 4 groups on long edges and 2 groups on short edges, sl st in top of ch-3, fasten off.

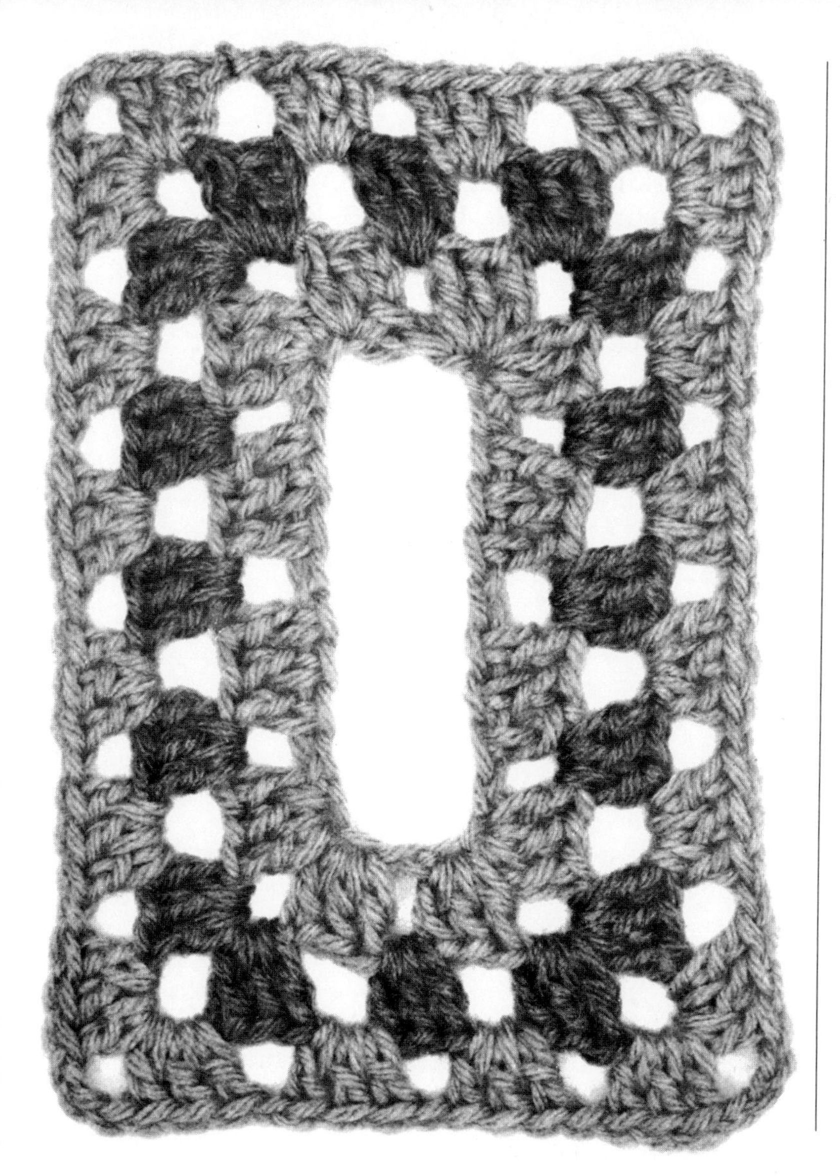

#B5 (Fig. 5-7)
Ch 28, join with sl st to form a ring, careful not to twist chain.

*Row 1:* Ch 3, 2 dc in same ch as sl st, ch 3, 3 dc in next ch, skip 1 ch, 1 dc in each of next 7 ch, skip 1 ch,* 3 dc in next ch, ch 3, 3 dc in next ch for a corner*, ch 1, repeat from* to* once, skip 1 ch, 1 dc in each of next 7 ch, skip 1 ch, repeat from* to* once, ch 1, skip 1 ch, sl st in top of ch 3.

*Rows 2 and 3:* Ch 3 to count as first dc, 1 dc in each dc with 3 dc, ch 3 and 3 dc in each corner ch-3 sp, sl st in top of ch-3, fasten off.

**Rectangles Using Filet Crochet**

Filet crochet, whose effect is achieved by working areas of open mesh in patterns with dense areas of double crochet worked in blocks, uses some special terms:

A *block* is basically 3 dc. It can be worked by (1) 2 dc in a ch-2 sp and 1 dc in dc of row below, or (2) 1 dc in each of 3 dc from row below.

A *mesh* is basically ch 2 and 2 dc. It can be worked by (1) ch 2 and 1 dc in next dc of row below, or (2) ch 2, skip 2 dc, 1 dc in next dc of row below.

The following two rectangular patches are worked in filet crochet.

Fig. 5-6 *Rectangular patch #B4*

Fig. 5-7 *Rectangular patch #B5*

#B6 (Fig. 5-8)

Ch 38.

*Row 1:* 1 dc in 8th ch from hook, 1 dc in each of next 12 ch, ch 2, skip 2 ch, 1 dc in each of next 13 ch, ch 2, skip 2 ch, 1 dc in last ch, ch 3, turn.

*Row 2:* 1 block, 1 mesh, 2 blocks, 3 mesh, 2 blocks, 1 mesh, 1 block, ch 3, turn.

*Row 3:* 2 blocks, 7 mesh, 2 blocks, ch 3, turn.

*Row 4:* 2 blocks, 2 mesh, 3 blocks, 2 mesh, 2 blocks, ch 3, turn.

*Row 5:* 1 block, 2 mesh, 1 block, 1 mesh, 1 block, 1 mesh, 1 block, 2 mesh, 1 block, ch 5, turn.

*Row 6:* 3 mesh, 2 blocks, 1 mesh, 2 blocks, 3 mesh, ch 3, turn.

*Rows 7, 8, 9, and 10:* Repeat Rows 5, 4, 3, and 2, ch 5 to turn at end of Row 10.

*Row 11:* 1 mesh, 4 blocks, 1 mesh, 4 blocks, 1 mesh, fasten off.

#B7 (Fig. 5-9)

Ch 56.

*Row 1:* 1 dc in 8th ch from hook, ch 2, skip 2 ch, 1 dc in each of next 4 ch,* (ch 2, skip 2 ch, 1 dc in next ch) 5 times, 1 dc in each of next 3 ch, repeat from* once more, (ch 2, skip 2 ch, 1 dc in next ch) twice, ch 5, turn.

*Row 2:* 1 dc in next dc, work 3 more mesh, 2 blocks, 1 mesh, 3 blocks, 1 mesh, 2 blocks, 4 mesh, with last dc in 5th st of turning ch, ch 3, turn.

*Row 3:* 1 block, 1 mesh, 4 blocks, 2 mesh, 1 block, 2 mesh, 4 blocks, 1 mesh, 1 block, ch 5, turn.

Fig. 5-8 *Rectangular filet crochet patch #B6*

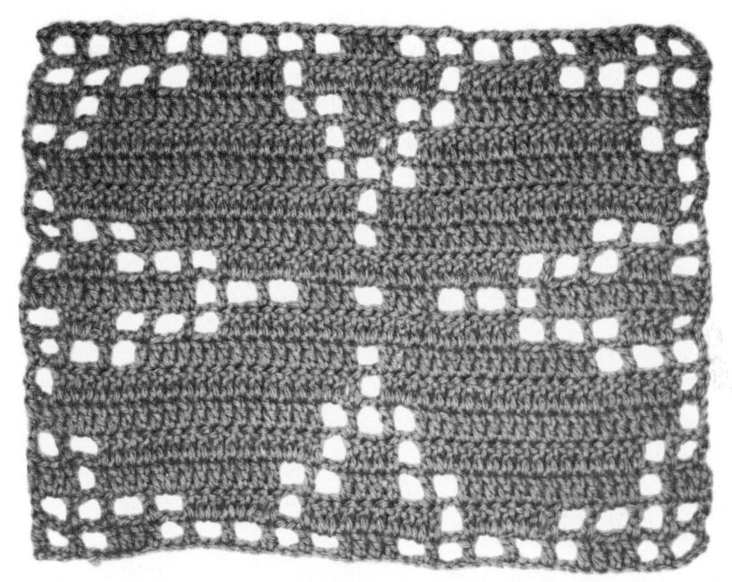

Fig. 5-9 *Rectangular filet crochet patch #B7*

*Row 4:* Skip first 3 dc, 1 dc in next dc, 1 mesh, 5 blocks, 1 mesh, 1 block, 1 mesh, 5 blocks, 2 mesh, ch 5, turn.

*Row 5:* 1 dc in next dc, 6 blocks, 3 mesh, 6 blocks, 1 mesh, ch 5, turn.

*Row 6:* 1 dc in next dc, 7 blocks, 1 mesh, 7 blocks, 1 mesh, ch 5, turn.

*Row 7:* 1 dc in next dc, 2 more mesh, 5 blocks, 1 mesh, 5 blocks, 3 mesh, ch 5, turn.

*Row 8:* 1 dc in next dc, 1 block, 3 mesh, 7 blocks, 3 mesh, 1 block, 1 mesh, ch 3, turn.

*Row 9:* 4 blocks, 3 mesh, 1 block, 1 mesh, 1 block, 3 mesh, 4 blocks, ch 5, turn.

*Row 10:* Repeat Row 8 across, ch 5 to turn.

*Rows 11, 12, and 13:* Repeat Rows 7, 6, and 5.

*Row 14:* Repeat Row 4, ch 3 to turn.

*Row 15:* Repeat Row 3.

*Row 16:* Repeat Row 2, ch 5 to turn.

*Row 17:* 1 dc in next dc, 1 more mesh, (1 block, 5 mesh) twice, 1 block, 2 mesh, fasten off.

## C. Triangles

#C1 (Fig. 5-10)

Ch 16.

*Row 1:* Starting in 2nd ch from hook, work 1 sc in each ch across, ch 1, turn. (15 sts)

*Row 2:* Dec 1 st at beg of row, work 1 sc in each sc across, ch 1, turn.

*Row 3:* Work 1 sc in each sc to last 2 sts, dec 1 st, ch 1, turn.

Repeat Rows 2 and 3 until 1 st remains, work 1 sc in last sc, fasten off.

Fig. 5-10 *Triangular patch #C1*

Fig. 5-11 *Triangular patch #C2*

#C2 (Fig. 5-11)

Ch 31.

*Row 1:* As Row 1 of #C1. (30 sts)

*Row 2:* Dec 1 st at beg of row, work 1 sc in each sc to last 2 sts, dec 1 st, ch 1, turn.

Repeat Row 2 until 1 st remains, work 1 sc in last sc, fasten off.

#C3 (Fig. 5-12)

Worked in 2 colors. With Color A, ch 2.

*Row 1:* Work 3 sc in 2nd ch from hook, ch 1, turn.

*Row 2:* 2 sc in first sc, 3 sc in next sc, 2 sc in last sc, ch 1, turn: 7 sc.

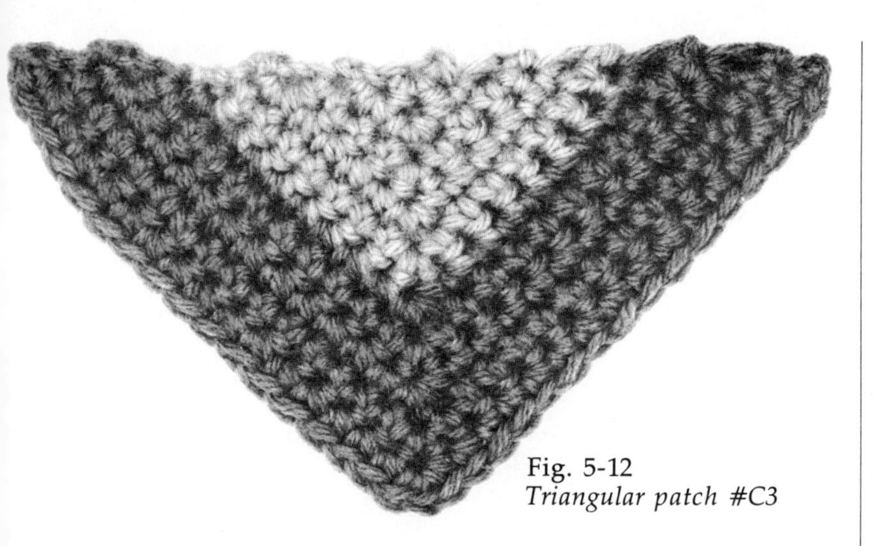

Fig. 5-12
*Triangular patch #C3*

*Rows 3 and 4:* 2 sc in first sc, 1 sc in each sc to center sc, 3 sc in center sc, 1 sc in each sc to last sc, 2 sc in last sc, ch 1, turn.

*Row 5:* 1 sc in each sc to center sc, 3 sc in center sc, 1 sc in each sc to end, break off Color A. Join Color B, ch 1, turn.

*Row 6, 7, and 8:* 2 sc in first sc, 1 sc in each sc to center sc, 3 sc in center sc, 1 sc in each sc to last sc, 2 sc in last sc, ch 1, turn.

*Row 9:* 1 sc in each sc to center sc, 3 sc in center sc, 1 sc in each sc to end, ch 1, turn.

*Row 10:* Repeat Row 6, fasten off.

#C4 (FIG. 5-13)
Exactly the same as #C3, alternating 2 rows of each color.

Fig. 5-13
*Triangular patch #C4*

#C5 (Not illustrated)
Exactly the same as #C3 for first five rows, starting with 3 rows of one color, and finishing with 2 rows of contrasting color, fasten off.

#C6 (FIG. 5-14)
Ch 4, join with sl st to form a ring.

*Row 1:* Ch 4, 1 dc in ring,* ch 2; 1 dc, ch 1 and 1 dc in ring, repeat from* 4 times more, ch 2, sl st in top of ch-4.

*Row 2:* 1 sc in first ch-1 sp,* 1 dc, ch 1, 1 dc, ch 1 and 1 dc in next ch-2 sp; 1 sc in next ch-1 sp, repeat from* around, end last repeat with sl st in first sc.

*Row 3:* Ch 4,* (1 sc in next ch-1 sp) twice, ch 1; 2 tr, ch 5 and 1 tr in next sc, (ch 1, 1 sc in next ch-1

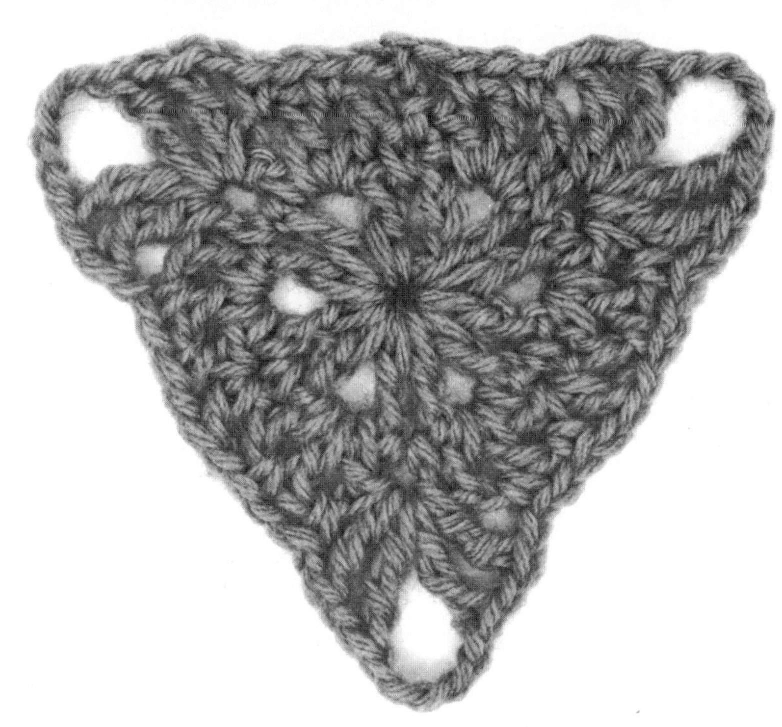

Fig. 5-14 *Triangular patch #C6*

sp) twice, ch 1, 1 dc in next sc, ch 1, repeat from * around, end last repeat with sl st in 3rd st of ch-4, fasten off.

### D. Miscellaneous Shapes

#D1—PENTAGON (FIG. 5-15)

Ch 6, join with sl st to form a ring.

*Row 1:* Ch 3 to count as 1 dc, 2 dc in ring, ch 2, (3 dc, ch 2) 4 times in ring. Join with sl st in top of ch-3. Fasten off when another color is used for next row.

To continue with same color, sl st across next 2 dc and into ch-2 sp. Ch 3 to count as first dc of next row.

Fig. 5-15 *Pentagonal patch #D1*

*All rows start and end the same.*

*Row 2:* With loop on hook work 3 dc, ch 2, 3 dc, and ch 1 in each space around. Join in top of first dc.

*Row 3:* With loop on hook,* 3 dc, ch 2, 3 dc in ch-2 sp, ch 1, 3 dc in next sp, ch 1, repeat from* around. Join.

*Row 4:* With loop on hook,* 3 dc, ch 2, 3 dc in ch-2 sp, ch 1, (3 dc in next sp, ch 1 to next ch-2 sp), repeat from* around. Join.

Repeat Row 4 to desired size.

#D2--HEXAGON (FIG. 5-16)

Ch 6, join with sl st to form a ring.

*Row 1:* Ch 5,* 1 dc in ring, ch 2, repeat from* 10 times more, sl st in 3rd st of ch-5.

*Row 2:* Ch 3, 2 dc in next ch-2 sp, 1 dc in next dc, ch 3,* 1 dc in next dc, 2 dc in next sp, 1 dc in next dc, ch 3, repeat from* 4 times more, sl st in top of ch-3.

*Row 3: Work in back loop only of each dc throughout:* Ch 3, 1 dc in same st, 1 dc in each of next 2 dc, 2 dc in next dc, ch 3,* 2 dc in next dc, 1 dc in each of next 2 dc, 2 dc in next dc, ch 3, repeat from* 4 times more, sl st in top of ch-3.

*Row 4:* Ch 3, 1 dc in same st, 1 dc in each of next 4 dc, 2 dc in next dc, ch 3,* 2 dc in next dc, 1 dc in each of next 4 dc, 2 dc in next dc, ch 3, repeat from* 4 times more, sl st in top of ch-3.

*Row 5:* Ch 3, 1 dc in each of next 7 dc, ch 4, 1 sc in next sp, ch 4,* 1 dc in each of next 8 dc, ch 4, 1 sc in next sp, ch 4, repeat from* 4 times more, sl st in top of ch-3.

*Row 6:* Sl st in next dc, ch 3, 1 dc in each of next 5 dc, ch 4, (1 sc in next sp, ch 4) twice,* skip 1 dc, 1 dc in each of next 6 dc, ch 4, (1 sc in next sp, ch 4) twice, repeat from* 4 times more, sl st in top of ch-3.

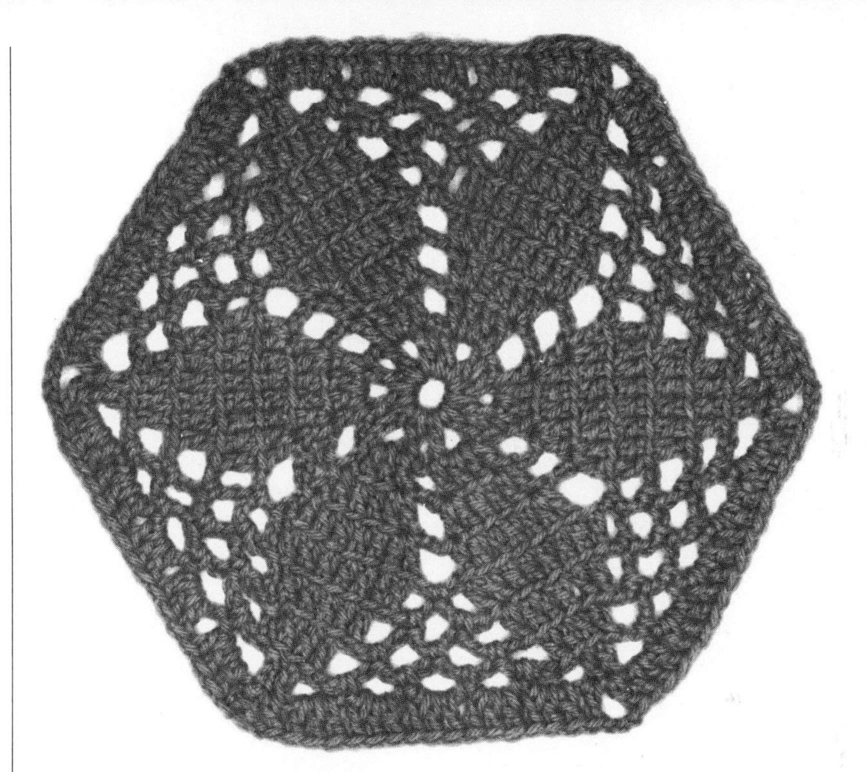

Fig 5-16 *Hexagonal patch #D2*

*Row 7:* Sl st in next dc, ch 3, 1 dc in each of next 3 dc, ch 4, (1 sc in next sp, ch 4) 3 times,* skip 1 dc, 1 dc in each of next 4 dc, ch 4, (1 sc in next sp, ch 4) 3 times, repeat from* 4 times more, sl st in top of ch-3.

*Row 8:* Sl st in next dc, ch 3, 1 dc in next dc, ch 4, (1 sc in next sp, ch 4) 4 times,* skip 1 dc, 1 dc in next 2 dc, ch 4, (1 sc in next sp, ch 4) 4 times, repeat from* 4 times more, sl st in top of ch-3.

*Row 9:* Ch 6, 1 dc in next dc, 3 dc in each of next 5 sps,* 1 dc in next dc, ch 3, 1 dc in next dc, 3 dc in each of next 5 sps, repeat from* 4 times more, sl st in 3rd st of ch-6.

#D3—Octagon (Not illustrated)

This is a simple octagon which is used for a rug in the next chapter (see Fig. 6-18).

Ch 4, join with sl st to form a ring.

*Row 1:* Ch 1, 8 sc in ring, sl st to first sc.

*Row 2:* Ch 1, 2 sc in each sc around, sl st in top of first sc (16 sc).

*Row 3:* Ch 1,* 1 sc in next sc, 2 sc in next sc, repeat from* around, sl st in top of first sc.

*Row 4:* Ch 1,* 1 sc in each of next 2 sc, 3 sc in next sc for a corner, repeat from* around, sl st in top of first sc, fasten off.

## Instructions for Joining the Patches

*Sewn Together*

For a smooth finish, always sew your motifs together. Use the same yarn for sewing up as you have used to make the patches. You will need a large-eyed, blunt-ended tapestry needle, a pair of embroidery scissors for clipping ends of the yarn, and the longest steel pins you can find.

Pin the patches together in the pattern you want, with their right sides together. Cut a piece of yarn about 20 to 22 inches long, and knot it at roughly one inch from the end. Thread your needle, and begin sewing by drawing the yarn carefully through the patches up to the knot. Do not pull the knot itself through. Now lay the one-inch end of yarn down along the seam you are going to sew. Begin to work along the seam using overcasting stitches, covering the end of yarn as you go. Keep checking to see that you are not pulling the stitches too tight, or creating an ugly and stiff ridge by working stitches too close together. A good rule is to work one sewn stitch for each crocheted stitch or row. When you come to the end of your thread, weave your needle in and out of the stitches just worked for an inch or so. Pull the remaining end through and clip off any excess yarn.

When you have finished sewing the patches together, give them a very light press, using a damp cloth. If you have a steam iron, spray the work with jets of steam, concentrating on the seams. Gently ease the crochet into shape, flattening bulges with your fingers while the work is still damp and hot. Leave it flat to dry out. Moving or hanging the work while it is still very damp will result in stretching and distortion.

Always try to avoid flattening the surface of crochet by pressing down hard with the iron. All crochet work is better steamed rather than pressed, and some stitches, such as the puff stitch, must *never* be pressed.

### *Crocheted Together*

If you like a ridged effect on the surface of your work, try crocheting patches together, but I would recommend this method for square or rectangular patches only. Other shapes are far too complicated for an average worker.

Lay out your patches in the pattern you want. You may find it helpful to pin pieces together, but strictly speaking this should not be necessary when crocheting. As you will be creating your ridges on the right side of the work, place the patches with their wrong sides together. Join the yarn to the right-hand side of the front patch. Work a row of single crochet or slip stitch along the "seam" by inserting the hook into the next stitch on the front patch, then into the corresponding stitch on the patch at the back before pulling the yarn through.

Work all the horizontal joins into rows first; then work the vertical "seams" in the same way. By doing this you will achieve a neat ridged pattern on the surface of the finished item, and not a hodge-podge of random top-stitching.

The use of single crochet for joining will create seams that "stand up" more than slip stitch, which lies almost flat, and looks like an extra chain stitch worked on the surface. If you want to accentuate the crocheted joins, try working them in a contrasting color.

# 6 Patchwork Crochet Projects

When working any of the crochet projects that follow, check your gauge before you begin by making a patch about 3 inches square in the stitch and with the yarn given in the instructions. If you have more stitches and rows to the inch than given, your gauge is tighter than the instructions require. Change to a size larger hook and check again. If you have fewer stitches and rows to the inch, change to a size smaller hook and make another square. Your gauge is too loose, and the smaller hook will help tighten the correct gauge. This will ensure that your finished item has the right dimensions, and that you will not use more yarn than given in the instructions.

Designs marked* are suitable for relative newcomers to crocheting.

**Cushion in Squares*** (Fig. 6-1)

FINISHED SIZE: Approx. 16″ × 16″

YOU NEED: 4-ply acrylic.

1 4-oz. skein in medium brown (Shade A)
1 4-oz. skein in scarlet (Shade B)
1 4-oz. skein in orange (Shade C)
A size-I aluminum crochet hook.

GAUGE: 6 sts and 7 rows to 2 inches over sc using a size-I hook.

THE CUSHION: based on patches #A2 and #A3 in Chapter 5.

*Square #1* (Make 12.)
Work #A2 in Shade A.

*Square #2* (Make 7.)
Work #A3 as follows:
*Rows 1–4:* in Shade B
*Row 5:* In Shade C
*Row 6:* In Shade A

*Square #3* (Make 6.)
Work #A3 as follows:
*Rows 1–4:* In Shade C
*Row 5:* In Shade A
*Row 6:* In Shade B

TO FINISH: Sew squares together as shown in Fig. 6-1. Attach Shade C to a corner, and work 1 row of sc around entire edge of cushion, working 3 sc to turn at each corner; break off C, join B, sl st in first st.

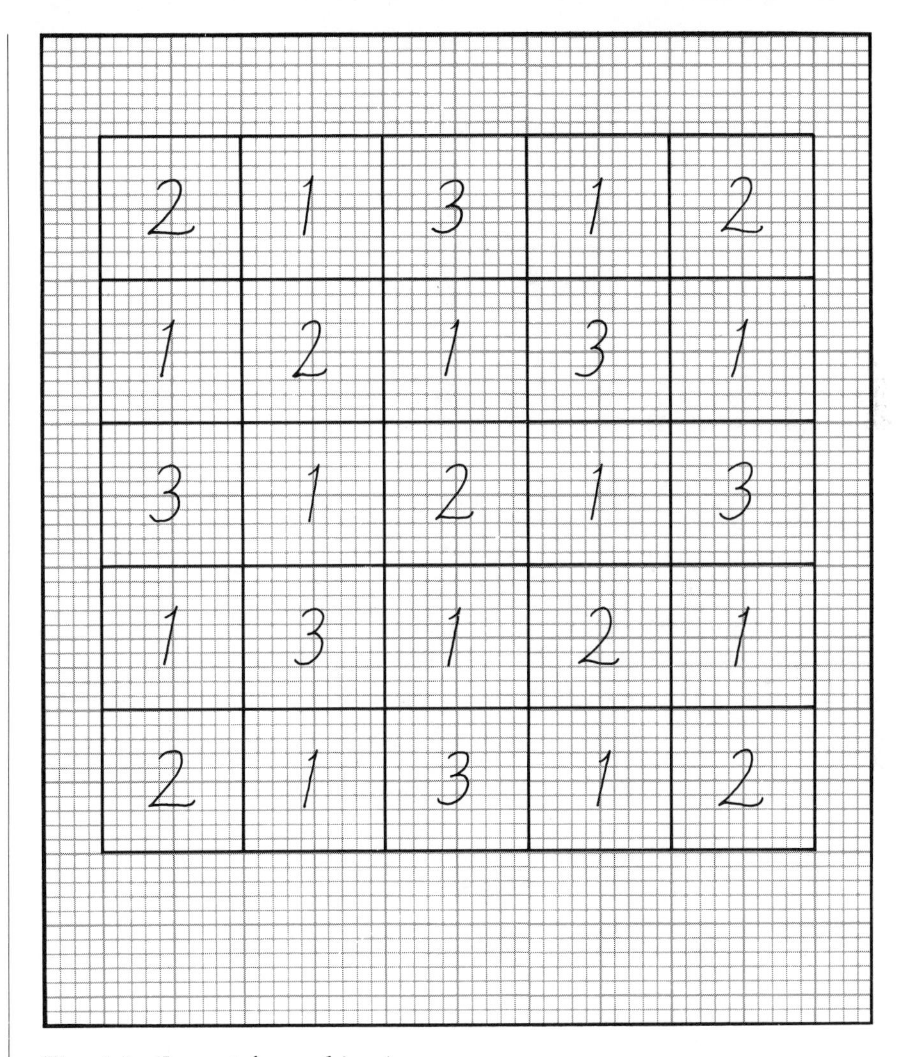


Fig. 6-1 *Layout for cushion in squares*

Work one round in Shade B and one in Shade A in the same manner, fasten off. You will have enough yarn to repeat the design for the back of the cushion if you so wish, or you can use a backing fabric if you prefer.

**Cushion in Triangles** (Fig. 6-2)

FINISHED SIZE: APPROX. 18½" × 18½"
YOU NEED: 4-ply acrylic.
1 4-oz. skein copper (Shade A)
1 4-oz. skein scarlet (Shade B)
A size-I aluminum crochet hook

GAUGE: A completed triangle measures 3 inches along its short sides and 4 inches along its longest side.
THE CUSHION: Based on the triangular patch #C5 from Chapter 5.

*Triangle #1* (Make 28.)
Work #C5 as follows:
*Rows 1 and 3:* Shade A
*Rows 4 and 5:* Shade B

*Triangle #2* (Make 28)
Work #C5 as follows:
*Rows 1–3:* Shade B
*Rows 4 and 5:* Shade A

*Filler triangles* are used for corners and sides, as shown in Fig. 6-2.

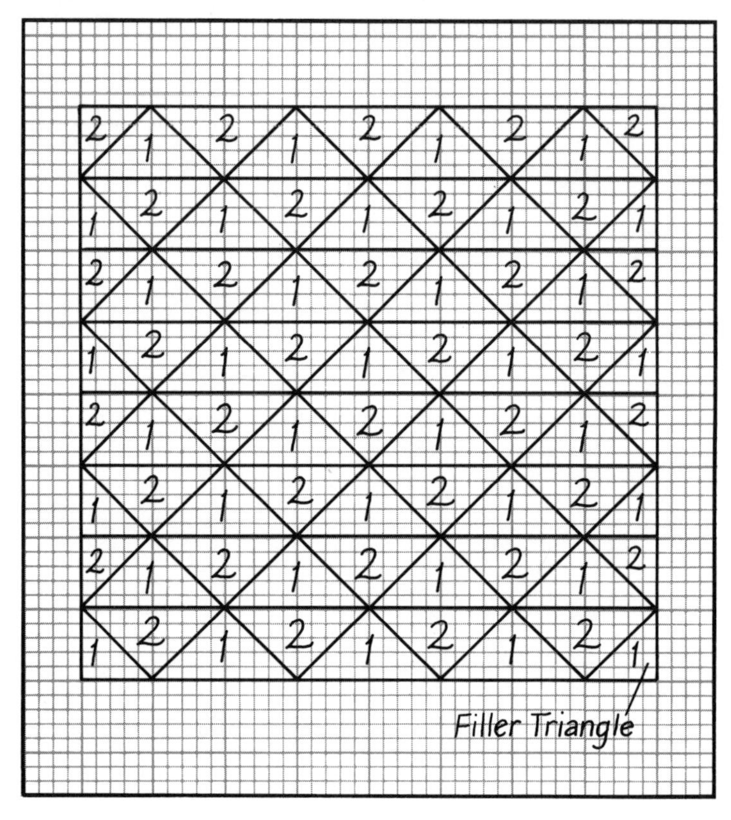


Fig. 6-2 *Layout for cushion in triangles*

*Filler #1* (Make 8.)
With Shade A, ch 2.
*Row 1:* 1 sc in 2nd ch from hook, ch 1, turn.
*Row 2:* 3 sc in sc, ch 1, turn.
*Row 3:* Work row in sc, inc by working 2 sc in first and last sc of row, break off A, join B, ch 1, turn.

*Rows 4 and 5:* As Row 3 but in Shade B, fasten off.

*Filler #2* (Make 8.)
Work as Filler #1 as follows:
*Rows 1–3:* Shade B
*Rows 4 and 5:* Shade A

To Finish: Sew triangles together as shown in Fig. 6-2. Attach Shade B to a corner, and work 1 row of sc around entire edge of cushion, working 3 sc to turn at each corner, break off B, join A, sl st in first sc.

Work two more rounds in the same manner in Shade A, fasten off.

You will have sufficient yarn left to repeat the design for the back of your cushion, or you can use a backing fabric if you prefer.

**Floor Cushion in Squares** (Fig. 6-3)

Finished Size: Approx. 28″ × 28″
You Need: 4-ply acrylic.
2 4-oz. skeins copper (Shade A)
1 4-oz. skein off-white (Shade B)
1 4-oz. skein brown (Shade C)
A size-I aluminum crochet hook

Gauge: A completed square measures 3 inches × 3 inches, and 4 inches across the diagonal.
The Cushion: Based on square patches #A2 and #A4 and triangle #C5, all from Chapter 5.

*Square #1* (Make 25.)
Work #A2 in Shade A.

*Square #2* (Make 36.)
Work #A4 as follows:
*Rows 1–3:* Shade B
*Rows 4 and 5:* Shade C
*Row 6:* Shade B

*Triangle #1* (Make 20.)
Work #C5 as follows:
*Rows 1–5:* Shade A

*Filler Triangle #2* (Make 4.)
Work as Filler #1 in "Cushion in Triangles," earlier in this chapter, working all five rows in Shade A.

To Finish: Sew squares and triangles together as shown in Fig. 6-3. Attach Shade B to a corner, and work 1 row of sc around entire edge of cushion, working 3 sc to turn at each corner, break off B, join C, sl st in first sc. Work two more rounds in Shade C in the same way, fasten off.

Because this cushion is to be used on the floor, it is suggested that you back the crocheted square with a closely woven cotton fabric. You will not have sufficient yarn to make a crocheted back.

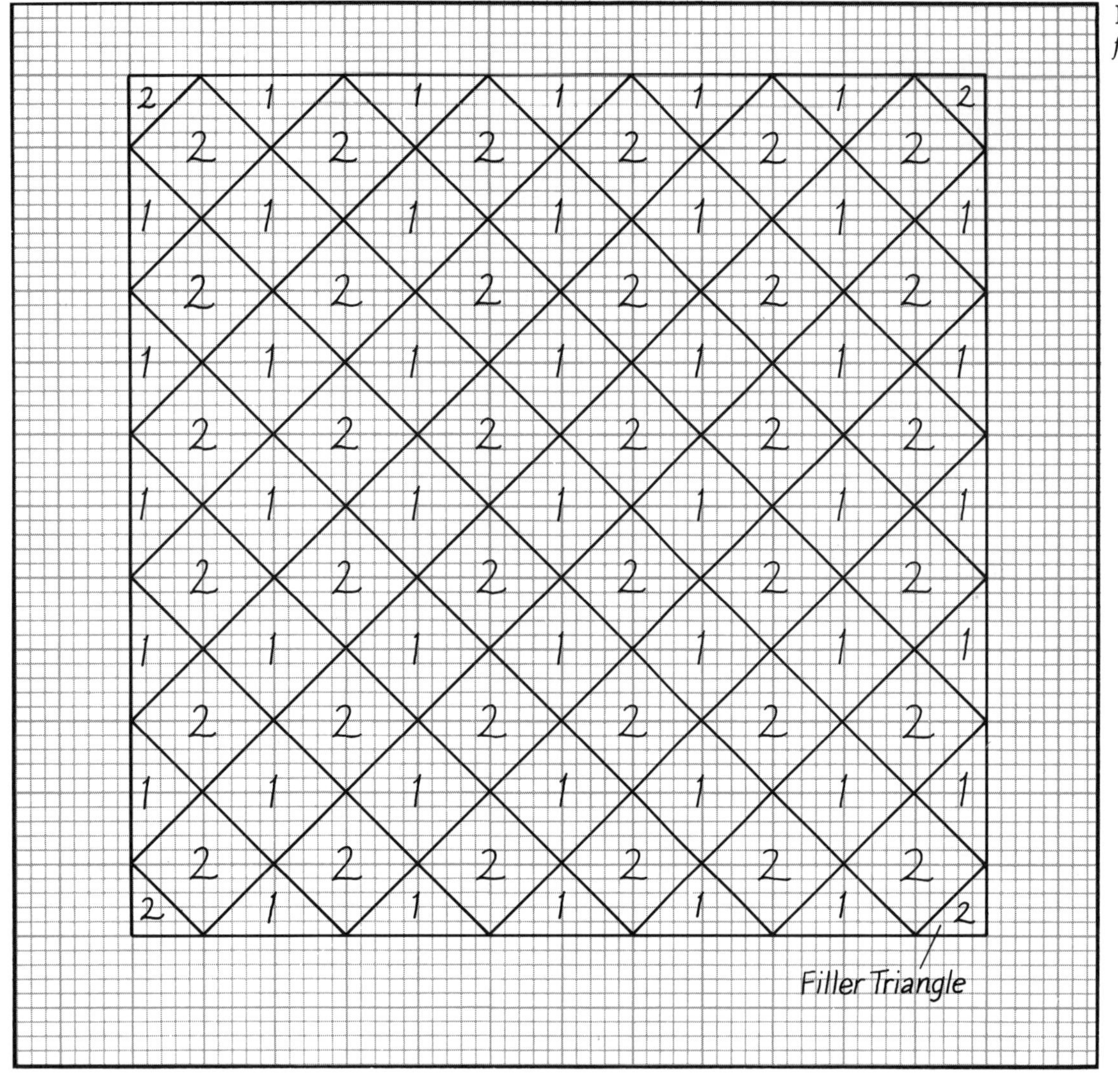


Fig. 6-3 *Layout for filler triangle floor cushion in squares*

Fig. 6-4 *Floor seat in squares and rectangles*

**Floor Seat in Squares and Rectangles***
(Fig. 6-4)

The floor seat consists of two oversize cushions, one measuring 3 feet × 3 feet for sitting on—forming the base of the seat—and the other measuring 2 feet × 3 feet for leaning against—forming the back of the seat. The front of each cushion is worked in a patchwork design (Fig. 6-5); the backs are crocheted in straight single crochet in the main color.

To make both cushions—

YOU NEED: 4-ply acrylic.
- 9 4-oz. skeins in medium brown (Shade A)
- 2 4-oz. skeins in off-white (Shade B)
- 2 3½-oz. skeins in brown ombré (Shade C)
- 3 4-oz. skeins in dark brown (Shade D)
- A size-I aluminum crochet hook

GAUGE: 6 sts and 7 rows to 2 inches over sc using a size-I hook.

THE CUSHIONS: To make both cushions you will require the following patches:

*Patch #1:* Measures 4″ × 4″.
Ch 15.
*Row 1:* Starting in 2nd ch from hook, work 1 sc in each ch across (14 sts), ch 1, turn.
Continue working in sc until 16 rows have been completed, fasten off.

*Make:*
30 in Shade B
30 in Shade C

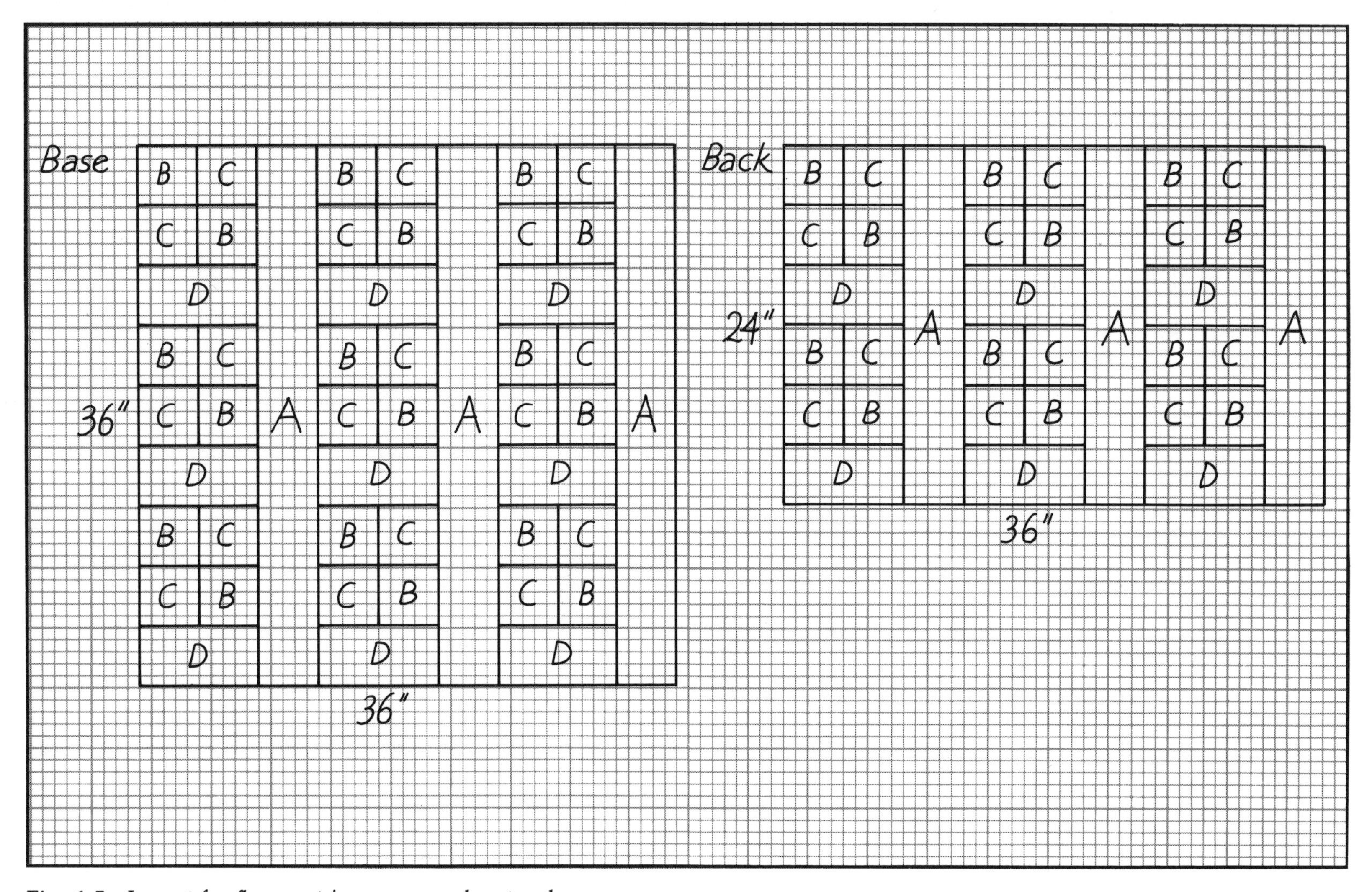


Fig. 6-5 *Layout for floor seat in squares and rectangles*

*Patch #2:* Measures 8″ × 4″.
Ch 29.
*Row 1:* Starting in 2nd ch from hook, work 1 sc in each ch across (28 sts), ch 1, turn.
Continue working in sc until 16 rows have been completed, fasten off.

*Make:*
15 in Shade D

*Patch #3:* Measures 4″ × 36″.
Work as for Patch #1, but continue in sc until 144 rows have been worked, fasten off.

*Make:*
3 in Shade A

*Patch #4:* Measures 4″ × 24″.
Work as for Patch #1, but continue in sc until 96 have been worked, fasten off.

*Make:*
3 in Shade A

BACKING FOR 3′ × 3′ CUSHION: Measures 36″ × 36″.
With Shade A, ch 127.
*Row 1:* Starting in 2nd ch from hook, work 1 sc in each ch across (126 sts), ch 1, turn.
Continue working in sc until 144 rows have been completed, fasten off.

BACKING FOR 2′ × 3′ CUSHION: Measures 24″ × 36″.
Work as other backing piece, but continue in sc until 96 rows have been worked, fasten off.

TO FINISH: Sew the patches together as shown in Fig. 6-5. Sew the backs to the fronts to make cushion covers.

**Patchwork Denim Sweater** (Fig. 6-6)

FINISHED SIZES: Small (6–8), medium (10–12). Instructions for the medium size appear in parentheses.

Fig. 6-6 *Patchwork denim sweater*

YOU NEED: 4-ply acrylic. These amounts apply for both small and medium sizes.

2 4-oz. skeins dark blue (Shade A)
2 4-oz. skeins blue ombré (Shade B)
2 4-oz. skeins light blue (Shade C)
2 4-oz. skeins medium blue (Shade D)
A size-I aluminum crochet hook
One dozen ½-inch buttons to match

GAUGE: 6 sts and 7 rows to 2 inches over sc using a size-I hook.

THE SWEATER

*Patch #1* (Basic square patch).
Ch 13 (15).
*Row 1:* Starting in 2nd ch from hook, work 1 sc in each ch across, ch 1, turn. 12 (14) sts.
Continue working in sc, until 14 (16) rows have been completed, fasten off.

*Make:*
9 in Shade A
11 in Shade B
10 in Shade C
8 in Shade D

LOWER ARMHOLE PATCH

Ch 10 (12). Work in sc on these 9 (11) sts for 3 rows.
*Row 4:* Dec 1 st at beg of row, work in sc to end, ch 1, turn.
*Row 5:* 1 sc in each sc across, ch 1, turn.
*Row 6:* As Row 4.
Continue working on these 7 (9) sts until 14 (16) rows of sc have been completed, fasten off.

*Make:*
2 in Shade A
2 in Shade D

UPPER ARMHOLE PATCH

Ch 8 (10). Work in sc on these 7 (9) sts for 14 (16) rows, fasten off.

*Make:*
2 in Shade C
2 in Shade D

FRONT NECK PATCH

Ch 13 (15). Work in sc on these 12 (14) sts for 9 (10) rows.
*Next Row:* 1 sc in each of next 4 (5) sc, ch 1, turn.
*Dec Row:* * Dec 1 sc at beg of next row at neck edge, complete row in sc, ch 1, turn.
Work 1 row in sc.
Repeat from* once more, fasten off.

*Make:*
1 in Shade A
1 in Shade B
Following Fig. 6-7, sew up the body of sweater as shown.

SLEEVES: (Made in two halves)
*First Half:* (Make 2.)
With Shade C, ch 13 (14).

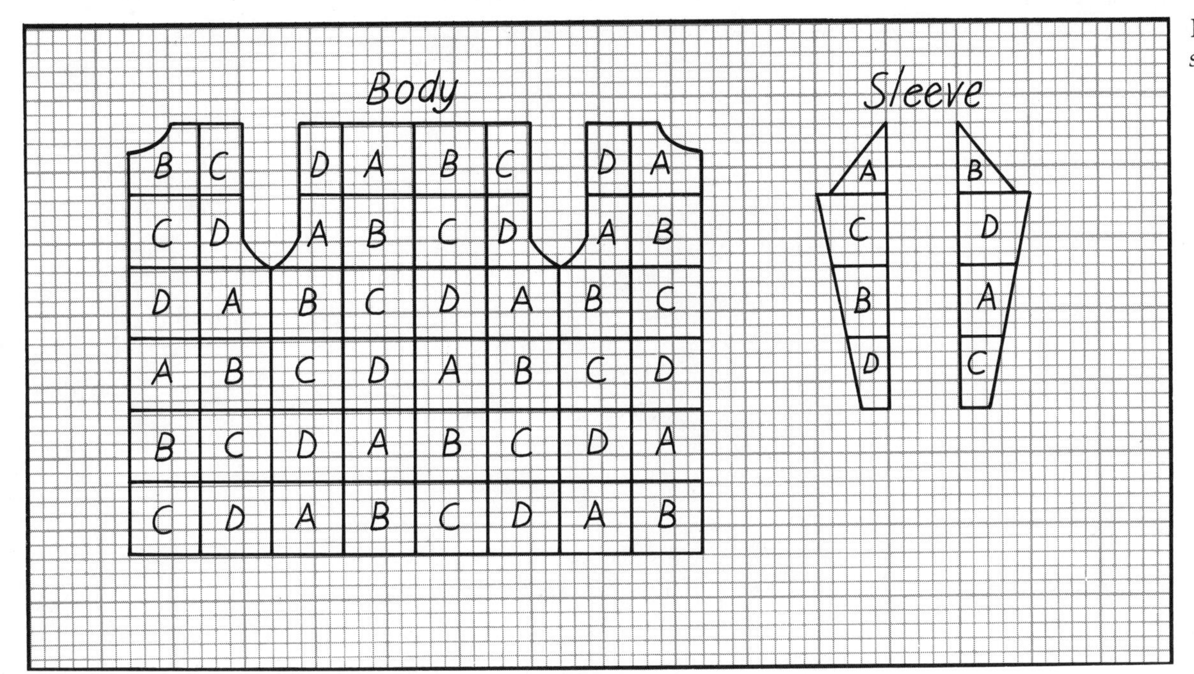


Fig. 6-7 *Layout for sweater in square patches*

*Row 1:* Starting in 2nd ch from hook, work 1 sc in each ch across, ch 1, turn.

Work 2 more rows in sc.

*Row 4—Increase Row:* Increase 1 st at beg of row.

Work one *Increase Row* on every 8th row until there are 20 (21) sts.

*At the same time:* Change color in the following sequence:

20 rows C
20 rows A
20 rows D, break off D.

*Sleeve Cap:* Join B in 4th st from beg of row, ch 1, 1 sc in same st, 1 sc in each st across, ch 1, turn.

Work 1 row in sc.

*Decrease Row:* Decrease 1 st at beg of row, work in sc across, ch 1, turn.

Repeat the last 2 rows until 7 sc remain, fasten off.

*Second Half:* (Make 2.)

Make the second half of the sleeve in exactly the same way as the first, changing color as follows:

20 rows D
20 rows B

20 rows C
Finish sleeve cap in A.

To Finish: Following Fig. 6-7, sew sleeve halves together. Sew sleeve and shoulder seams of body of sweater. Set in sleeves.

Border: With right side of work facing you, attach Shade B to bottom of sweater on right-hand side, and begin working a row of sc across bottom of sweater. Work 3 sc to turn the corner, then work up right front of sweater, working 3 more sc at front neck-edge corner. Work around neck, then complete other side to match, and end with a sl st in first sc.

*Row 2:* Tie contrasting yarn markers to sts at equal intervals to mark the position of twelve buttonholes which must be worked on the right-hand front on this row. A buttonhole is worked by ch 2 and skipping 2 sc. Work around entire sweater in sc, making 3 sc to turn at corners as before.

*Row 3:* Work another row of sc around sweater, making 2 sc in each ch-2 buttonhole space.

*Row 4:* 1 row sc, sl st in first sc, fasten off. Sew buttons on left front to correspond to buttonholes.

**Irish Patch Afghan** (Fig. 6-8)

Finished Size: Approx. 37″ × 60″

You Need: 4-ply acrylic.

9 4-oz. skeins off-white

A size-I aluminum crochet hook

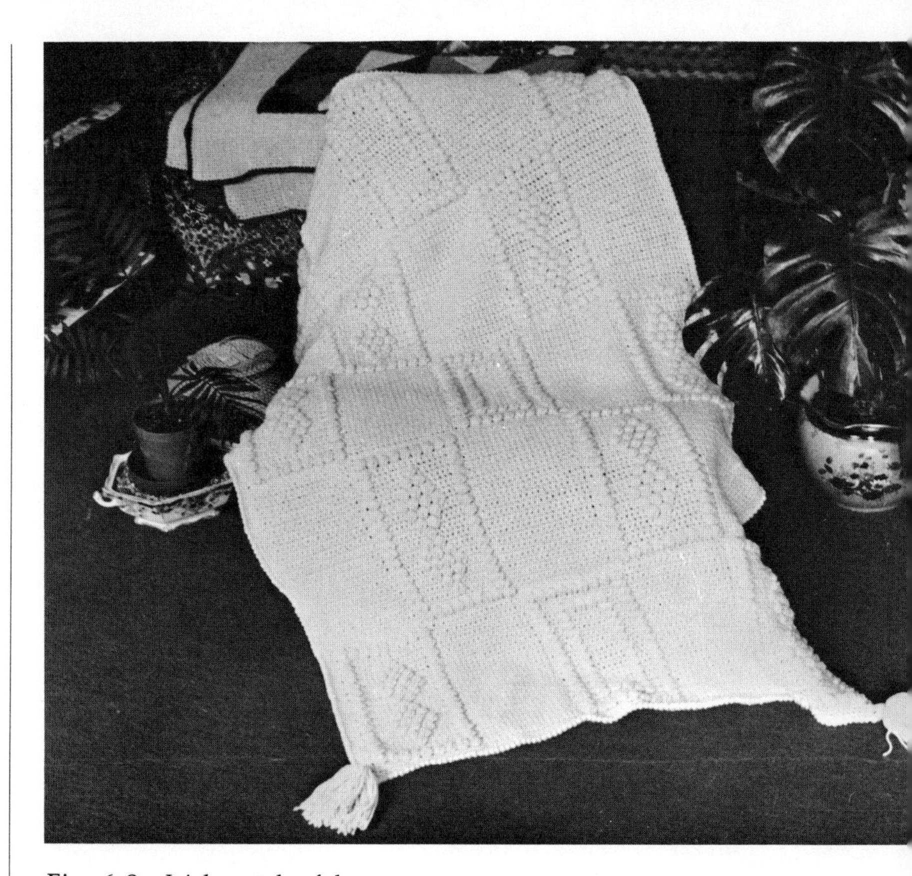

Fig. 6-8 *Irish patch afghan*

GAUGE: 6 sts and 7 rows to 2 inches over sc using a size-I hook.
THE AFGHAN: Based on the rectangular patches #B1, #B2, and #B3 from Chapter 5. The patchwork effect in this design is not achieved by contrasting colors, but by juxtaposing different textures.
*Patch #B1:* Make 12.
*Patch #B2:* Make 3.
*Patch #B3:* Make 10.

TO FINISH: Sew the patches together as shown in Fig. 6-9, taking care to place the foundation ch at the bottom of each patch, so that all the stitches run the same way. Attach yarn to bottom corner, to work along the foundation chains of the five patches. Work a row of sc around entire afghan, working 3 sc in each corner to turn, sl st in first sc.
*Row 2:* Ch 1, 1 sc in each sc around, sl st in first sc.
*Row 3:* As first row.
*Row 4:* Ch 1, with same side of work facing, begin working a row of sc from left to right, instead of from right to left. This creates the rippled edge which you can see in Fig. 6-8. Finish with a sl st in first sc worked, fasten off.

Do not press the finished afghan; pressing it would completely flatten and spoil the puff stitches. Instead, gently steam out any bulges or distortions along the seams. Finish by making four tassels following the method described under "Making a Cushion" in Chapter 9. Instead of using folded cardboard, wind the yarn around a small hard-cover book about 5½ inches wide. Wind the yarn around 60 times rather than 50, to create a thicker tassel. Attach one tassel to each of the four corners of the afghan.

### Log Cabin Afghan* (Fig. 6-10)

This design is worked entirely in very simple single crochet. Based on the traditional American quilt design of the same name, the pieces are worked separately, then sewn together. As there are no awkward shapes or corners to cope with, this afghan would be a highly suitable project for a recent beginner in crochet. The fact that it is worked in strips makes it easy to carry around while in progress.

FINISHED SIZE: APPROX. 41" × 60"
YOU NEED: Yarn as follows:
- 8 2-oz. skeins tweed in charcoal gray (Shade A)
- 3 4-oz. skeins 4-ply worsted-weight wool in black (Shade B)
- 2 4-oz. skeins 4-ply worsted-weight wool in white (Shade C)
- A size-I aluminum crochet hook

GAUGE: 6 sts and 7 rows to 2" over sc using a size-I hook.
THE AFGHAN: Before actually starting work, take a careful look at Fig. 6-11, which shows the layout of the different sections. We are going to start in the center with piece #1, worked in Shade A, and work out to the edges.

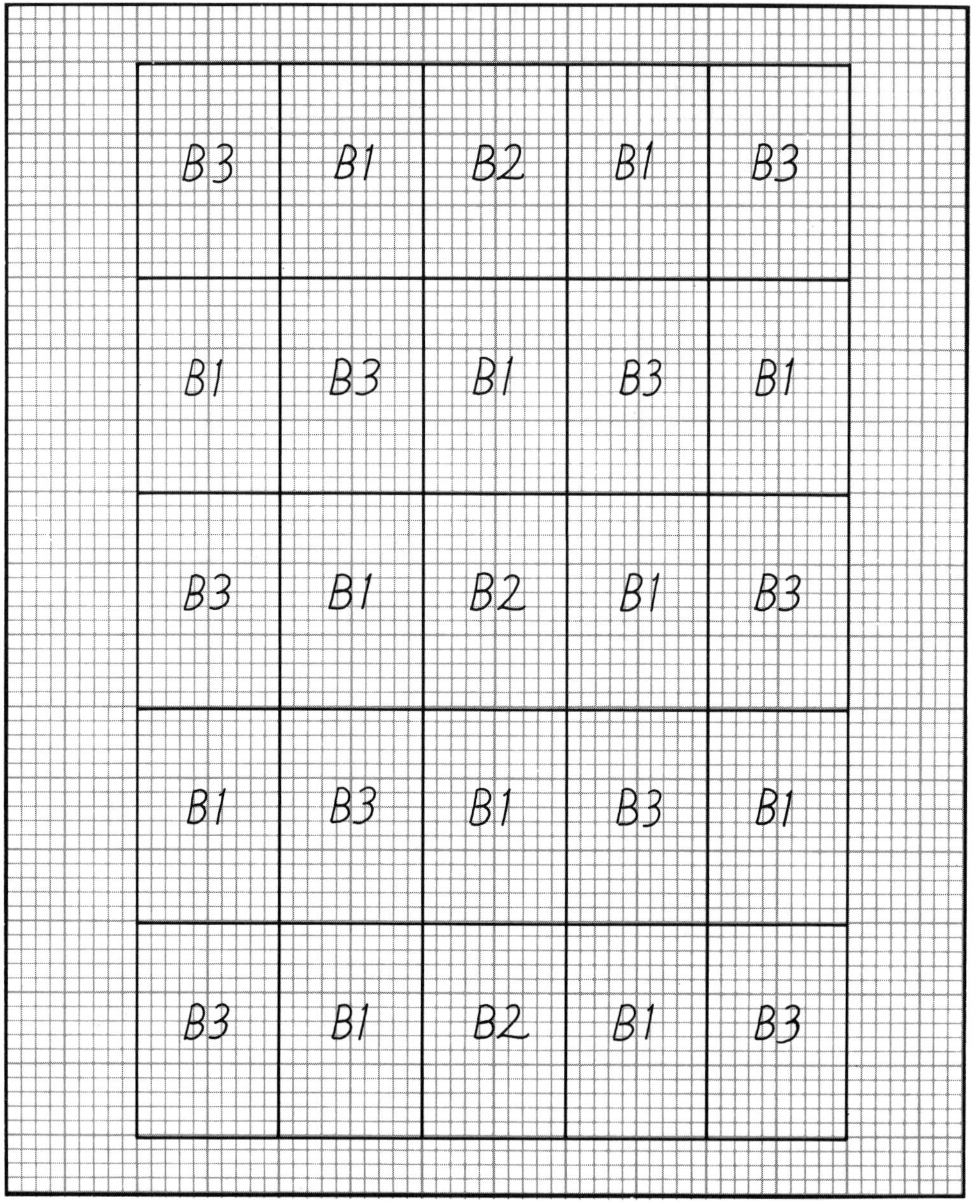

| B3 | B1 | B2 | B1 | B3 |
|---|---|---|---|---|
| B1 | B3 | B1 | B3 | B1 |
| B3 | B1 | B2 | B1 | B3 |
| B1 | B3 | B1 | B3 | B1 |
| B3 | B1 | B2 | B1 | B3 |

Fig. 6-9 *Layout for Irish patch afghan*

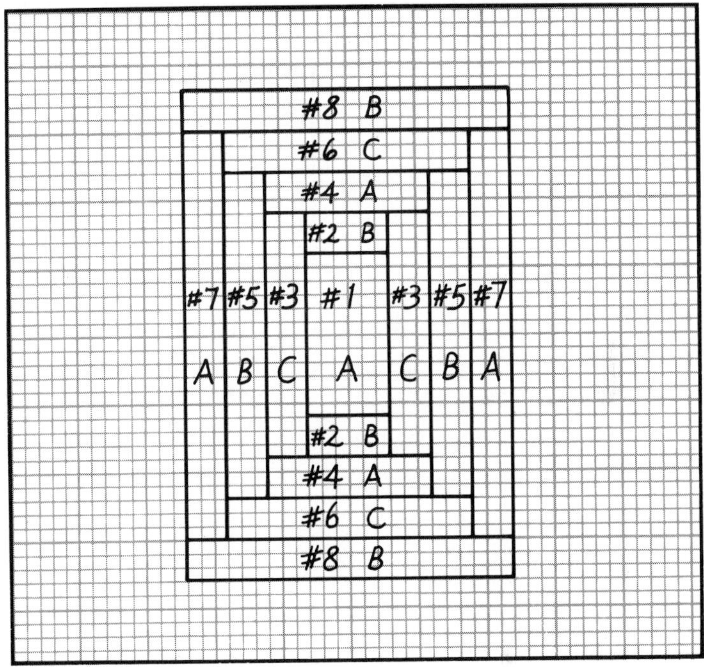


Fig. 6-11 *Layout for "Log Cabin" afghan*

Fig. 6-10 *"Log Cabin" afghan*

*Piece #1* (Make one.)
With A and a size-I hook, ch 31.
*Row 1:* 1 sc in 2nd ch from hook, 1 sc in each ch across (30 sts), ch 1, turn.
*Row 2:* 1 sc in each sc across, ch 1, turn.
Repeat Row 2 until 70 rows have been worked in all.
Fasten off.

*Piece #2* (Make 2.)
With Shade B and a size-I hook, work as Piece #1 to end of Row 2.
Repeat Row 2 until 18 rows have been worked in all.
Fasten off.

*Piece #3* (Make 2.)
With Shade C and a size-I hook, ch 16.
*Row 1:* 1 sc in 2nd ch from hook, 1 sc in each ch across (15 sts), ch 1 turn.
*Row 2:* 1 sc in each sc across, ch 1, turn.
Repeat Row 2 until 105 rows have been worked in all. Fasten off.

*Piece #4* (Make 2.)
With Shade A and a size-I hook, ch 61.
Work as Piece #1 to end of Row 2 (you will have 60 sts).
Repeat Row 2 until 18 rows have been worked in all. Fasten off.

*Piece #5* (Make 2.)
With Shade B and a size-I hook, ch 16.
Work as Piece #3 until 140 rows have been worked in all. Fasten off.

*Piece #6* (Make 2.)
With Shade C and a size-I hook, ch 91.
Work as Piece #1 to end of Row 2 (you will have 90 sts).
Repeat Row 2 until 18 rows have been worked in all. Fasten off.

*Piece #7* (Make 2.)
With Shade A and a size-I hook, ch 16.
Work as Piece #3 until 175 rows have been worked in all. Fasten off.

*Piece #8* (Make 2.)
With Shade B and a size-I hook, ch 121.
Work as Piece #1 to end of Row 2 (you will have 120 sts).
Repeat Row 2 until 18 rows have been worked in all. Fasten off.

To FINISH: Following Fig. 6-11, lay out all the pieces on the floor or a bed, anywhere that you can leave them for the time it will take you to sew them up. Having put all the pieces in place, check to see that the foundation chain row is at the bottom of each piece. This will ensure that the crochet is all running in the same direction.

Begin sewing by taking Piece #1 (in Shade A) from the center of your layout. Attach Pieces #2 at the top and bottom, that is, along the short edges of Piece #1. Attach Pieces #3 on either side, that is, along the long edges. Continue applying strips in this manner, following the numerical order of the pieces, and referring to Fig. 6-11 whenever a problem arises.

Attach Shade A to the bottom of the afghan, so that you can begin working an edging along the foundation chain of Piece #8. Make sure that you have the right side of the work facing you as you start. Work one row of sc around the entire afghan, making 3 sc in each corner to turn, sl st to top of first sc.
*Row 2*: As first row, fasten off.

**Multi-Patched Afghan or Wall Hanging** (Fig. 6-12)

FINISHED SIZE: APPROX. 41" × 63"

YOU NEED: 4-ply worsted-weight wool.

3 4-oz. skeins tan (Shade A)
5 4-oz. skeins off-white (Shade B)
2 4-oz. skeins tangerine (Shade C)
2 4-oz. skeins copper (Shade D)
A size-I aluminum crochet hook

GAUGE: 6 sts and 7 rows to 2 inches over sc using a size-I hook.

THE AFGHAN (OR WALL HANGING): Uses the square shape #A1, and triangular shapes #C1 and #C2, all explained in Chapter 5, in addition to the new shapes described in detail below.

*Piece #1:* The square at the center of the design (see Fig. 6-13).
With Shade A, ch 31.
*Row 1:* Starting in 2nd ch from hook, work 1 sc in each ch across, ch 1, turn.
Continue working in sc until 35 rows have been completed, fasten off.

*Piece #2:* Right-angle triangle (see Fig. 5-10).
Follow the instructions for #C1 in Chapter 5.

*Make:*

16 in Shade A
8 in Shade D

Fig. 6-12 *Multi-patched afghan*

*Piece #3:* Isosceles triangle (see Fig. 5-11).
Follow the instructions for #C2 in Chapter 5.

*Make:*

10 in Shade B
10 in Shade C
8 in Shade D

*Piece #4:* square (see Fig. 5-1).
Follow the instructions for #A1 in Chapter 5.

*Make:*

4 in Shade C

*Piece #5:* L-shaped patches.
With Shade A, ch 31.
*Row 1:* Starting in 2nd ch from hook, work 1 sc in each ch across, ch 1, turn.
Continue working in sc until 18 rows have been completed.
*Row 19:* 1 sc in each of next 15 sc, ch 1, turn.
Continue working on these 15 sts until 35 rows have been completed from the beginning, fasten off.
Make 4 in Shade A.

*Piece #6:* Long side strips.
Follow the instructions for Piece #7 in "Log Cabin Afghan."
Make 2 in Shade B.

*Piece #7:* Top and bottom strips.
Follow the instructions for Piece #8 in "Log Cabin Afghan."
Make 2 in Shade B.

To Finish: Following Fig. 6-13, lay out all the pieces on the floor or on a bed, somewhere you can leave them undisturbed for the time it will take to sew them up. As far as possible, keep the crochet stitches running in the same direction. This will not be entirely possible with this particular design. Just make sure that the patches are arranged in a manner that satisfies your eye. Starting with Piece #1, the center square, add patches according to the diagram.

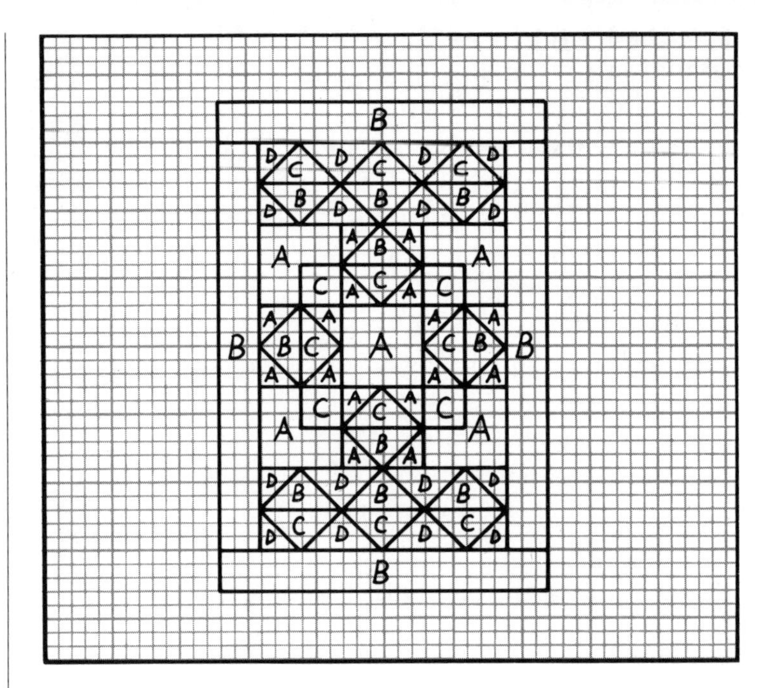


Fig. 6-13 *Layout for multi-patched afghan or wallhanging*

When all the patches are sewn together, join Shade B to the foundation chain at the bottom corner of the afghan. Make sure that you have the right side of the work facing you. Work one round of sc around the entire edge of the afghan, making 3 sc in each corner to turn, break off B, join D, sl st to top of first sc.
*Row 2:* Work 1 sc in each sc around, sl st to top of first sc, fasten off.

**Star-Patched Afghan or Wall Hanging** (Fig. 6-14)

FINISHED SIZE: Approx. 41″ × 58″

YOU NEED: 4-ply worsted-weight wool.
4 4-oz. skeins in black (Shade A)
5 4-oz. skeins in white (Shade B)
A size-I aluminum crochet hook.

GAUGE: 6 sts and 7 rows to 2 inches over sc using a size-I hook.

THE AFGHAN (OR WALL HANGING): Uses the square shape #A1, and triangular shapes #C1 and #C2, all from Chapter 5, in addition to other shapes from the "Multi-Patched Afghan" in this chapter.

*Piece #1:* As Piece #1 in "Multi-Patched Afghan" (see Figs. 6-12 and 6-13)

*Make:*
4 in Shade A

*Piece #2:* Right-angle triangle (see Fig. 5-10)
Follow the instructions for #C1 in Chapter 5.

*Make:*
32 in Shade A

*Piece #3:* Isosceles triangle (see Fig. 5-11)
Follow the instructions for #C2 in Chapter 5.

Make:
16 in Shade B

*Piece #4:* Square (see Fig. 5-1)
Follow the instructions for #A1 in Chapter 5.

*Make:*
16 in Shade B

Fig. 6-14 *Star-patched afghan*

*Piece #5:* Horizontal strips
Follow the instructions for Piece #8 in "Log Cabin Afghan" earlier in this chapter.

*Make:*
3 in Shade B

To Finish: Following Fig. 6-15, lay out all the pieces on the floor or on a bed, somewhere you can leave them undisturbed for the time it will take to sew them up. Try to keep the crochet stitches running in the same direction as far as possible. Start with Piece #1 at the center of each star, and build the other pieces around it.

When the sewing is completed, attach Shade B to the foundation chain at the bottom corner of the afghan. Make sure that you have the right side of the work facing you. Work one row of sc around the entire edge of the afghan, making 3 sc in each corner to turn, break off B, join A, sl st to top of first sc.

*Row 2:* Work 1 sc in each sc around, sl st to top of first sc.

*Row 3:* As first row, fasten off.

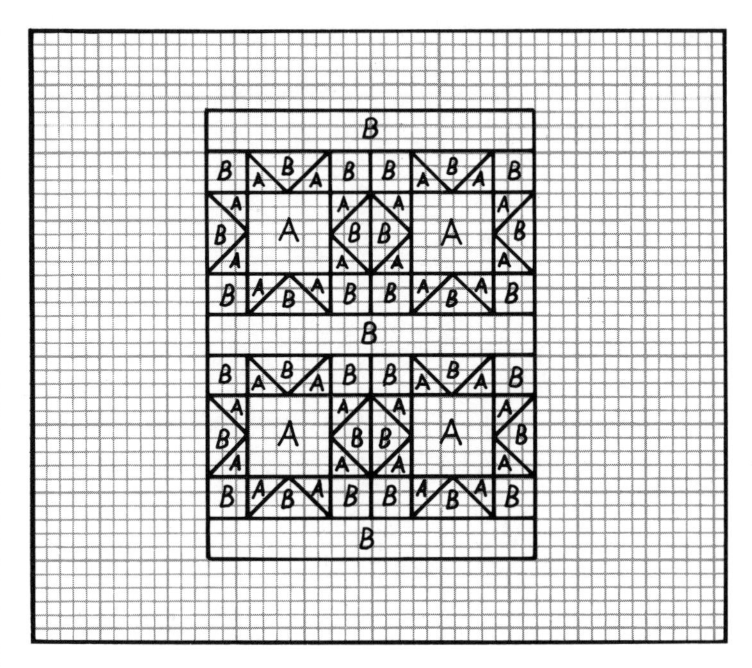


Fig. 6-15 *Layout for star-patched afghan*

### **Granny Square Rug** (Fig. 6-16)

Finished Size: Approx. 25″ × 55″

You Need: Bulky acrylic.

3 2-oz. skeins heather (Shade A)
4 2-oz. skeins pure blue (Shade B)
3 2-oz. skeins turquoise (Shade C)
2 2-oz. skeins bright avocado (Shade D)
3 2-oz. skeins light avocado (Shade E)
A size-J aluminum crochet hook

Gauge: One granny square of 3 rounds measures 5″ × 5″, worked on a size-J hook.

The Rug: Composed of large and small granny patches as shown in Fig. 6-17.

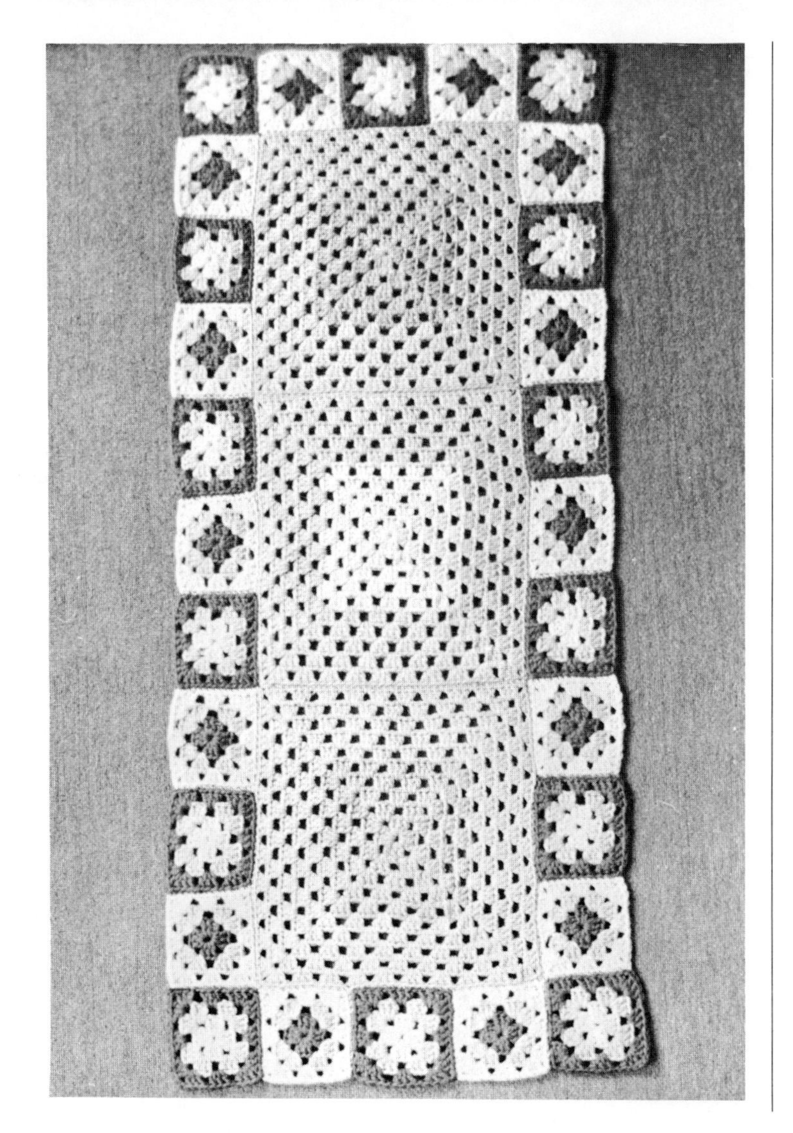

| 1 | 2 | 1 | 2 | 1 |
|---|---|---|---|---|
| 2 | | | | 2 |
| 1 | | 3 | | 1 |
| 2 | | | | 2 |
| 1 | | | | 1 |
| 2 | | 4 | | 2 |
| 1 | | | | 1 |
| 2 | | | | 2 |
| 1 | | 3 | | 1 |
| 2 | | | | 2 |
| 1 | 2 | 1 | 2 | 1 |

Fig. 6-17 *Layout for granny square rug*

Fig. 6-16 (Left) *Granny square rug*

*Square #1:* (Make 14.)
With Shade C, ch 4, join with sl st to form a ring.
*Row 1:* Ch 3, 2 dc in ring, ch 2, (3 dc in ring, ch 2) 3 times, join with sl st in top of ch-3, break off C.
*Row 2:* Join Shade B in a ch-2 sp. ch 3, 2 dc, ch 2 and 3 dc in same sp, ch 1, (3 dc, ch 2 and 3 dc in next ch-2 sp, ch 1) 3 times, join with sl st in top of ch-3, break off B.

*Row 3:* Join Shade A in a ch-2 sp, ch 3, 2 dc, ch 2 and 3 dc in same sp, ch 1, 3 dc in next ch-1 sp, ch 1, (3 dc, ch 2 and 3 dc in next ch-2 sp, ch 1, 3 dc in next ch-1 sp, ch 1) 3 times, join with sl st to top of ch-3, fasten off.

*Square #2:* (Make 14.)
Work exactly the same as Square #1, but using these colors:
*Row 1:* Shade A
*Row 2:* Shade B
*Row 3:* Shade C

*Square #3:* (Make 2.)
With Shade D, work exactly as Square #1, keeping the same color throughout. Instead of breaking off the color at the end of each row, sl st across dcs into corner ch-2 sp, then work exactly as for next row of Square #1. Continue working the granny square by making 3 dc and ch 1 in each ch-1 sp along the sides, and 3 dc, ch 2 and 3 dc in each ch-2 sp at the corners.
Work 5 rows in Shade D, break off D and join Shade E in a ch-2 sp.
Work 5 rows in Shade E, fasten off.

*Square #4:* (Make one.)
Follow the instructions for Square #3, but using these colors:
*Rows 1–5:* Shade E
*Rows 6–10:* Shade D

To Finish: Following Fig. 6-17, sew the squares together.

**Rug in Octagons and Squares*** (Fig. 6-18)

Finished Size: Approx. 28″ × 40″
You Need: Bulky acrylic.
8 2-oz. skeins black (Shade A)
3 2-oz. skeins white (Shade B)
A size-J aluminum crochet hook

Fig. 6-18 *Detail of rug in squares and octagons*

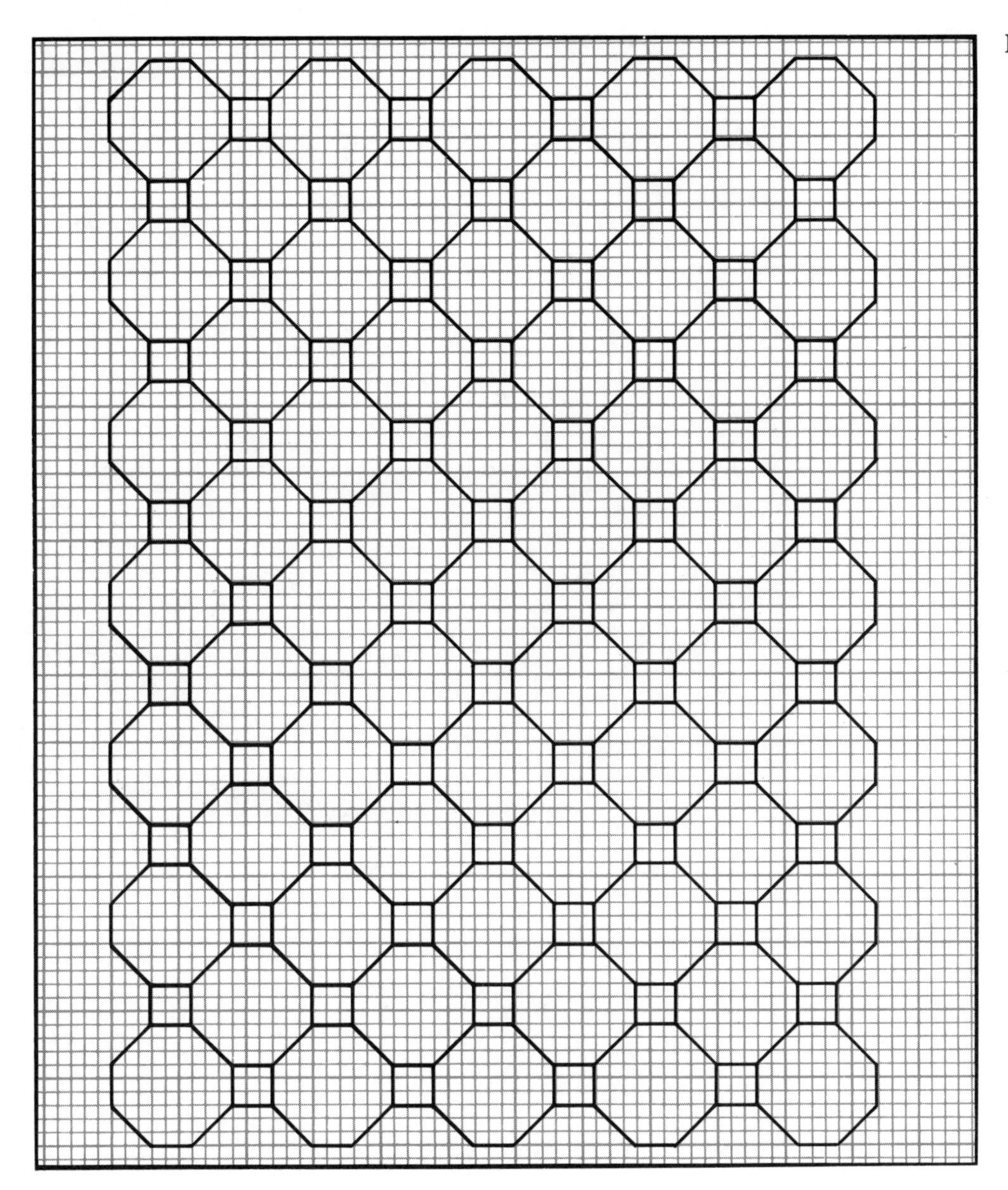

Fig. 6-19 *Layout for rug in squares and octagons*

GAUGE: A finished square measures 2″ × 2″, worked on a size-J hook.
THE RUG: Based on the square shape, #A2, and the octagon, #D3, in Chapter 5.

*The Square:* (Make 58 in Shade B.)
Follow the instructions for #A2 to the end of Row 2, fasten off.

*The Octagon:* (Make 59 in Shade A.)
Follow the instructions for #D3 in Chapter 5.

TO FINISH: Lay out the pieces as shown in Fig. 6-19. Sew them together in rows.

**Hexagonal Striped Cushion** (Fig. 6-20)

FINISHED SIZE: Approx. 18½″ across widest part
YOU NEED: 4-ply acrylic.
1 4-oz. skein in orange (Shade A)
1 4-oz. skein in scarlet (Shade B)
2 4-oz. skeins in cocoa brown (Shade C)
A size-I aluminum crochet hook
A round pillow form, 18″ in diameter.

GAUGE: 6 sts and 7 rows to 2″ worked over a flat sc square with a size-I hook.
THE CUSHION:

*Front:* (Make one.)
With Shade A, ch 4, join with sl st to first ch to form a ring.
*Row 1:* Ch 1, 6 sc in ring, sl st in first sc.
*Row 2:* Ch 1, 2 sc in each sc, break off A, join B, sl st in first sc.

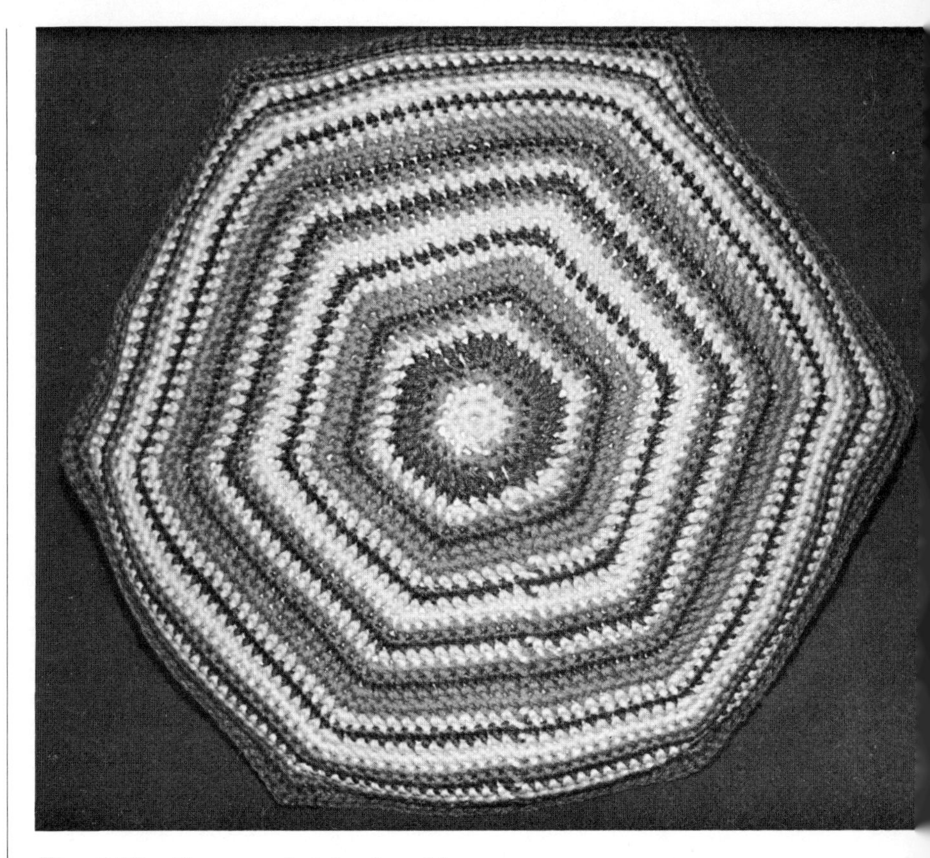

Fig. 6-20 *Hexagonal striped cushion*

*Row 3:* Ch 1, 1 sc in first sc,* 3 sc in next sc for a corner, 1 sc in next sc, repeat from* around, end 3 sc in last sc, break off B, join C, sl st in first sc.

*Row 4:* Ch 3 (stands for first dc), 1 dc in next sc,* 3 dc in next sc for a corner, 1 dc in each of next 3 sc, repeat from* around, end 3 dc in next sc, 1 dc in last sc, break off C, join A, sl st in top of ch-3.

*Row 5:* Ch 1, 1 sc in each of next 3 sts,* 3 sc in next st for a corner, 1 sc in each of next 5 sts, repeat from* around, end 3 sc in next st, 1 sc in each of last 2 sts, break off A, join B, sl st in first sc.

*Row 6:* Ch 1, 1 sc in each sc around, break off B, join C, sl st in first sc.

*Row 7: Increase Row:* Ch 1,* 1 sc in each sc to center st of a corner, 3 sc in next sc for a corner, repeat from* around, end 1 sc in each of last scs to beg of row, break off C, join B, sl st to first sc.

Rows 6 and 7 are alternated to keep the correct rate of increase in size. The colors are changed as follows:

*Rows 8 and 9:* B
*Row 10:* A
*Row 11:* C
*Rows 12 and 13:* A
*Row 14:* B
*Row 15:* C
*Row 16:* A
*Row 17:* B
*Row 18:* C

Repeat Rows 8 through 18 once more, fasten off.

*Back:* (Make one.)

Work exactly the same as for front but using Shade C throughout.

To Finish: Place the two hexagons with the wrong sides together, and the front facing you. Join Shade C along a side. Working through corresponding scs on front and back at same time, crochet the two pieces together by making a row of sc around edge. Insert pad before completing the join. Sl st in first sc, fasten off.

# 7 Crocheted Appliqués

The first part of this chapter contains instructions for making a variety of appliqué shapes, which can be used on cushions, bedspreads, afghans, wall hangings, pictures, and garments. Suggestions for projects incorporating some of these appliqués follow, together with more detailed instructions for specific items. Many of the crocheted patches appearing in Chapter 5 can also be used in the same way as the appliqués that follow.

**A. Medium-sized Appliqués**

#A1 (Fig. 7-1)

Ch 6, join with sl st to form a ring.

*Row 1:* Ch 5,* 1 dc in ring, ch 2, repeat from* 4 times more, sl st in 3rd st of ch-5.

*Row 2:* In each ch-2 sp, work 1 sc, ch 6 and 1 sc, sl st to first sc.

*Row 3:* In each ch-6 sp, work 2 sc, 3 dc, ch 3, 3 dc and 2 sc, sl st in first sc.

Fig. 7-1 *Crocheted appliqué #A1*

*Row 4:* * Ch 5; in ch-3 sp, work 1 sc, ch 3 and 1 sc, ch 5, skip 5 sts, 1 sc in next st, repeat from* around. Fasten off.

#A2 (Fig. 7-2)
Ch 8, join with sl st to form a ring.

Fig. 7-2 *Crocheted appliqué #A2*

*Row 1:* Work 16 sc in ring, sl st in first sc:
*Row 2:* Ch 9, 1 tr in same place as sl st,* skip 1 sc, in next sc work 1 tr, ch 5 and 1 tr, repeat from* around, end skip 1 sc, sl st in 4th st of ch-9.
*Row 3:* 1 sc in same place as sl st,* 1 sc in each of

next 2 ch, 3 sc in next ch, 1 sc in each of next 2 ch, 1 sc in each of next 2 tr, repeat from* around, end last repeat with 1 sc in last tr, sl st in first sc. Fasten off.

#A3 (FIG. 7-3)
Ch 6, join with sl st to form a ring.
*Row 1:* Ch 3 to count as 1 dc, work 11 more dc in ring, sl st in top of ch-3.
*Row 2:* Ch 6,* 1 dc in next dc, ch 3, repeat from* 10 times more, sl st in 3rd st of ch-6.
*Row 3:* Sl st in first ch-3 sp, work 3 sc in each ch-3 sp around, sl st in first sc.
*Row 4:* Sl st in next sc; in same sc work ch 3, 2 dc, ch 6 and 3 dc,* skip 2 sc, 1 sc in next sc, skip 2 sc; in next sc work 3 dc, ch 6 and 3 dc, repeat from* 4 times more, skip 2 sc, 1 sc in next sc, sl st in top of ch-3.
*Row 5:* Ch 1, work 1 sc in next 2 dc,* 7 sc in ch-6 sp, 1 sc in each of next 3 dc, skip 1 sc, 1 sc in each of next 3 dc, repeat from* 5 times more, end last repeat with sl st in first ch-1.
*Row 6:* Work 1 sc in each sc and 1 sc, ch 2 and 1 sc in each sc at point, sl st in first sc, fasten off.

#A4 (FIG. 7-4)
Ch 6, join with sl st to form a ring.
*Row 1:* Work 12 sc in ring, sl st in first sc.
*Row 2:* Ch 5,* 1 dc in next sc, ch 2, repeat from* around, sl st in 3rd st of ch-5.

Fig. 7-3 *Crocheted appliqué #A3*

*Row 3:* Ch 1, 1 sc in same place as sl st; 2 sc in each ch-2 sp with 1 sc in each dc around, sl st in first sc.
*Point:* Ch 1, 1 sc in same place as sl st,* 1 sc in each of next 6 sc, ch 1, turn, 1 sc in each of next 4 sc,

skip 1 sc, 1 sc in last sc, ch 1, turn, continue to work 1 sc less by skipping next to last sc on every row until 2 sc remain. Ch 1, turn.

Draw up a loop in each of 2 sc, yo and through all 3 loops to complete point, fasten off.

Repeat from* 5 times more.

Fig. 7-4 *Crocheted appliqué #A4*

#A5 (Fig. 7-5)

Ch 12, join with sl st to form a ring.

*Row 1:* Ch 3 to count as 1 dc, work 31 more dc in ring, sl st in top of ch-3.

*Row 2:* Ch 5,* skip 1 dc, 1 dc in next dc, ch 2, repeat from* around, sl st in 3rd st of ch-5.

Fig. 7-5 *Crocheted appliqué #A5*

*Row 3:* Sl st in first sp, ch 3, 4 dc in same sp,* ch 7, skip next ch-2 sp, 5 dc in next sp, repeat from* around. End ch 7, sl st in top of ch-3.

*Row 4:* Sl st in each of next 2 dc, ch 1, 1 sc in same place as last sl st,* 7 dc, ch 2 and 7 dc in next ch-7 sp, skip 2 dc, 1 sc in next dc, repeat from* around, end last repeat with sl st in first sc, fasten off.

#A6 (FIG. 7-6)

Ch 8, join with sl st to form a ring.

*Row 1:* Work 24 sc in ring, sl st to first sc.

*Row 2:* Ch 1, 1 sc in next sc,* ch 14, 1 dc in 6th ch from hook, (ch 2, skip 2 ch, 1 dc in next ch) twice, ch 2, 1 sc in next sc on ring, ch 3, turn, (2 sc in next ch-2 sp, 1 sc in next dc) 3 times, 5 sc in end space, work on other side: (1 sc in next dc, 2 sc in ch-2 sp) 3 times*, sl st to next sc, ch 2, turn, working in back loops only for each sc, 1 sc in each of next 12 sc, 3 sc in next sc, 1 sc in each sc down other side, 1 sc in next sc in ring.

A petal has been worked over 4 sc. Make another petal: 1 sc in each of next 2 sc in ring, work as for first petal from* to*, sl st to sc in ring, ch 2, turn, working in back loops only of each sc, 1 sc in each of next 5 sc, join to previous petal by making 1 dc in 6th sc from base of previous petal, finish as other petal. Work 3 more petals as for 2nd petal, then work 6th petal to 2nd side of petal, attach with a dc to first petal as in other petals, finish rest of petal as before. Fasten off.

Fig. 7-6 *Crocheted appliqué #A6*

#A7 (Fig. 7-7)
Worked in 2 colors.
With first color ch 10, join with sl st to form a ring.
*Row 1:* Ch 3 to count as first dc, 2 more dc in ring,* ch 2, 3 dc in ring, repeat from* 6 times more, ch 2, sl st in top of ch-3, fasten off.
*Row 2:* Join 2nd color in a ch-2 sp. Ch 3 to count as first dc; 2 dc, ch 2 and 3 dc in same ch-2 sp; in each ch-2 sp work 3 dc, ch 2 and 3 dc, sl st in top of ch-3, fasten off.
*Row 3:* Join first color in a ch-2 sp. Ch 3, 2 dc, ch 2 and 3 dc in same ch-2 sp,* 1 dc between next 2 groups of dcs; in next ch-2 space work 3 dc, ch 2 and 3 dc, repeat from* 6 times more, 1 dc between last 2 groups, sl st in top of ch-3, fasten off.

#A8 (Fig. 7-8)
Ch 2, work 1 sc in 2nd ch from hook, ch 1, turn.
*Row 2:* Work 3 sc in the sc, ch 1, turn. Inc 1 sc at each side of next 2 rows then every other row until there are 13 sc, ch 1, turn. Work 4 rows on the 13 sc, ch 1, turn.
*Next row:* Work 6 sc, ch 1, turn. Dec 1 sc at beg of next 2 rows: *To Dec:* Draw up a loop in each of 2 sc, yo and through all 3 loops on hook.
Dec 1 sc st each side of next row—2 sc remain, fasten off.
Skip 1 sc at center on last long row and work other side.

Fig. 7-7 *Crocheted appliqué #A7*

Fig. 7-8 *Crocheted appliqué #A8*

Fig. 7-9 *Crocheted appliqué #B1*

### B. Larger Motifs

#B1 (Fig. 7-9)

Ch 10, join with sl st to form a ring.

*Row 1:* 16 sc in ring, join with sl st to first sc.

*Row 2:* Ch 4, holding back on hook the last loop of each tr, work 2 tr in joining, yo and through all loops on hook—*cluster made,** ch 5, skip 1 sc, 3-tr cluster in next sc, repeat from*, ending ch 5, sl st in top of first cluster; 8 clusters.

*Row 3:* Work 7 sc in each ch-5 sp around. Do not join.

*Row 4:* * 1 sc in each of next 7 sc, ch 1, repeat from* around. Join with sl st to first sc.

*Row 5:* Ch 1, 1 sc in joining, 1 sc in each of next 6 sc,* ch 4, 1 sc in each of next 7 sc, repeat from*, end ch 4, join with sl st to first sc.

*Row 6:* * 1 sc in each of next 5 sc, ch 3, 5 dc in next ch-4 sp for corner, ch 3, skip 1 sc, 1 sc in each of next 5 sc, ch 4, skip 1 sc, ch 1 and 1 sc, repeat from*, end sl st in first sc.

*Row 7:* * 1 sc in each of next 3 sc, ch 5, 1 dc in each of next 2 dc; 1 dc, ch 3 and 1 dc in next dc at corner, 1 dc in each of next 2 dc, ch 5, skip 1 sc, 1 sc in each of next 3 sc, ch 1, 5 dc in next ch-4 sp, ch 1, skip 1 sc, repeat from*, end sl st in first sc.

*Row 8:* * 1 sc in next sc, ch 6, 1 dc in each of next 3 dc; 1 dc, ch 5 and 1 dc in ch-3 sp at corner, 1 dc in each of next 3 dc, ch 6, skip 1 sc, 1 sc in next sc, ch 2, 1 dc in each of next 2 dc; 1 dc, ch 3 and 1 dc in next dc, 1 dc in each of next 2 dc, ch 2, skip 1 sc, repeat from*, end sl st in first sc. Fasten off.

#B2 (Fig. 7-10)

Ch 10, join with sl st to form a ring.

*Row 1:* Ch 4, 2-tr cluster in ring, ch 6,* 3-tr cluster in ring, ch 6, repeat from* 6 times more, sl st in top of first cluster.

*Row 2:* Sl st to 3rd st of first ch-6 sp, ch 1, 1 sc in same sp,* ch 7; in next sp work (3-tr cluster, ch 5) twice and 1 more 3-tr cluster; ch 7, 1 sc in next ch-6 sp, repeat from* around, end last repeat with sl st in first sc.

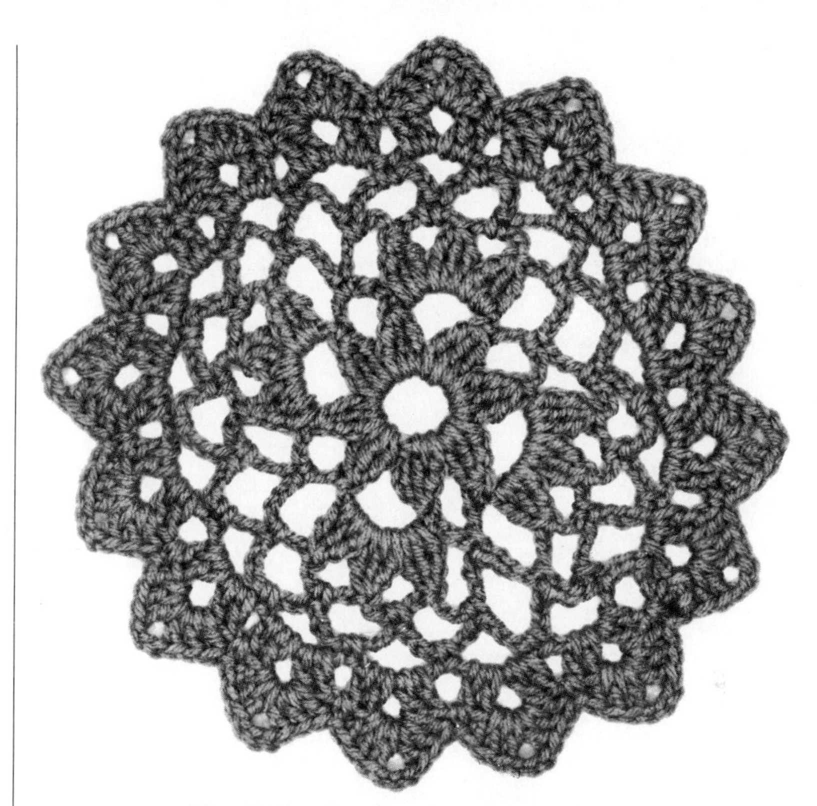

Fig. 7-10 *Crocheted appliqué #B2*

*Row 3:* Sl st to 4th st of first ch-7 sp, ch 1, 1 sc in same sp,* ch 7, 1 sc in next sp, repeat from* around, end last repeat with sl st in first sc.

Fig. 7-11 *Crocheted appliqué #B3*

*Row 4:* Sl st to 4th st of first ch-7 sp, ch 1, 1 sc in same sp,* ch 5, 1 sc in next ch-7 sp, repeat from* around, end last repeat with sl st in first sc.

*Row 5:* Sl st to 3rd st of first ch-5 sp, ch 3; 1 dc, ch 3 and 2 dc in same sp,* 2 dc, ch 3 and 2 dc in next ch-5 sp for a *shell,* repeat from* around, sl st in top of ch-3.

*Row 6:* Sl st to first ch-3 sp, ch 3; 2 dc, ch 3 and 3 dc in same sp,* 1 sc between next 2 shells; 3 dc, ch 3 and 3 dc in next ch-3 sp, repeat from* around, end 1 sc between last 2 shells, sl st to top of ch-3, fasten off.

#B3 (Fig. 7-11)

Ch 8, join with sl st to form a ring.

*Row 1:* Ch 3 to count as 1 dc, work 23 more dc in ring, sl st in top of ch-3.

*Row 2:* Ch 3, 1 dc in each of next 2 dc, ch 3,* 1 dc in each of next 3 dc, ch 3, repeat from* 6 times more, sl st in top of ch-3.

*Row 3:* Ch 3, 1 dc in each of next 2 dc, ch 8,* 1 dc in each of next 3 dc, ch 8, repeat from* 6 times more, sl st in top of ch-3.

*Row 4:* Ch 3, 1 dc in each of next 2 dc,* ch 4, 1 sc in next ch-8 sp, ch 4, 1 dc in each of next 3 dc, repeat from* 6 times more, end ch 4, 1 sc in last ch-8 sp, ch 4, sl st in top of ch-3.

*Row 5:* Ch 3, 1 dc in each of next 2 dc,* ch 4, 1 sc in next ch-4 sp, 1 sc in sc, 1 sc in next ch-4 sp, ch 4, 1 dc in each of next 3 dc, repeat from* 6 times more, end ch 4, 1 sc in next ch-4 sp, 1 sc in sc, 1 sc in last ch-4 sp, ch 4, sl st in top of ch-3.

*Row 6:* Ch 3, 1 dc in each of next 2 dc,* ch 4, 1 sc in next ch-4 sp, 1 sc in each of next 3 sc, 1 sc in next ch-4 sp, ch 4, 1 dc in each of next 3 dc, repeat from* 7 times more, end last repeat with 1 sc in last ch-4 sp, ch 4, sl st in top of ch-3.

*Row 7:* Ch 3, 1 dc in each of next 2 dc,* ch 5, skip 1 sc, 1 sc in each of next 3 sc, ch 5, 1 dc in each of next 3 dc, repeat from* 7 times more, end last repeat with ch 5, sl st in top of ch-3.

*Row 8:* Ch 3, 1 dc in each of next 2 dc,* ch 7, 1 sc in center sc, ch 7, 1 dc in each of next 3 dc, repeat from* 7 times more, end last repeat with ch 7, sl st in top of ch-3.

*Row 9:* Ch 1, 1 sc in each dc and 8 sc in each ch-7 sp, sl st in first sc, fasten off.

#B4 (FIG. 7-12)

Ch 10, join with sl st to form a ring.

*Row 1:* Ch 5, 2 dc, ch 2 and 2 dc in ring for a *shell,* ch 4, 15 tr in ring, ch 4, 1 shell in ring, ch 5, turn.

*Row 2:* 1 shell in ch-2 sp of next shell, ch 4; 1 tr and ch 1 in each of next 14 tr, 1 tr in last tr; ch 4, 1 shell in ch-2 sp of last shell, ch 5, turn.

*Row 3:* 1 shell in ch-2 sp of next shell, ch 4, 1 sc in next ch-1 sp, (ch 3, 1 sc in next ch-1 sp) 13 times, ch 4, 1 shell in ch-2 sp of last shell, ch 5, turn.

Fig. 7-12 *Crocheted appliqué #B4*

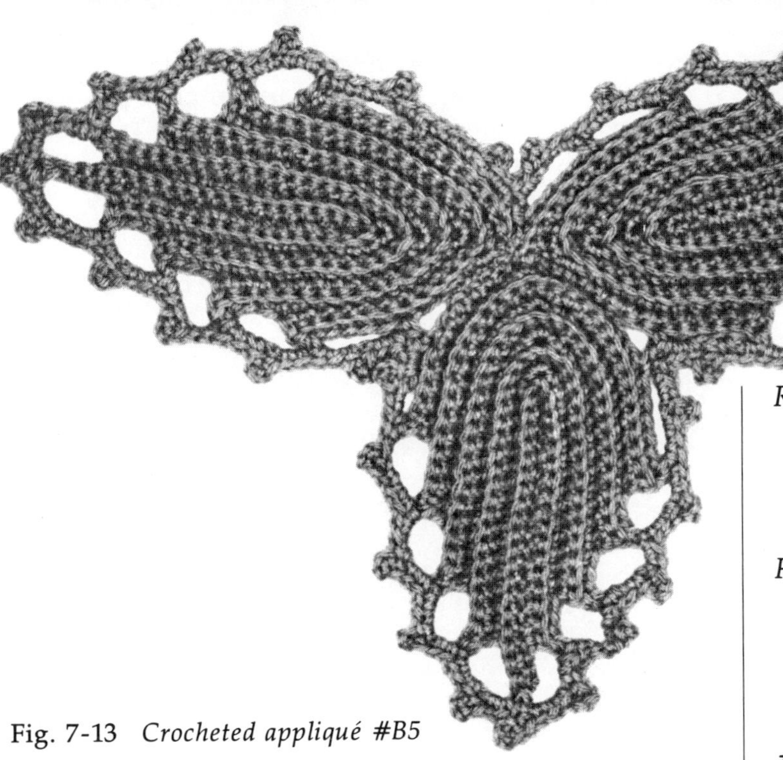

Fig. 7-13 *Crocheted appliqué #B5*

*Row 4:* 1 shell in ch-2 sp of next shell, ch 4, 1 sc in ch-3 sp, (ch 3 & 1 sc in next sp) 12 times, ch 4, 1 shell in ch-2 sp of last shell, ch 5, turn. Continue working Row 4 with 1 less ch-3 sp on each row until 1 ch-3 sp remains, ch 5, turn.

*Final row:* 1 shell in ch-2 sp of next shell, ch 4, 1 sc in ch-3 sp, ch 4, 2 dc in ch-2 sp of last shell, ch 1, sl st in ch-2 sp of shell at beg of row, ch 1, 2 dc in ch-2 sp of last shell, ch 5, turn, sl st in join of 2 shells, fasten off.

#B5 (Fig. 7-13)

Ch 22.

*Row 1:* 1 sc in 3rd ch from hook, 1 sc in each of next 18 ch, 3 sc in last ch and mark for base of leaf: along other side of foundation ch, work 1 sc in each sc to last 4 sc, ch 2, turn.

*Row 2: Work in back loops only from now on.* 1 sc in each sc to base of leaf, 3 sc in center sc at base of leaf, 1 sc in each sc to last 4 sc, ch 2 turn, forming a tip.

Repeat Row 2 six times more.

*Row 9:* 1 sc in each sc to base of leaf, fasten off. Work 3 leaves the same. Sew tog as shown in photograph, joining 4 sts at each side of center leaf.

*Edging:* Join yarn to first tip from lower point on right-hand side of center leaf, 1 sc in same tip, (ch 5, 1 sc in next tip) 8 times, ch 5, skip 5 sc, 1 sc in next sc, 1 sc in corresponding sc in next leaf, (ch 5, 1 sc in next tip) 9 times, ch 5, skip 5 sc, 1 sc in next sc, 1 sc in corresponding sc on next leaf, (ch 5, 1 sc in next tip) 9 times, ch 5, skip 5 sc, 1 sc in next sc, ch 5, 1 sc in join between 2 leaves, ch 5, skip 5 sc, 1 sc in next sc, ch 5, sl st in first sc.

*Row 2:* In each ch-5 sp around, work 3 sc, ch 3, 1 sc in 3rd ch from hook for a *picot* and 2 more sc, working an extra picot at top of each leaf; sl st in first sc, fasten off.

#B6 (Fig. 7-14)

Ch 6, join with sl st to form a ring.

*Row 1:* Ch 3 to count as 1 dc, work 15 more dcs in ring, sl st in top of ch-3.

*Row 2:* Ch 3, 1 dc in same place as ch-3; 2 dc in each dc around, sl st in top of ch-3.

*Row 3:* Ch 3, 1 dc in each of next 2 dc,* ch 6, skip 1 dc, 1 dc in each of next 3 dc, repeat from* 6 times more, ch 6, sl st in top of ch-3.

*Row 4:* Ch 3, 1 dc in each of next 2 dc,* ch 4, 1 sc, ch 4 and 1 dc in next ch-6 sp, 1 dc in each of next 3 dc; 1 dc, ch 4 and 1 sc in next ch-6 sp, ch 4, 1 dc in each of next 3 dc, repeat from* around, end last repeat with 1 sc, ch 4, sl st in top of ch-3.

*Row 5:* Ch 3, 1 dc in each of next 2 dc,* ch 4, 1 sc in ch-4 sp, 1 sc in sc, 1 sc in next ch-4 sp, ch 4, 1 dc in each of next 5 dc, ch 4, 1 sc in next ch-4 sp, 1

Fig. 7-14 *Crocheted appliqué #B6*

sc in sc, 1 sc in next ch-4 sp, ch 4, 1 dc in each of next 3 dc, repeat from* around, end last repeat with 1 sc in last sp, ch 4, sl st in top of ch-3.

*Row 6:* Ch 3, 1 dc in each of next 2 dc,* ch 4, 1 sc in next ch-4 sp, 1 sc in each of next 3 sc; 1 sc, ch 4 and 1 dc in next ch-4 sp, 1 dc in each of next 5 dc; 1 dc, ch 4 and 1 sc in next ch-4 sp, 1 sc in each of next 3 sc, 1 sc in next ch-4 sp, ch 4, 1 dc in each of next 3 dc, repeat from* around, end last repeat with 1 sc in last sp, ch 4, sl st in top of ch-3.

*Row 7:* Ch 3, 1 dc in each of next 2 dc,* ch 6, skip 1 sc of next group, 1 sc in each of next 3 sc, ch 6, 1 dc in each of next 7 dc, ch 6, skip first sc of next group, 1 sc in each of next 3 sc, ch 6, 1 dc in each of next 3 dc, repeat from* around, ending last repeat with 3 sc, ch 6, sl st in top of ch-3.

*Row 8:* Ch 3, 1 dc in each of next 2 dc,* ch 8, 1 sc in center sc of next group, ch 8, skip first dc of next group, 1 dc in each of next 5 dc, ch 8, 1 sc in center sc of next group, ch 8, 1 dc in each of next 3 dc, repeat from* around, end last repeat with 1 sc, ch 8, sl st in top of ch-3.

*Row 9:* Ch 3, 1 dc in each of next 2 dc,* ch 10, 1 sc in next sc, ch 10, skip first dc of next group, 1 dc in each of next 3 dc, ch 10, 1 sc in next sc, ch 10, 1 dc in each of next 3 dc, repeat from* around, end last repeat with ch 10, sl st in top of ch-3.

*Row 10:* Ch 4, skip next sc, 1 sc in next dc,* (12 sc in next ch-10 sp) twice, 1 sc in next dc, ch 4, skip 1 dc, 1 sc in next dc, repeat from* 6 times more, (12 sc in next ch-10 sp) twice, sl st in 3rd st of ch-4, fasten off.

#B7 (FIG. 7-15)

Ch 10, join with sl st to form a ring.

*Row 1:* Work 24 sc in ring, sl st in first sc.

*Row 2:* Ch 1, 1 sc in same place as sl st, ch 6,* skip 2 sc, 1 sc in next sc, ch 6 repeat from* around, sl st in first sc.

*Row 3:* In each ch-6 sp work 8 sc.

*Row 4:* Ch 5, skip 1 sc,* 1 dc in back loop of next sc, ch 2, skip 1 sc, repeat from* around, end sl st in 3rd st of ch-5.

*Row 5:* 2 sc in each ch-2 sp around.

*Row 6:* 1 sc in back loop of each sc around.

*Row 7:* Through both loops, work* 2 sc in next sc, 1 sc in next sc, repeat from* around.

*Row 8:* Repeat Row 6.

*Row 9:* Repeat Row 4.

*Row 10:* Sl st in first ch-2 sp; ch 3, 1 dc, ch 2 and 2 dc in same sp,* ch 6, skip 2 ch-2 sps; 2 dc, ch 2 and 2 dc in next ch-2 sp, repeat from* around, end ch 6, sl st in top of ch-3.

*Rows 11 and 12:* Sl st to first ch-2 sp, ch 3; 1 dc, ch 2 and 2 dc in same sp, ch 6,* 2 dc, ch 2 and 2 dc in next ch-2 sp, ch 6, repeat from* around, sl st in top of ch-3.

Fig. 7-15 *Crocheted appliqué #B7*

*Row 13:* Sl st to first ch-2 sp, ch 3; 1 dc, ch 2 and 2 dc in same sp,* ch 4, 1 sc over the ch-6 loops of Rows 10, 11, and 12, ch 4; 2 dc, ch 2 and 2 dc in next ch-2 sp, repeat from* around, end ch 4, 1 sc over the ch-6 loops as before, ch 4, sl st in top of ch-3, fasten off.

**Project Suggestions**

The medium- and large-sized appliqués described above can be used in any number of interesting ways. Try applying one large appliqué to a background fabric and making a pillow. These large motifs look stunning on either square or round pillows. Make your appliqué in a brightly contrasting or subtly blended shade. The medium-sized appliqués can be used on larger projects such as wall hangings. Choose a strong and firm background fabric, and arrange your appliqués to suit your own taste. You can also use these smaller appliqués in groups on cushions. There are endless possibilities for experimentation with the wide selection of shapes here.

*Making and Sewing on Appliqués*

If you have chosen to make an appliquéd wall hanging, I suggest you choose a fairly lightweight yarn for making the motifs. Heavy yarn will most likely cause the background fabric to sag instead of allowing it to lie smooth. You can use an ordinary 4-ply yarn for such items as cushions, where extra body is desirable and no hanging is involved. Suit the weight of yarn you choose to your purpose. Choose the lightest possible weights where any free-hanging is involved, that is, for unmounted wall hangings, or clothing. For any item that is supported, such as a cushion with its cushion pad, you can use a heavier yarn. This also applies to pictures. You can mount a bold motif on a piece of contrasting fabric, which is then stretched over a piece of cork or board. This is an excellent way of making simple but effective appliqué pictures. The motif will stand out more boldy if made with a heavier yarn, such as a 4-ply.

Sewing motifs to a backing fabric is quick and easy, if it is done correctly. Lay your backing fabric, right side up, on the floor or a table. Place your appliqué piece or pieces exactly in the position you have chosen. Pin each motif to the backing in its center and around its outer perimeter with long pins. Use the same yarn in which the motif is made for sewing. If you have made the motif in a very thick yarn and have a closely woven background fabric, you may have to substitute a sewing thread in the same color.

Start in the center of a motif if it is worked from a center ring outward. Work a row of fine running stitches around the center ring. For small motifs that are not basically circular in shape, such as the heart (#A8), you will not need to work any stitches in the center of the motif. Work another row of running stitches around the border of the motif. If it has a "solid" last row, you can embroider around the edge using a contrasting yarn and working in blanket stitch. However, if it has a delicate, lacy edge, the fine running stitch will not detract from the effectiveness of a pretty pattern, indeed, done properly, it will be almost invisible on the right side.

### *Sticking on Appliqués*

If you choose to mount appliqués on a piece of painted board, you can use a transparent glue for fixing them in place. Mark the center of the appliqué on the board with a small pencil dot. Place a small amount of glue on the wrong side of the appliqué, taking care not to be too liberal with it. If you put too much on, it will squeeze out through the crocheting. Now place the motif very gently onto the painted board, lining up the center of your motif with the pencil dot. When you are certain that the appliqué is in the position you like, press it firmly onto the board and leave it flat to dry.

Figs. 7-16 and 7-17 show two crochet flower pictures created by Joan Chatterton. Mounting with glue is particularly suited to small flower motifs, which would be very fiddly to sew onto

Fig. 7-16 *"Floral Bouquet," by Joan Chatterton*

Fig. 7-17 *"Floral Bouquet," by Joan Chatterton*

a background. Make up some flower shapes of your own and try out some of these floral pictures, using up tiny scraps of yarn. In Fig. 7-16, a bright color scheme of orange-yellow-gold was used. In Fig. 7-17, pastel shades of blue and green alone were used, creating a look reminiscent of Wedgwood china. Choose your own color schemes and enjoy the pleasure of experimenting in appliqué.

Clothing of all kinds can be brightened up by the addition of crocheted appliqués. Here, of course, one is mostly limited to the smaller pieces—those that will fit on a sweater, a pair of jeans, or whatever you have in mind. Clusters of flowers, such as those used in the appliquéd pictures in Figs. 7-16 and 7-17, can look equally attractive on a plain sweater or hat. Try some of the medium-sized motifs shown at the beginning of this chapter as center pieces on a plain sweater. Choose a brightly contrasting color, and sew your motif onto the sweater. You can easily remove the appliqué without doing any damage to the basic garment, and you can keep changing the appliquéd motifs to match a new color scheme or simply to create a different sweater. For those of you who prefer the security of charted waters, instructions for an appliqué project follow.

**Tank Top with Appliquéd Hearts** (Fig. 7-18)

SIZES: Small (6–8) and medium (10–12). Instructions for the medium size appear in parentheses.

YOU NEED: Sports yarn. These amounts apply for both small and medium sizes.

- 3 2-oz. skeins in tangerine (Shade A)
- 1 2-oz. skein in royal blue (Shade B)
- 1 2-oz. skein in green (Shade C)
- A size-F aluminum crochet hook

GAUGE: 8 sts and 5 rows to 2 inches over dc using a size-F hook.

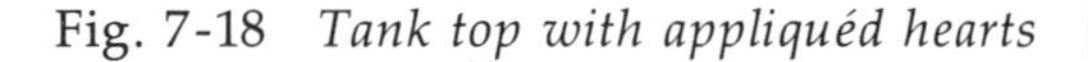

Fig. 7-18 *Tank top with appliquéd hearts*

THE SWEATER

*Back:* Ch 59 (63).

*Row 1:* Starting in fourth ch from hook, work 1 dc in each ch across, ch 3 turn.

*Row 2:* 1 dc in each dc across, ch 3, turn.

Continue working straight in dc until work measures 11″ from beginning.

*Armhole shaping:* Sl st over next 4 sts, sl st into next st, ch 3, 1 dc in each dc across to within last 4 sts, ch 3, turn.

Dec 1 dc at each end of next 2 rows.

Continue working straight in dc until work measures 6½ inches from beg of armhole shaping.

*Shoulder:* Work 1 dc in each of next 9 dc (10 sts including ch-3 at beg of row), fasten off.

Attach yarn to other side 10 sts from the end of the row, ch 3, work 1 dc in each of next 9 sts, fasten off.

*Front:* Work as for back until armhole measures 4½ inches from beg.

*Shape neck:* Work 1 dc in each of next 12 dc (13 sts including ch-3 at beg of row), ch 3, turn.

Dec 1 st at neck edge on each row until there are 10 sts.

Work straight until armhole measures same as for back, fasten off.

Work other side of neck in same way.

*Appliqués:*

Follow instructions for #A8 in Chapter 7.

*Make:*

2 in Shade B

1 in Shade C

Sew the appliqués to the front of the sweater as shown in Fig. 7-18.

TO FINISH: Sew side and shoulder seams together. Work the following border around lower, neck, and armhole edges.

*Border:* Attach Shade A to edge, work 1 row of sc around, break off A, join C, sl st in first sc.

*Rows 2 and 3:* As first row using Shade C.

*Rows 4 and 5:* As first row using Shade B, fasten off.

# 8 Patchwork Knitting

Knitting for patchwork presents an entirely different problem from crochet. Whereas it is relatively simple to create any shape one wants with crochet, the art of medallion, or motif, knitting disappeared as common practice with the fading of the era of Victorian leisure. It is an extremely difficult art, and I do not propose to discuss it here. It would be an easier task to learn to crochet from the beginning than to struggle with the intricacies of medallion knitting. Delicate, lacy patterns and complex shapes are far easier to create in crochet. My approach to patchwork knitting is therefore from a different angle entirely.

## Very Easy Projects

This section is primarily for use by those who have just learned the basic techniques of knitting. However, many of these projects may be

attractive enough to tempt even the more experienced knitter. All the projects suitable for beginners will be marked*. For helpful hints on finishing knitted garments, refer to the section "Finishing Patchwork Knitting" at the end of this chapter.

ABBREVIATIONS

| | | | |
|---|---|---|---|
| K | = knit | st(s) | = stitch(es) |
| P | = purl | tog | = together |
| beg | = beginning | st st | = stockinette stitch |
| pat | = pattern | sl | = slip |

For instructions on how to achieve the correct gauge, refer to the section "Planning a Patchwork Crochet Project" in Chapter 5. The procedure is the same for knitting as for crochet.

**Cushion in Squares and Rectangles*** (Fig. 8-1)

FINISHED SIZE: APPROX. 16″ × 16″
YOU NEED: 4-ply worsted-weight wool.
1 4-oz. skein in dusty rose (Shade A)
1 4-oz. skein in magenta (Shade B)
A pair of size-10½ needles

GAUGE: 4 sts and 5 rows to 1 inch over st st on size-10½ needles.

THE CUSHION

*Patch #1* (Make one.)
With B, cast on 32 sts.
Work 8″ in st st, bind off.

*Patch #2* (Make 2.)
With A, cast on 32 sts.
Work 4″ in st st, bind off.

*Patch #3* (Make 2.)
With A, cast on 16 sts.
Work 8″ in st st, bind off.

*Patch #4* (Make 4.)
With B, cast on 16 sts.
Work 4″ in st st, bind off.

TO FINISH: Sew the patches together as shown in Fig. 8-1. Should you wish to make a knitted back for your cushion, you will have sufficient yarn to do so. Otherwise you can use a suitably strong backing fabric.

**Log Cabin Cushion*** (Fig. 8-2)

FINISHED SIZE: APPROX. 16″ × 16″
YOU NEED: 4-ply worsted-weight wool.
1 4-oz. skein copper (Shade A)
1 4-oz. skein dark tan (Shade B)
1 4-oz. skein light tan (Shade C)
A pair of size-10½ needles

GAUGE: 4 sts and 5 rows to 1 inch over st st on size-10½ needles.

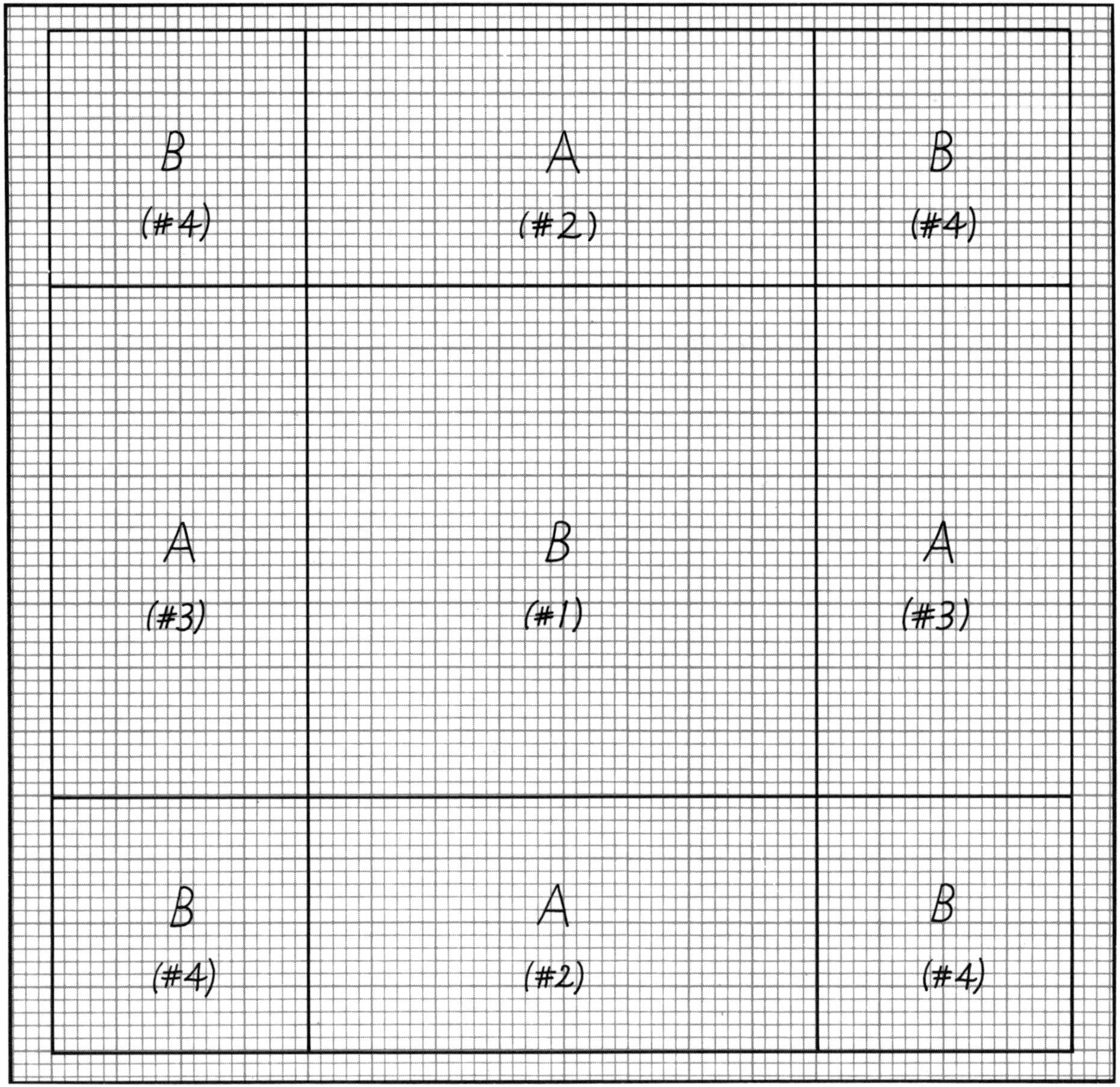

B (#4) | A (#2) | B (#4)

A (#3) | B (#1) | A (#3)

B (#4) | A (#2) | B (#4)

Fig. 8-1 *Layout for cushion in squares and rectangles*

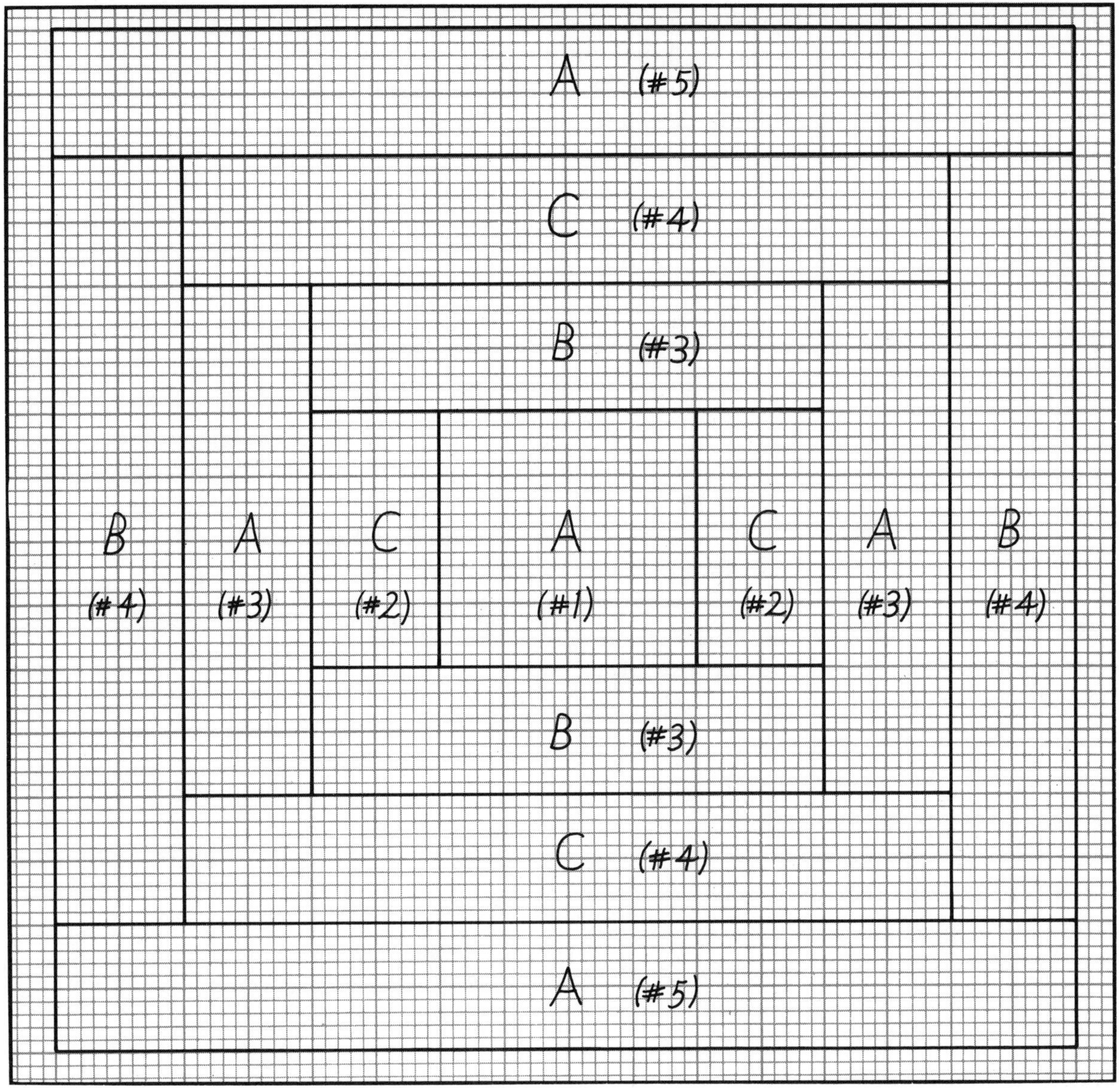

A (#5)

C (#4)

B (#3)

B (#4) A (#3) C (#2) A (#1) C (#2) A (#3) B (#4)

B (#3)

C (#4)

A (#5)

Fig. 8-2 *Layout for "Log Cabin" cushion*

THE CUSHION

*Patch #1* (Make one.)
With A, cast on 16 sts.
Work 4" in garter st, bind off.

*Patch #2* (Make 2.)
With C, cast on 16 sts.
Work 2" in garter st, bind off.

*Patch #3* (Make 2 in B, and 2 in A.)
With A or B, cast on 32 sts.
Work 2" in garter st, bind off.

*Patch #4* (Make 2 in C, and 2 in B.)
With B or C, cast on 48 sts.
Work 2" in garter st, bind off.

*Patch #5* (Make 2.)
With A, cast on 64 sts.
Work 2" in garter st, bind off.

TO FINISH: Sew patches together as shown in Fig. 8-2. You will have enough yarn left over to make a knitted backing for your cushion, or you can use a fabric back if you prefer.

**Checkerboard Cushion*** (Not illustrated)

This design consists of four simple garter-stitch squares, made in two contrasting colors, which are then arranged to alternate, with two squares in the top half and two in the bottom half of the cushion.

FINISHED SIZE: APPROX. 20" × 20"
YOU NEED: 4-ply worsted-weight wool.
1 4-oz. skein in black (Shade A)
1 4-oz. skein in white (Shade B)
A pair of size-10½ needles

GAUGE: 4 sts and 5 rows to 1 inch over st st on size-10½ needles.
THE CUSHION: Made in 4 equal squares, each 10" × 10".
THE SQUARE PATCH: (Make 2 in A, and 2 in B.)
Cast on 40 sts.
Work in garter st for 10 inches, bind off.

TO FINISH: Alternating black and white patches, sew squares together to make a larger square measuring 20" × 20".
To back the cushion, you may either knit another square or use a fabric.

**Afghan in Brilliant Colors*** (Fig. 8-3)

FINISHED SIZE: APPROX. 44" × 60"
YOU NEED: 4-ply worsted-weight wool.
1 4-oz. skein white (Shade A)
2 4-oz. skeins bright tangerine (Shade B)
1 4-oz. skein black (Shade C)
2 4-oz.skeins turquoise (Shade D)
1 4-oz. skein tangerine (Shade E)
1 4-oz. skein kelly green (Shade F)
1 4-oz. skein royal blue (Shade G)
A pair of size-10½ needles

Fig. 8-3 *Afghan in brilliant colors*

GAUGE: 4 sts and 5 rows to 1 inch over st st on size-10½ needles.
THE AFGHAN: Study Fig. 8-4 carefully before starting work. The center panel of the afghan is worked all in one piece. The patched effect is achieved by alternating colors. The other pieces are all worked as separate patches; each shape is numbered.

*Center Panel*
With A, cast on 80 sts.
Work 2″ in st st, break off A, join B.

Change color as follows, working 2 inches in each shade:

| | |
|---|---|
| * A (just worked) | E |
| B | F |
| C | G |
| D | |

Repeat from * 3 times more (work measures 56 inches from beg). Bind off.

*Patch #1*
Cast on 16 sts.
Work 14 inches in st st, bind off.

*Make:*

| | |
|---|---|
| 3 in Shade A | 2 in Shade E |
| 2 in Shade B | 2 in Shade F |
| 2 in Shade C | 3 in Shade G |
| 2 in Shade D | |

*Patch #2*
Cast on 8 sts.
Work 56 inches in st st, bind off.

*Make:*
2 in Shade B
2 in Shade D

*Patch #3*
Cast on 176 sts.
Work 2 inches in st st, bind off.

*Make:*
2 in Shade B

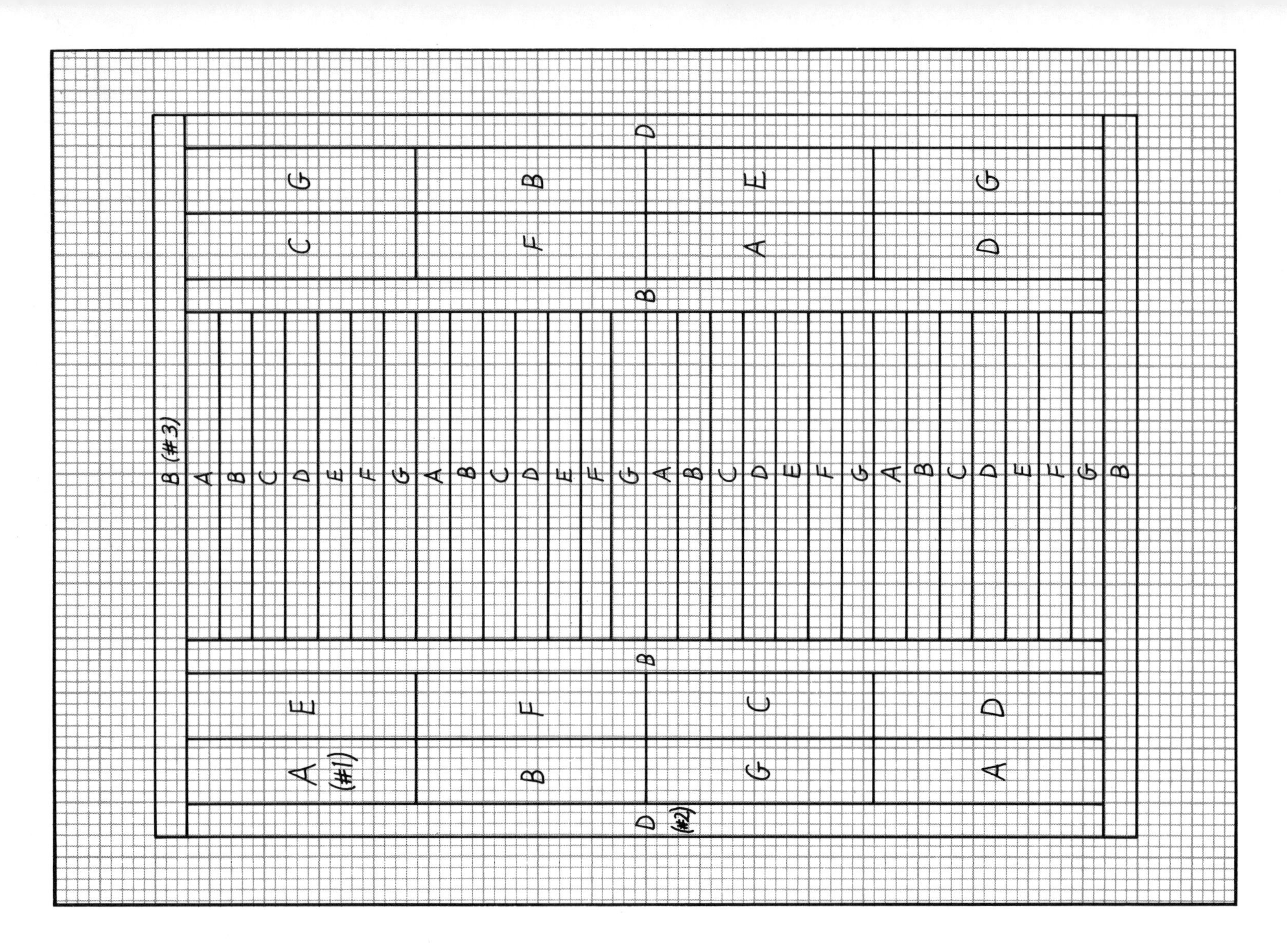

B (#3)
A B C D E F G A B C D E F G A B C D E F G A B C D E F G B
A (#1)
D (#2)

TO FINISH: Lay out the patches as shown in Fig. 8-4. Try to find a place in the house where you can leave the patches undisturbed while you sew. This will make it much easier to see exactly how far along you are, and which piece to attach next.

**Golden Afghan*** (Fig. 8-5)

FINISHED SIZE: APPROX. 37″ × 59″

YOU NEED: 4-ply worsted-weight wool.

| | |
|---|---|
| 3 4-oz. skeins in light yellow-gold | (Shade A) |
| 1 4-oz. skein in yellow-gold | (Shade B) |
| 1 4-oz. skein in canary | (Shade C) |
| 1 4-oz. skein in brown | (Shade D) |
| 1 4-oz. skein in white | (Shade E) |

A pair of size-10½ needles

GAUGE: 4 sts and 5 rows to 1 inch over st st on size-10½ needles.

THE AFGHAN: Worked in three very simple patches (see Fig. 8-6). The interest is given to the design by making one of the patches striped.

*Patch #1:* (Make 7.)
With A, cast on 156 sts.
Work 3 inches in st st, bind off.

*Patch #2:* (Make 30.)
With A, cast on 12 sts.
Work 6 inches in st st, bind off.

Fig. 8-4 *Layout for afghan in brilliant colors*

Fig. 8-5 *Golden afghan*

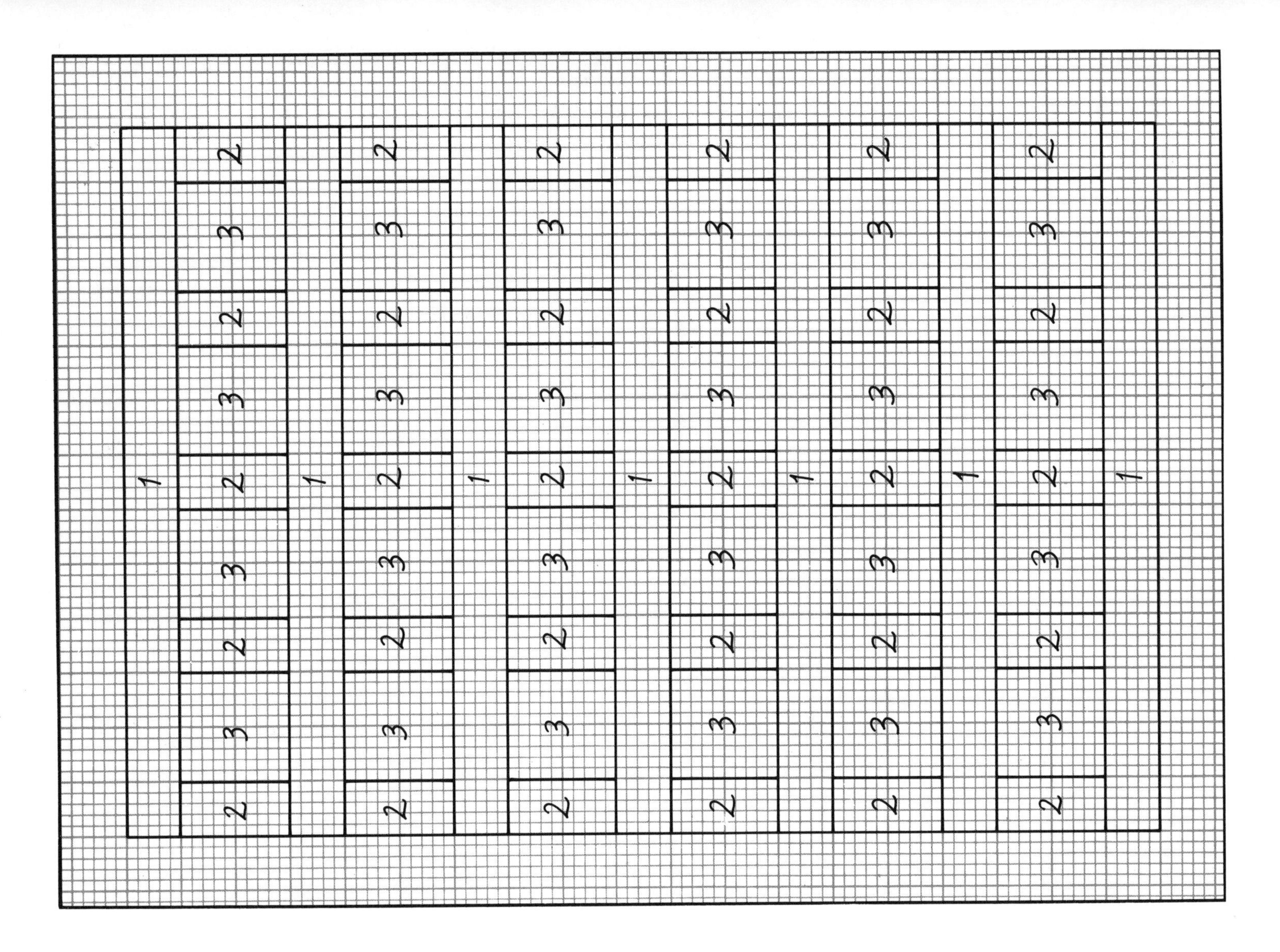
1
2
3
2
3
2
3
2
3
2
1
2
3
2
3
2
3
2
3
2
1
2
3
2
3
2
3
2
3
2
1
2
3
2
3
2
3
2
3
2
1
2
3
2
3
2
3
2
3
2
1
2
3
2
3
2
3
2
3
2
1

*Patch #3:* (Make 24.)
With B, cast on 24 sts.
Work 4 rows in st st in shade B, break off B, join E.

Continue working in st st, changing color as follows:

| | |
|---|---|
| 4 rows E | 4 rows D |
| 2 rows B | 2 rows B |
| 4 rows D | 4 rows E |
| 4 Rows C | 4 rows B |

Bind off.

To Finish: Lay out the pieces as shown in Fig. 8-6. Try to find a place where you can leave the pieces undisturbed as you sew.

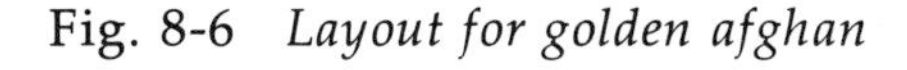

Fig. 8-6 *Layout for golden afghan*

**Diamond Spread*** (Fig. 8-7)

This design can be used as either a bedspread or a blanket for a single bed. Although it is made in three colors here, the pattern could easily be applied as a basis for using up any old scraps of yarn. The entire cover is made in very simple 5″ × 5″ garter stitch squares.

Finished Size: Approx. 70″ × 90″
You Need: 4-ply acrylic.

| | |
|---|---|
| 8 4-oz. skeins in off-white | (Shade A) |
| 8 4-oz. skeins in copper | (Shade B) |
| 8 4-oz. skein in avocado green | (Shade C) |

A pair of size-10½ needles.

Fig. 8-7 *Diamond spread*

Gauge: 4 sts and 5 rows to 1 inch over st st on size-10½ needles.
The Cover: Worked in one basic square throughout.

*The Square:* Cast on 20 sts.
Work 5 inches in garter st, bind off.

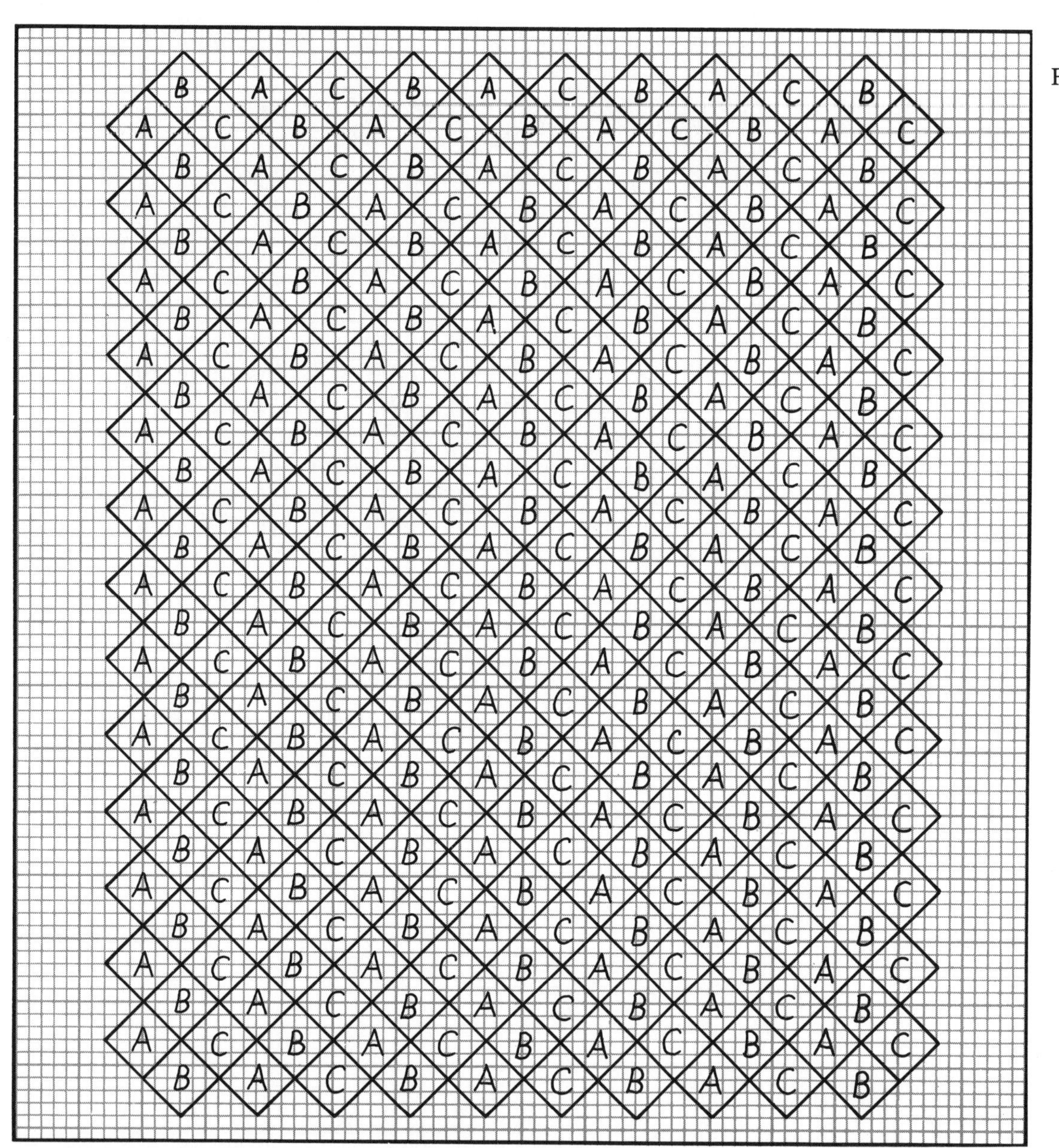


Fig. 8-8 *Layout for diamond spread*

*Make:*

94 in A
95 in B
94 in C

TO FINISH: Sew the patches together in rows on the diagonal as shown in Fig. 8-8.

**Double Bedspread*** (Fig. 8-9)

Although large, this is an extremely simple project, worked in stockinette stitch throughout.

FINISHED SIZE: APPROX. 90″ × 96″ (for a double bed 4′6″ wide)
YOU NEED: 4-ply acrylic.

| | |
|---|---|
| 7 4-oz. skeins in white | (Shade A) |
| 7 4-oz. skeins in gold | (Shade B) |
| 6 3½-oz. skeins in gold ombré | (Shade C) |
| A pair of size-10½ needles | |

GAUGE: 4 sts and 5 rows to 1 inch over st st on size-10½ needles.
THE BEDSPREAD: Made in five basic patches, which are repeated to make the pattern (see Fig. 8-10).

*Patch #1:* Measures 6″ × 18″
Cast on 24 sts.
Work 18 inches in st st, bind off.

*Make:*

12 in A
12 in B
11 in C

Fig. 8-9 *Double bedspread*

*Patch #2:* Measures 12″ × 12″
Cast on 48 sts.
Work 12 inches in st st, bind off.

*Make:*
12 in A
12 in B

*Patch #3:* Measures 6″ × 36″
Cast on 24 sts.
Work 36 inches in st st, bind off.

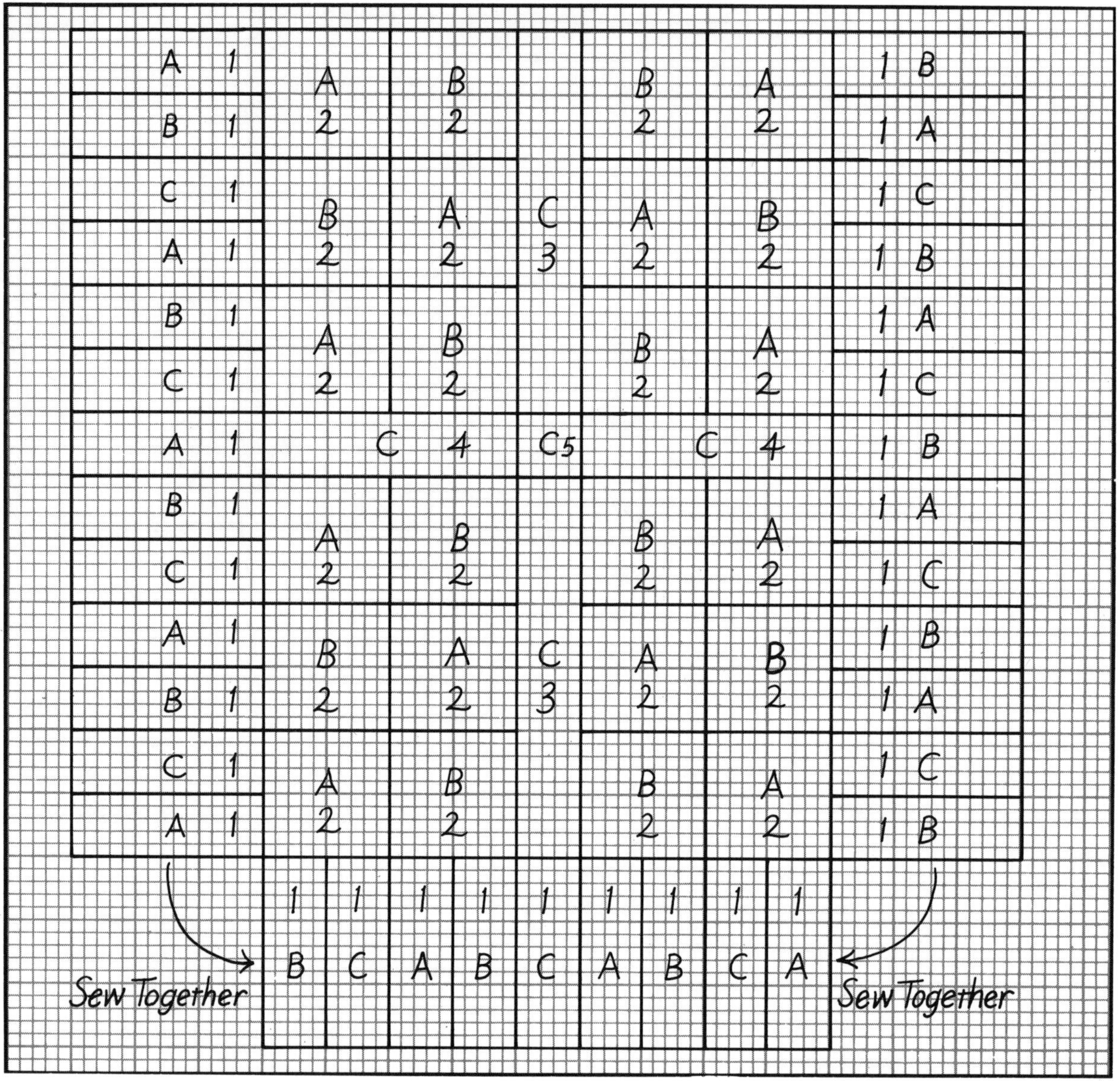

Fig. 8-10
*Layout for double bedspread*

*Make:*
2 in C

*Patch #4:* Measures 24″ × 6″
Cast on 96 sts.
Work 6 inches in st st, bind off.

*Make:*
2 in C

*Patch #5:* Measures 6″ × 6″ (Make one.)
With C, cast on 24 sts.
Work 6 inches in st st, bind off.

To Finish: Following Fig. 8-10, lay out the patches on the floor, preferably where they can remain undisturbed while sewing is in progress. When you have sewn all the patches together as shown on the diagram, sew the two seams indicated by the arrows.

Fig. 8-11 *Double blanket*

## More Knitted Patches

The patches that now follow are all used in the patchwork double blanket, shown in Fig. 8-11, and the single blanket, in Fig. 8-12. Detailed instructions are not given for these blankets, since they are patchwork projects in the true tradition of using scrap materials. Of course, with projects this size it would be highly unlikely that you would have that amount of yarn just lying around. However, I think the projects are much more fun if you buy the yarn only as you need it, choosing the colors as you work. Just remember not to use yarns of different weights in the same project. To give you the maximum freedom in creating your own blankets, I have provided two very simple layout diagrams: one for a double blanket (Fig. 8-13) and one for a single (Fig. 8-14). These blankets are based on a 10-inch square, and all the instructions for the patches that follow are given in those dimensions.

Fig. 8-12 *Single blanket*

The single blanket in Fig. 8-12 was worked entirely in garter stitch in 10-inch squares. I managed to use up nearly all my small remnants of yarn by striping the squares, sometimes in a pattern, sometimes at random. I strongly recommend this project for anyone who has a rather large store of leftover yarns.

The single blanket discussed above and the patches that now follow are worked in a 4-ply yarn on size-10½ needles. You should have a gauge of 4 stitches and 5 rows to 1 inch over stockinette.

*Patch #1:* Tile stitch (Fig. 8-15)
Cast on 41 sts.
*Rows 1, 3, and 5:* K.
*Rows 2 and 4:* K 1,* P 4, K 1, repeat* across.
*Row 6:* K.
These 6 rows form the pattern. Repeat them until the patch measures 10 inches, bind off.

*Patch #2:* Hurdle stitch (Fig. 8-16)
Cast on 42 sts.
*Rows 1 and 2:* K.
*Rows 3 and 4:** K 1, P 1, repeat from* across.
These 4 rows form the pattern. Repeat them until the patch measures 10 inches, bind off.

*Variations of Patch #2*

1. Try alternating a contrasting color after every fourth row has been completed.
2. Change to a different color after every fourth row has been worked. This will create a striped effect.

Fig. 8-13
*Layout for double blanket, worked in 10-inch squares*

| 1 | 2 | 3 | 4 | 5 | 6 | 7 | 8 | 9 |
|---|---|---|---|---|---|---|---|---|
| 10 | 11 | 12 | 13 | 14 | 15 | 16 | 17 | 18 |
| 19 | 20 | 21 | 22 | 23 | 24 | 25 | 26 | 27 |
| 28 | 29 | 30 | 31 | 32 | 33 | 34 | 35 | 36 |
| 37 | 38 | 39 | 40 | 41 | 42 | 43 | 44 | 45 |
| 46 | 47 | 48 | 49 | 50 | 51 | 52 | 53 | 54 |
| 55 | 56 | 57 | 58 | 59 | 60 | 61 | 62 | 63 |
| 64 | 65 | 66 | 67 | 68 | 69 | 70 | 71 | 72 |
| 73 | 74 | 75 | 76 | 77 | 78 | 79 | 80 | 81 |
| 82 | 83 | 84 | 85 | 86 | 87 | 88 | 89 | 90 |

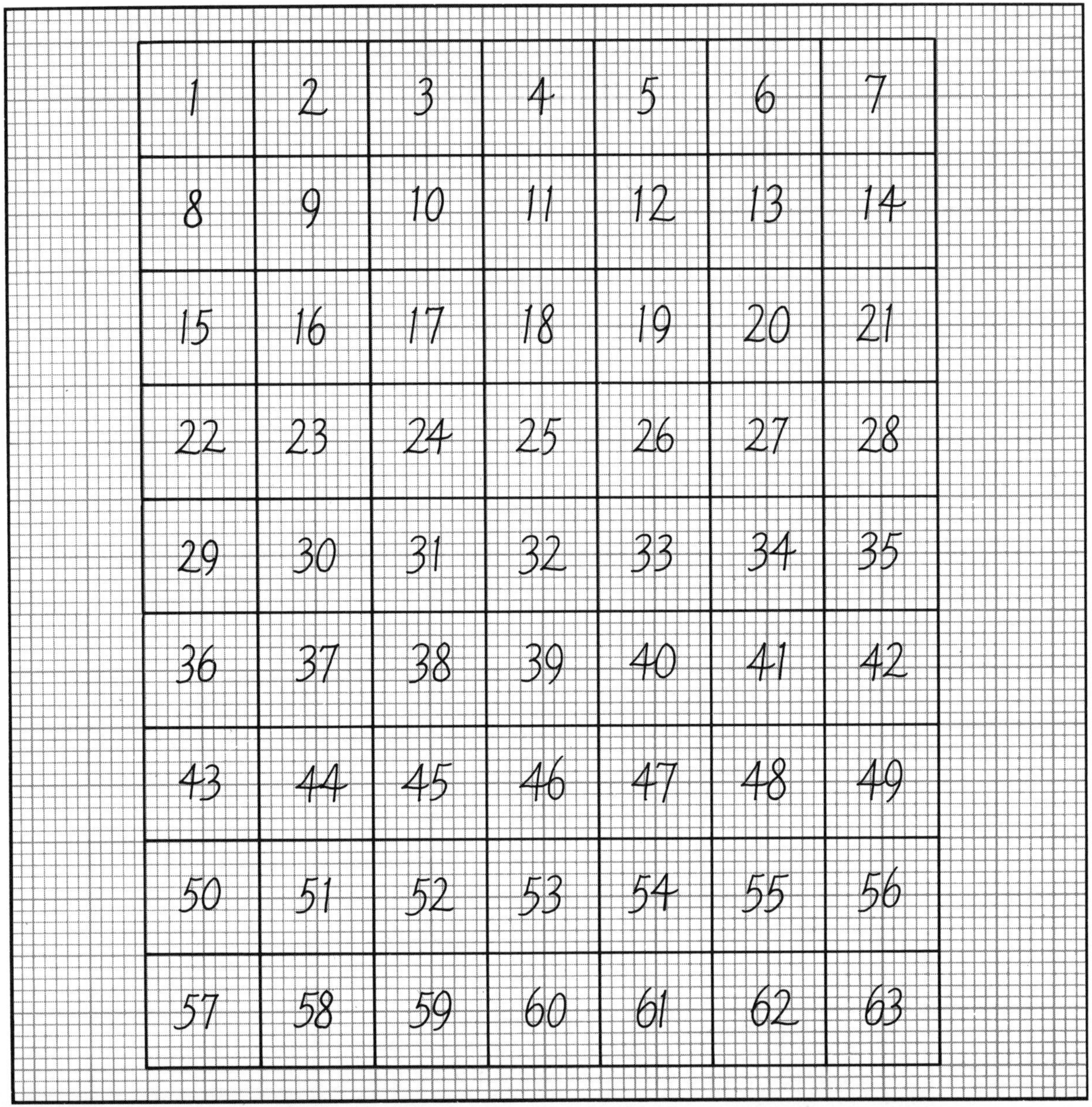

| 1 | 2 | 3 | 4 | 5 | 6 | 7 |
|---|---|---|---|---|---|---|
| 8 | 9 | 10 | 11 | 12 | 13 | 14 |
| 15 | 16 | 17 | 18 | 19 | 20 | 21 |
| 22 | 23 | 24 | 25 | 26 | 27 | 28 |
| 29 | 30 | 31 | 32 | 33 | 34 | 35 |
| 36 | 37 | 38 | 39 | 40 | 41 | 42 |
| 43 | 44 | 45 | 46 | 47 | 48 | 49 |
| 50 | 51 | 52 | 53 | 54 | 55 | 56 |
| 57 | 58 | 59 | 60 | 61 | 62 | 63 |

Fig. 8-14 *Layout for single blanket, worked in 10-inch squares.*

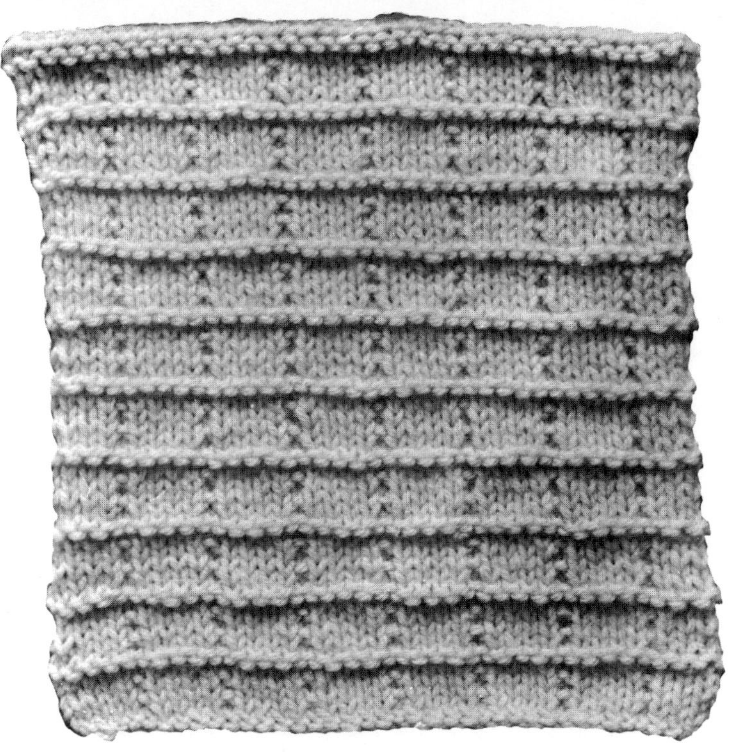

Fig. 8-15 *Knitted patch #2—tile stitch*

Fig. 8-16 *Knitted patch #2—hurdle stitch*

*Patch #3:* Block stitch (Fig. 8-17)
Cast on 42 sts. Keep a 1 st selvage at each side of work.
Instructions are given for working center 40 sts.
*Rows 1 to 4:* * K 4, P 4, repeat from* across.
*Rows 5 to 8:* * P 4, K 4, repeat from* across.

These 8 rows form the pattern. Repeat until the patch measures 10 inches, bind off.

*Variations on Patch #3.*

1. Work with blocks of K 5, P 5, instead of 4.
2. Work with blocks of K 8, P 8, instead of 4.
3. Try changing color after every fourth row.

Fig. 8-17 *Knitted patch #3—block stitch*

Fig. 8-18 *Knitted patch #4—basket stitch*

*Patch #4:* Basket stitch (Fig. 8-18)
Cast on 42 sts.
*Row 1:* K.
*Row 2:* P.
*Row 3:* K.
*Row 4:** K 3, P 3, repeat from* across.
*Row 5:* K.
*Row 6:* As Row 4.
*Row 7:* K.
*Row 8:* As Row 4.
*Row 9:* K.
*Row 10:* P.
*Row 11:* K.
*Row 12:** P 3, K 3, repeat from* across.

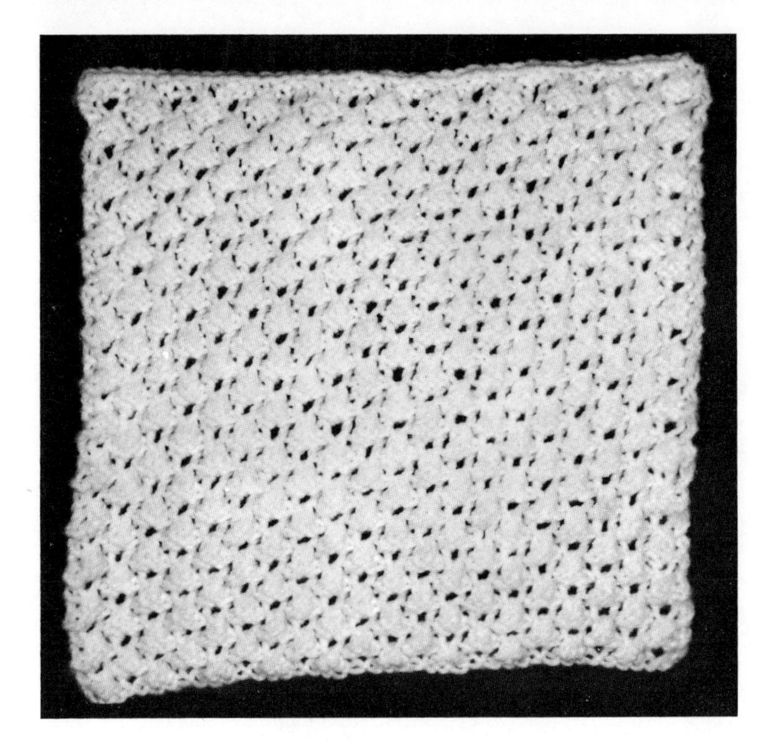

Fig. 8-19 *Knitted patch #5—blackberry stitch*

*Row 13:* K.
*Row 14:* As Row 12.
*Row 15:* K.
*Row 16:* As Row 12.
These 16 rows form the pattern.
Repeat them until the patch measures 10 inches, bind off.

*Patch #5:* Blackberry stitch (Fig. 8-19)
Cast on 42 sts.
*Row 1:* K 1,* into next st work K 1, P 1, and K 1, then P 3, repeat from* across to last st, K 1.
*Row 2:* K 1,* P 3 tog, K 3, repeat from* across to last st, K 1.
*Row 3:* K 1,* P 3, then into next st work K 1, P 1, and K 1, repeat from * across to last st, K 1.
*Row 4:* K 1,* K 3, P 3 tog, repeat from* across to last st, K 1.
These 4 rows form the pattern. Repeat them until the patch measures 10 inches, bind off.

*Variations of Patch #5:*
1. Change color every two rows.
2. Change color every four rows.

### Jacquard Patches

When more than one color appears in the same row, a jacquard pattern is created. To work such a pattern, carry the unused color loosely across the back of the work, catching it on every fourth stitch.

Figs. 8-20 through 8-25 contain diagrams for making the 10-inch squares needed for the double and single bedspreads above. Each of these jacquard patches is based on 44 stitches and 50 rows. Because jacquard has the tendency to tighten the gauge widthways, an extra few stitches have been added to compensate. Use 4-ply yarn and size-10½ needles. The contrasting colors are indicated in the diagrams by the symbols "×" and ".". The main, or

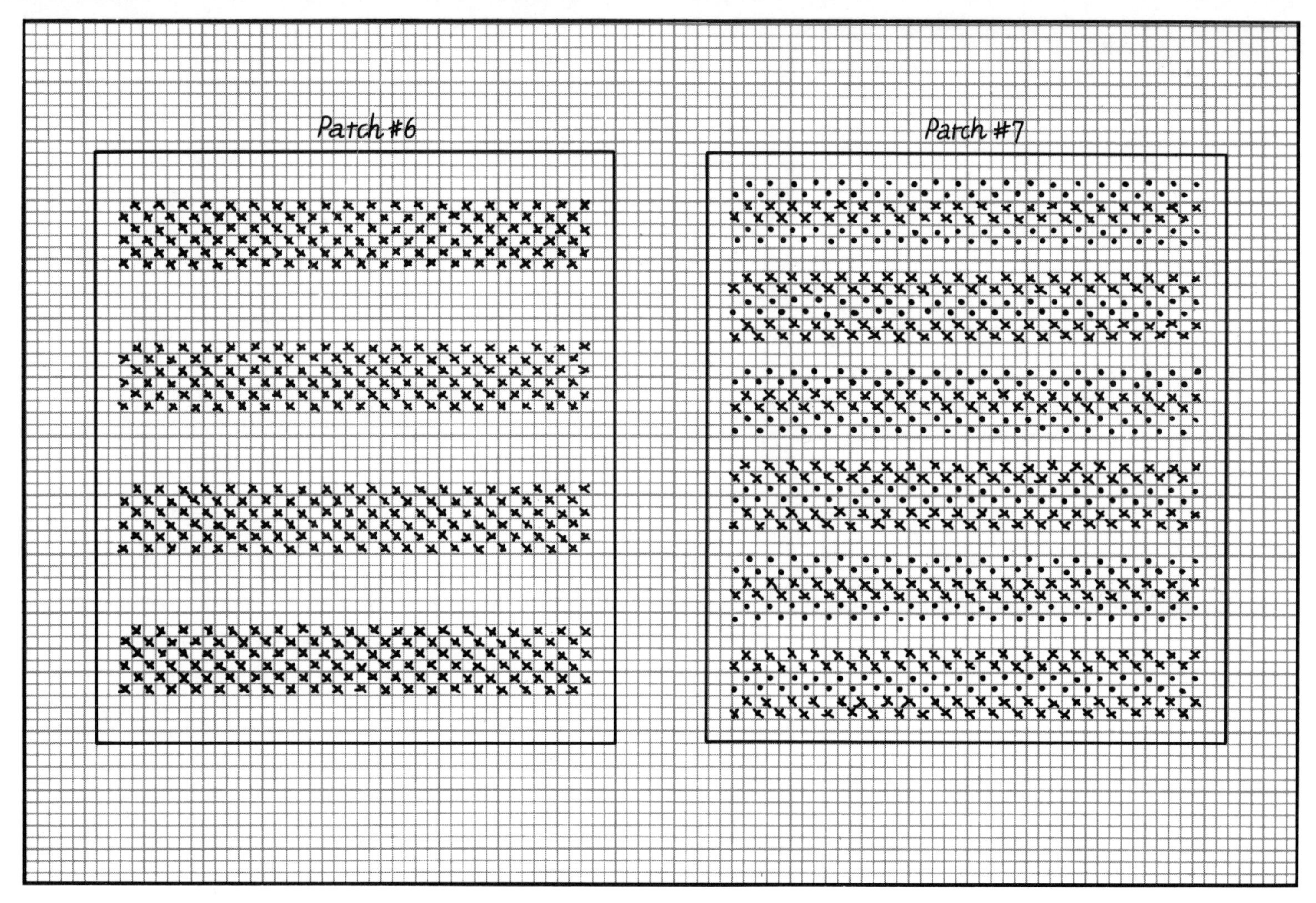


Fig. 8-20 *Jacquard patches #6 and #7*

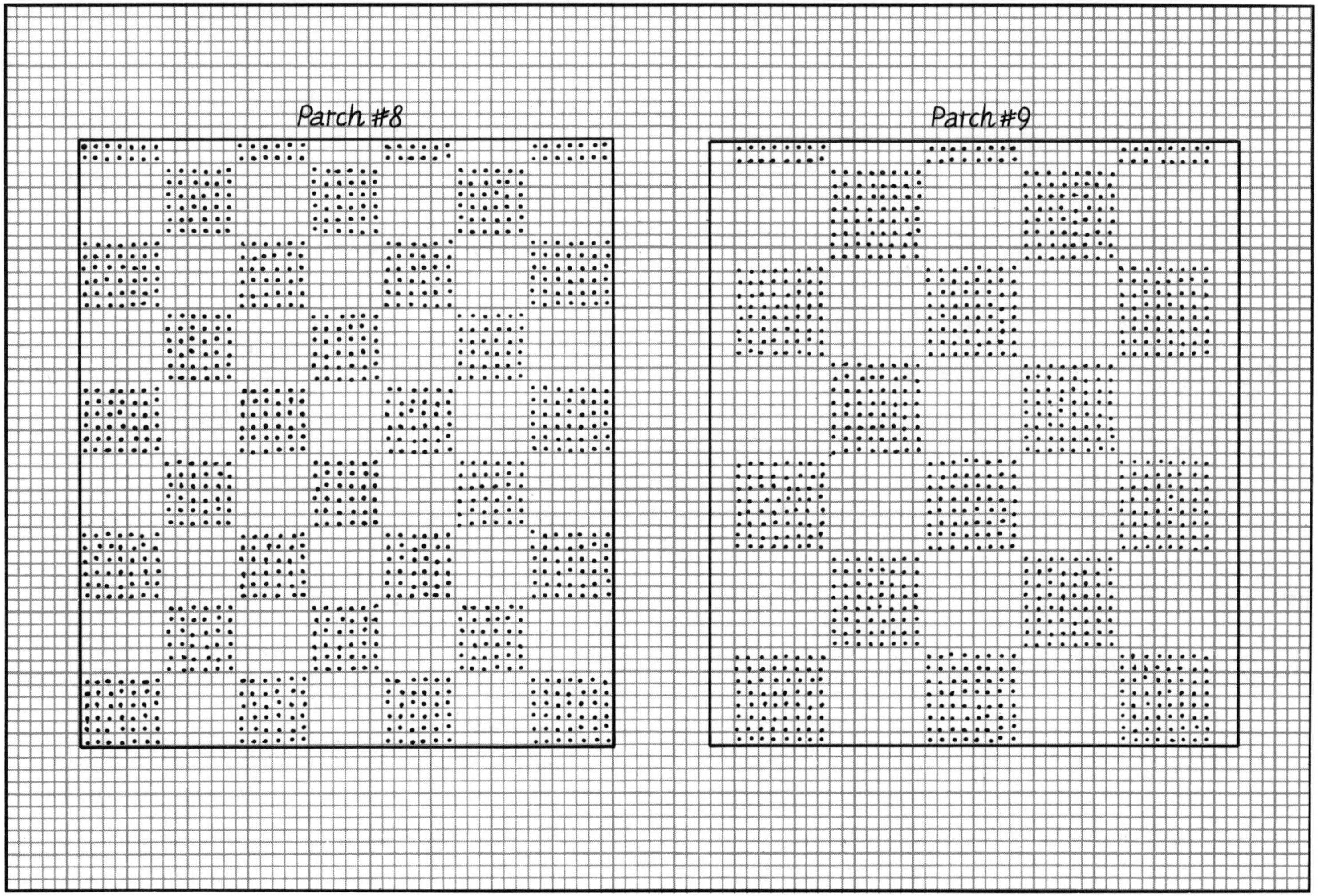

Parch #8

Parch #9

Fig. 8-21 *Jacquard patches #8 and #9*

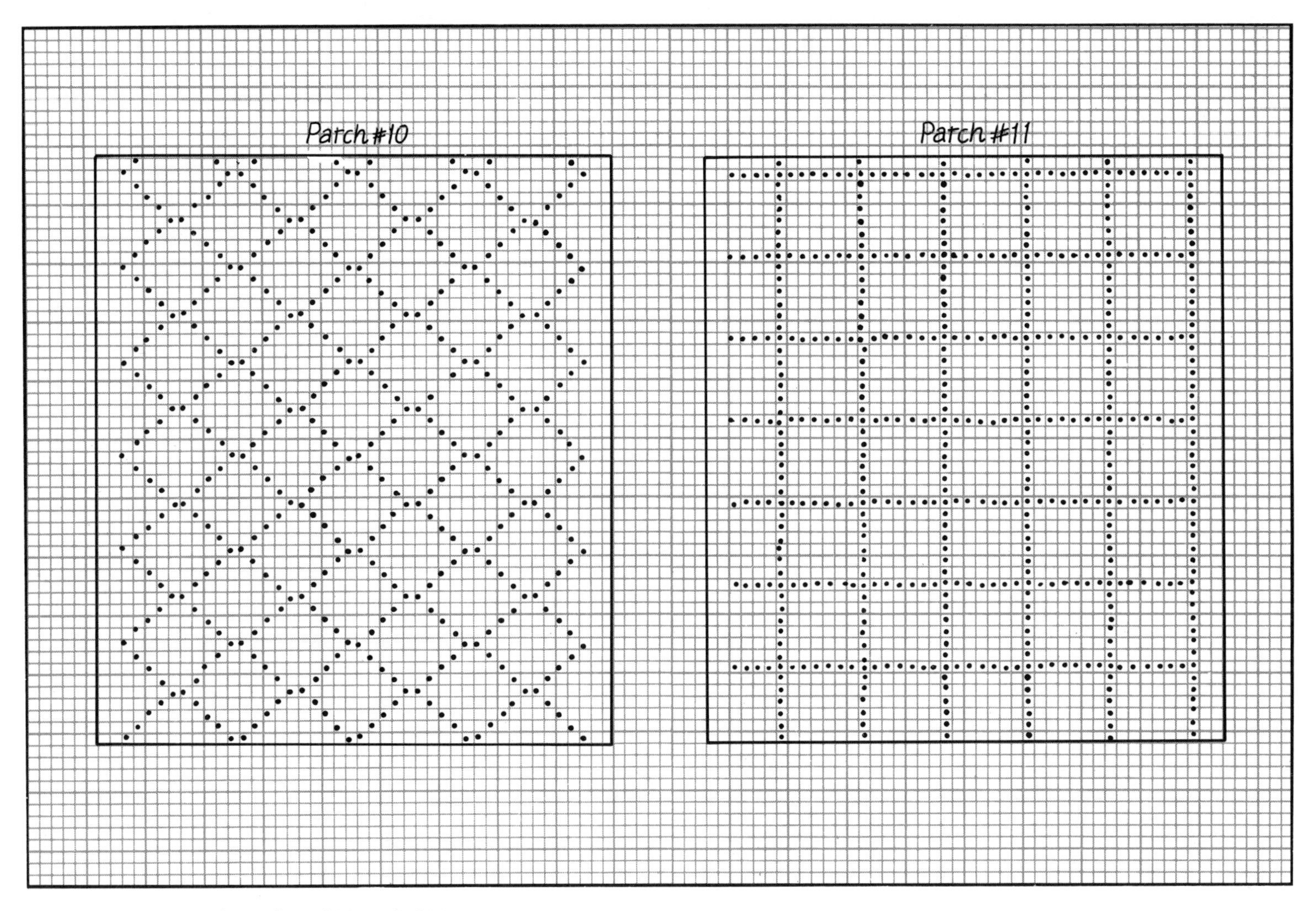


Fig. 8-22 *Jacquard patches #10 and #11*

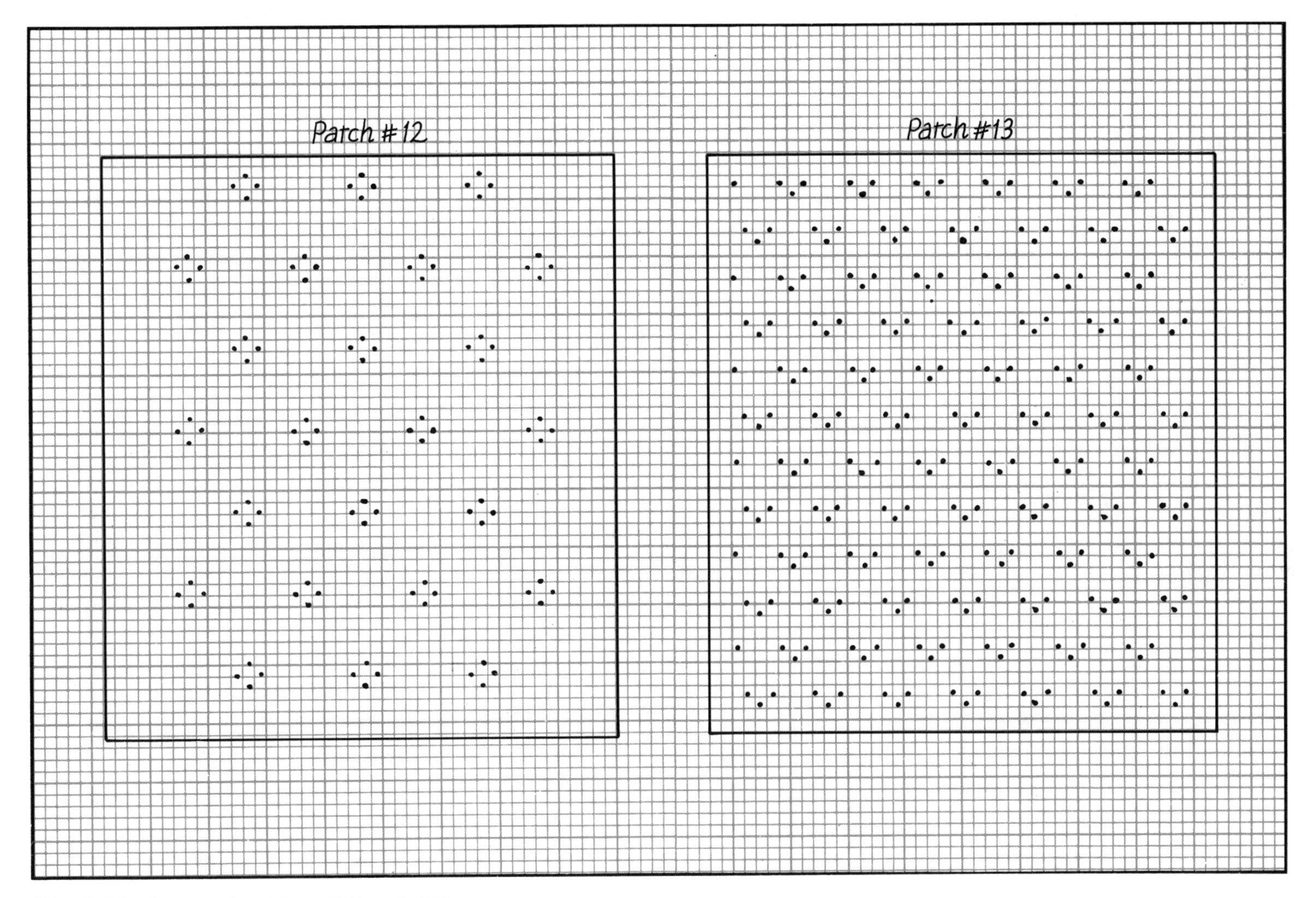


Fig. 8-23 *Jacquard patches #12 and #13*

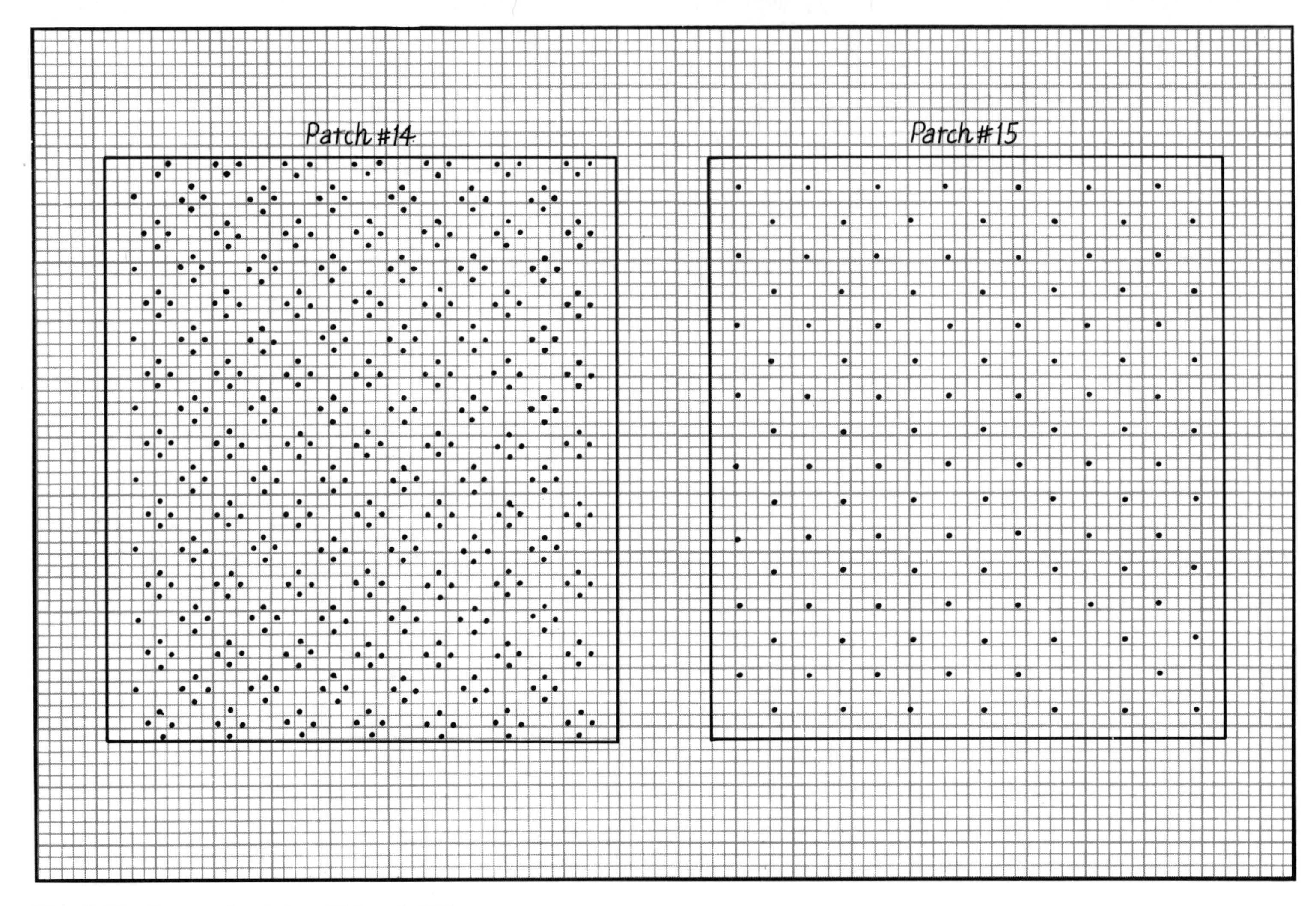


Fig. 8-24 *Jacquard patches #14 and #15*

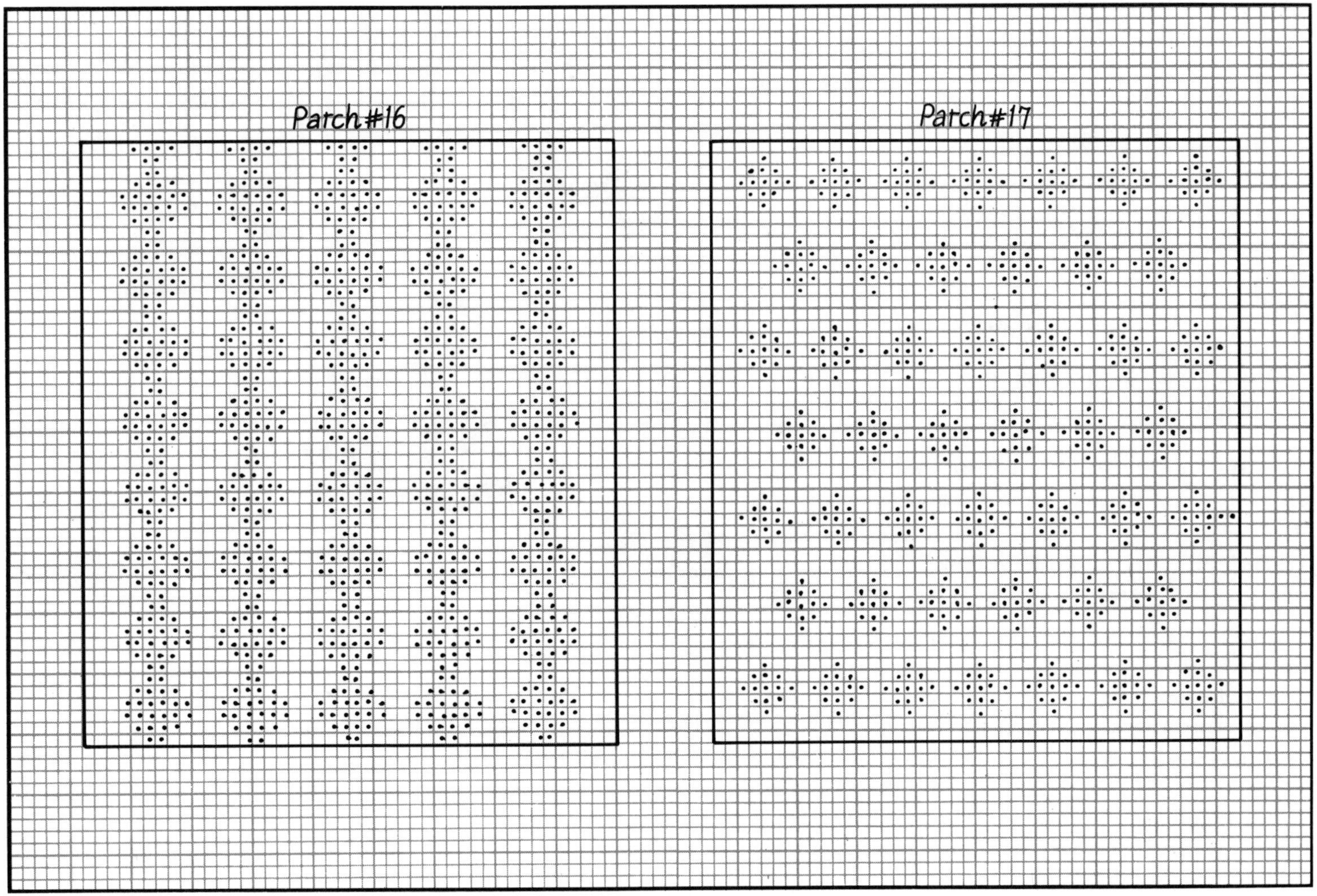

Parch #16

Parch #17

Fig. 8-25 *Jacquard patches #16 and #17*

background, color is left blank on the charts. One square equals one stitch throughout.

## Project Suggestions

**Patch Tunic** (Fig. 8-26)

FINISHED SIZE: Will fit small to medium.
YOU NEED: 4-ply worsted-weight wool.
2 4-oz. skeins in black (Shade A) and
4 2-oz. skeins in charcoal gray tweed (Shade B)
A pair of size-10½ needles
A size-I aluminum crochet hook

GAUGE: 4 sts and 5 rows to 1 inch over st st using size-10½ needles.
THE TUNIC: Before starting, study the layout of the pieces as shown in Fig. 8-27. The front and back are the same, each being worked in two halves. The sleeves and yoke are worked in one long piece.

*Right half:* (Front and back) Make 2.
With B, cast on 48 sts.
Work 12 rows in garter st.
*Row 13* (and every following tenth row):
Dec 1 st at beg of row, work to end.
Continue working in garter st, decreasing on every tenth row until 84 rows have been completed, break off B, join A.
Continue decreasing as before, until 36 sts remain. Work straight until 60 rows have been worked in A, bind off.

Fig. 8-26 *Patchwork tunic*

*Left half:* (Front and back) Make 2. Work as for the right half, starting with A and changing to B after 84 rows.
Work all decreases at the *end* of the row.
Sew the two halves of the front and back together, but leave the side seams open.

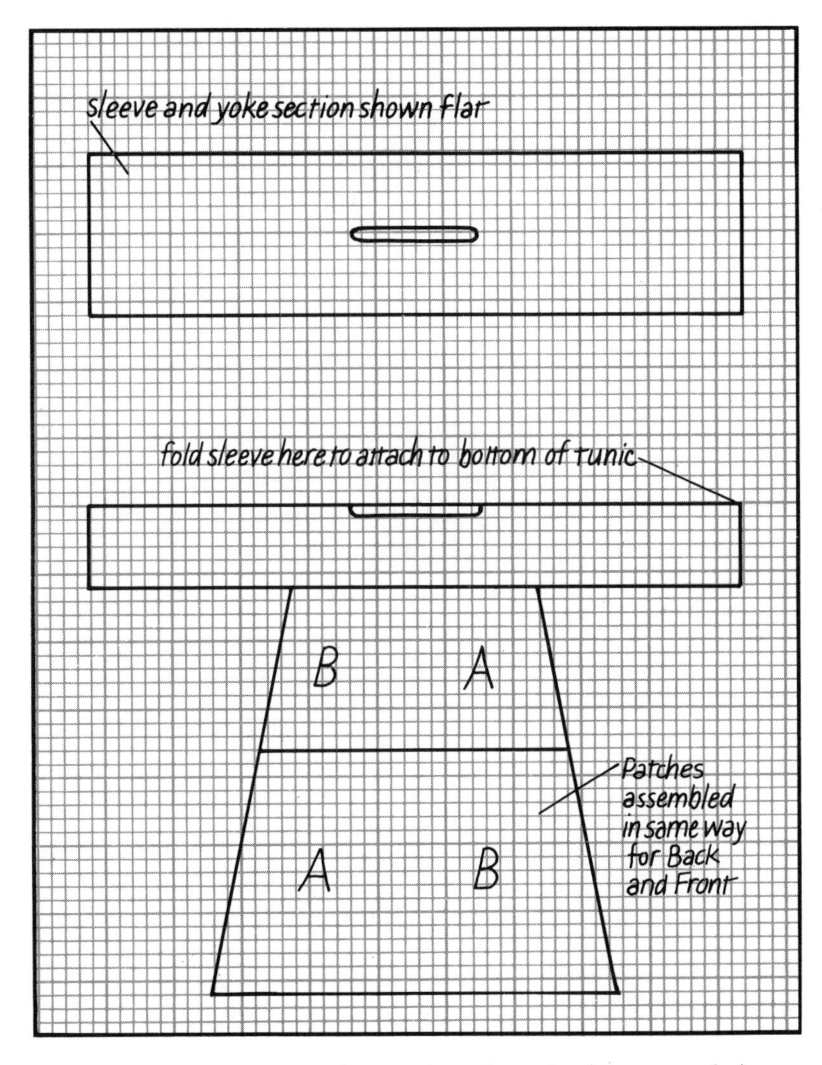


Fig. 8-27 *Layouts for patchwork tunic. (Not to scale.)*

*Sleeves and yoke:* (Make one.)
With A, cast on 64 sts.
Work 4 rows in garter st, do not break off A but carry unused yarn at side of work, join B.
Work in garter st:

2 rows B
2 rows A

until sleeve measures 20 inches from start. This striping is worked over entire sleeve and yoke.

*Shape neck:*
K 32 sts, turn.
*Decrease* 1 st at neck edge on next 6 rows (26 sts).
Continue on these 26 sts until 9 inches have been worked from beg of neck shaping.
*Increase* 1 st at neck edge on next 6 rows (32 sts).
*Make sure to start and finish shaping with the same color stripe.*
Leave these stitches on a spare needle, return to other side of neck and work the same as for first side.
Now work across entire row, and continue straight until work measures 19½ inches from neck edge (or 4 rows less than other sleeve). *End with a stripe in Shade B.*

Work last 4 rows in A, bind off.

*Neck edge:* With A, and size-I crochet hook, work 2 rows sc around entire neck edge.

To Finish: Mark center front and back on yoke. Sew back and front to yoke placing join of two halves at center marker on yoke in each case. Sew side and sleeve seams.

### Patch Blankets

Figs. 8-28 and 8-29 offer two further suggestions for patterns in which a patchwork blanket or cover can be made. But remember, the possibilities are endless, and I strongly recommend that you try out your own design ideas on squared or graph paper. The hints on planning a patchwork crochet project in Chapter 5 will be helpful in this respect.

## Finishing Patchwork Knitting

The basic methods of sewing and crocheting together patches are discussed in Chapter 5, as they apply to crochet. Knitting should be treated in a similar fashion.

However, knitting differs in one respect from crochet. When you are working in stockinette stitch, you will find it much easier to press the patches *before* sewing. They curl up after binding off, and are very awkward to handle as they are. They should be pinned out to the cor-

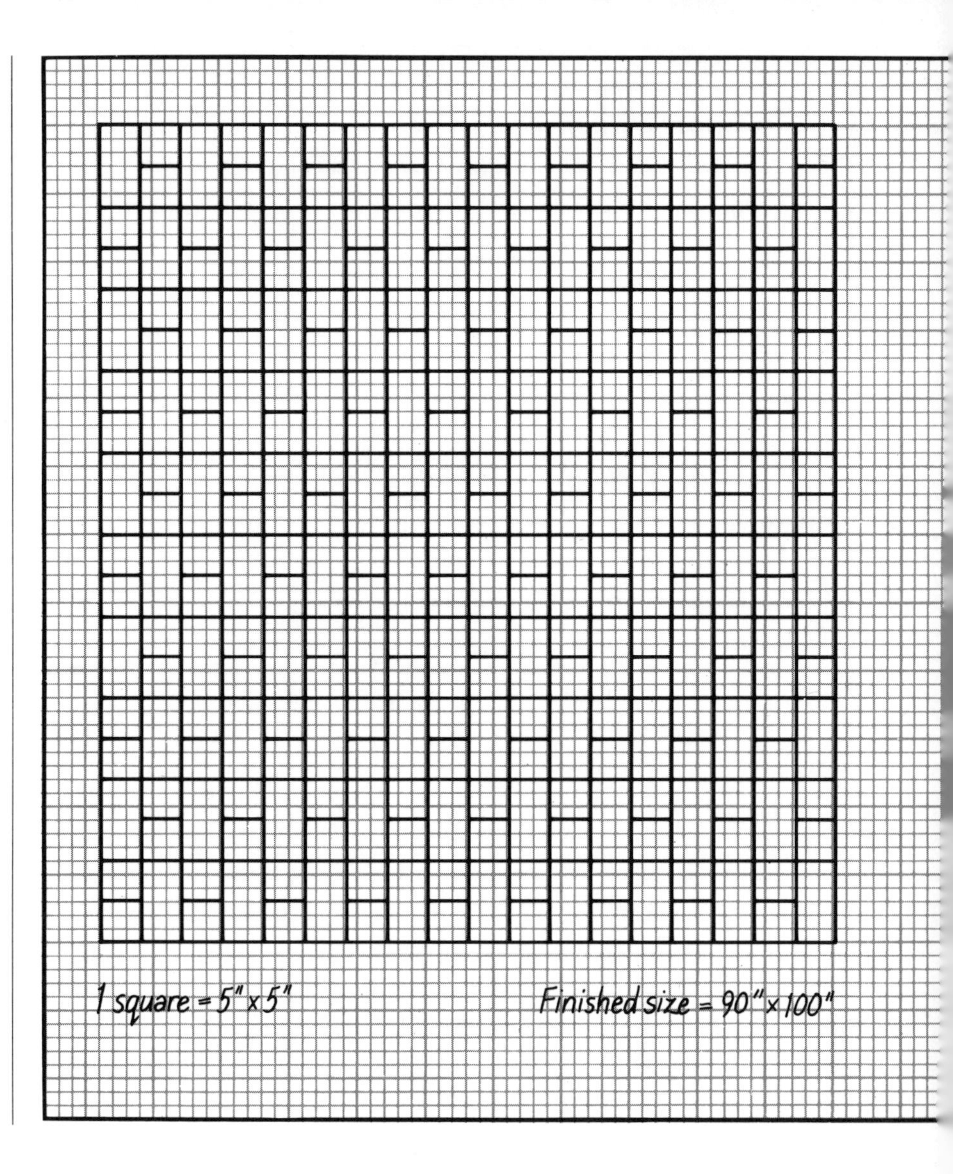


Fig. 8-28 *Layout for double blanket*

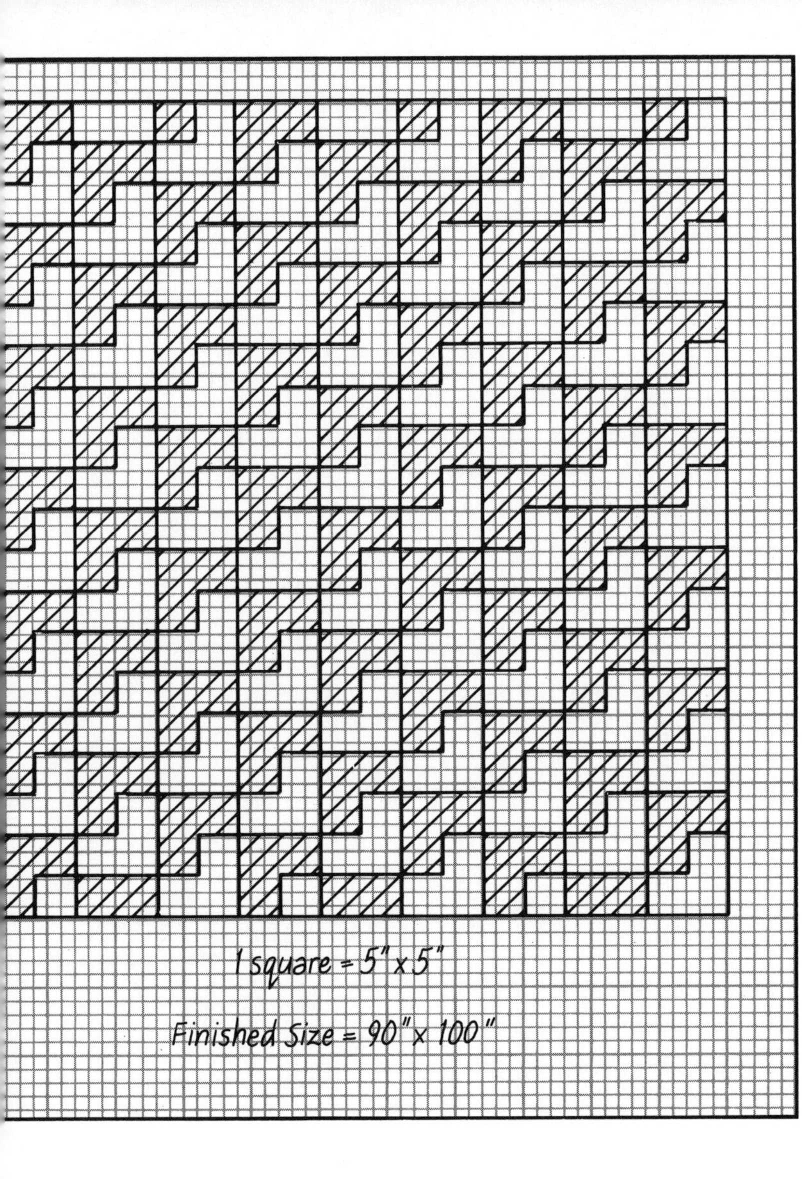


rect size on an ironing board and, with a damp cloth between them and the iron, pressed firmly. Dry the pieces flat, if possible, after pressing. Never use clothespins to hang them on a line at this point, or you will have ugly marks in the corners. The seams can be lightly pressed again, also with a damp cloth, after the sewing has been completed.

Some knitting stitches, like crochet, are best never pressed. For all raised stitches, such as ribs and garter stitch, steam the seams into shape after sewing. This type of stitch will not curl up after working, so you should find no difficulty in sewing the patches together before the final steaming.

### *Borders*

If you can crochet, many of the projects in this chapter would look better with a thin border of single crochet around them, which finishes off the raw edges.

Fig. 8-29 *Layout for double blanket in two colors*

# 9 Basic Bargello and Patchwork

Known alternatively as Hungarian point, Florentine needlepoint, or simply Bargello, this easy and quick stitch has been growing in popularity over the past few years. One of the reasons for this is undoubtedly the extraordinary versatility of such an easily mastered technique. There is basically only one stitch, which, when lengthened, shortened, and arranged in groups affords an almost endless range of effects. This chapter will give a brief, but comprehensive, survey of all you will need to know to start working in Bargello even if you have never done so before. It also provides a detailed guide to the techniques used in the projects, which follow in the next chapter. There is also a discussion of those particular elements in Bargello that lend themselves so well to creating patchwork designs.

## Materials for Bargello

The canvas used for Bargello is called "mono," meaning that it is woven with one thread (see Fig. 9-1), unlike Penelope or rug canvas which generally have two. Although Bargello can be successfully worked on Penelope canvas, mono is always preferred because it is easier to count the meshes without the confusion of the double weave. Widths of canvas vary from 27 inches to about 40 inches, one-yard widths being the most common. The fineness or coarseness of a canvas is measured by the number of holes, or meshes, there are to one inch. The most useful canvases to use for Bargello work are those with 14, 12, or 10 mesh to 1 inch.

Some canvas is produced in a beige or coffee color, some in pale yellow, while most is pure white. The advantage of a less than brilliant white background is that it tends to blend in better with the covering yarn. White canvas has a tendency to show through the work—especially when you are using dark colors.

There is a new type of canvas now on the market called "leno." It has an interlocking weave which prevents fraying, perhaps one of the most frequent hazards of working with a

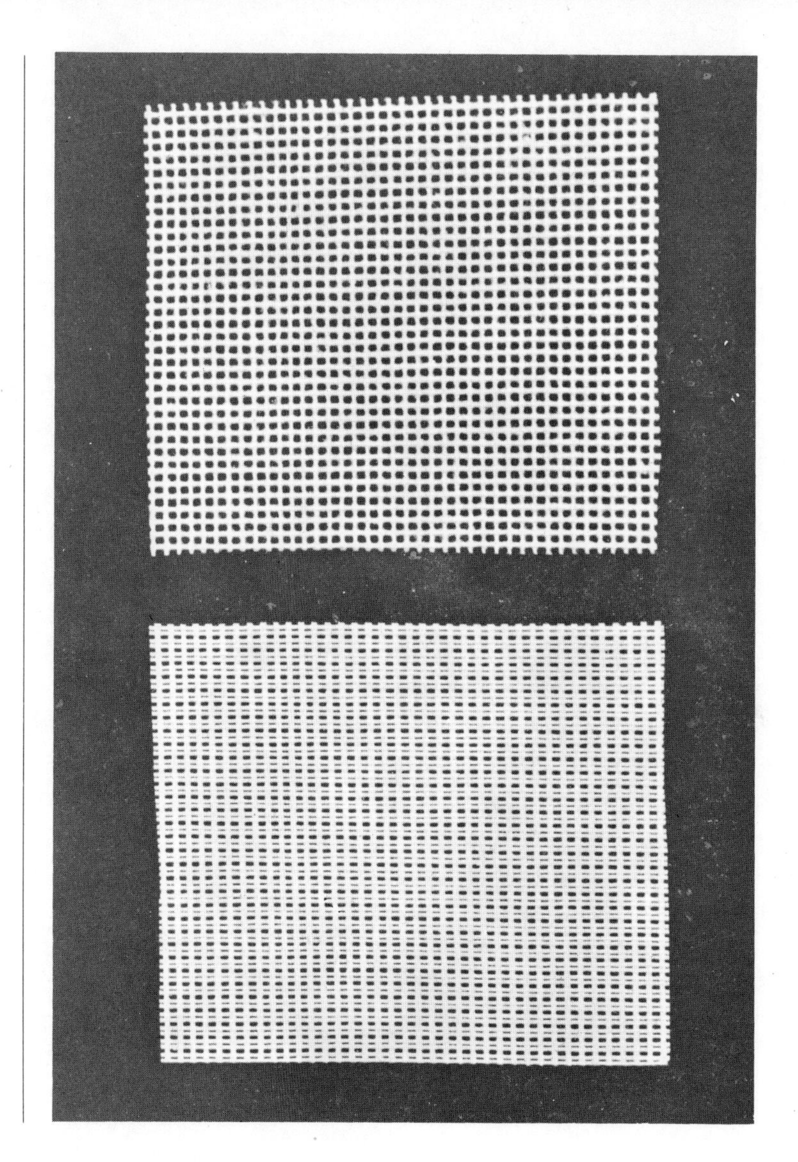

Fig. 9-1 *Penelope and mono canvases*

mono canvas. If you cannot buy the new leno weave, be sure to leave a generous border around the area of the canvas that you are actually going to work. The canvas measurements given in the project chapters allow for a border of 2 inches on each side. When you make up your finished canvas into a cushion, picture, or such, you will need to trim away the excess. However, make sure that you never trim your canvas closer than ½ inch from the edge of your work, unless there is a line of machine stitching holding the meshes in place. This is particularly important when dealing with the larger mesh of the mono canvases, such as 10 mesh to 1 inch. A finer-mesh canvas will obviously be more closely woven and ravel less. This is also true of the Penelope and other double-weave canvases.

If you are lucky enough to purchase an interlocking canvas, you can cut the required border down to 1 inch on each side, thus reducing the amount of canvas you will need by 2 inches on each measurement. However, even with the interlocking canvas, it is unadvisable to trim your canvas down closer than ½ inch from the beginning of the Bargello.

Faced with a piece of ordinary, non-interlocking mono canvas and the problem of fraying borders, there is a relatively simple solution. You can bind all four edges of your work with masking tape before you begin. To do this, press the edge of the canvas onto the sticky side of the tape firmly, leaving half the width of the tape to fold over. For this reason it is advisable to use a fairly wide tape, and certainly not one narrower than 1 inch. Having folded the tape over the edge of the canvas, run the handle end of a large pair of scissors firmly back and forth across the tape until the imprint of the meshes is clearly visible through it. This will help the tape to stick to the canvas. Repeat the same process for the other three sides. Should the tape begin to peel off as you work, remove it, and apply a fresh strip in the same way.

There is a wide range of yarns available for use in Bargello. Any needlepoint yarn can be used. The quality of yarn you choose will depend on the fineness of your canvas. The projects in this book, with the exception of the two rugs, use a canvas of 10 mesh to 1 inch. For that canvas, I have chosen an ordinary 4-ply knitting yarn, as it is both readily available and relatively inexpensive when compared with the special needlepoint yarns. It is always a good idea to start with a yarn that you wouldn't mind pulling out and throwing away if necessary. When you feel more confident in your abilities, perhaps you would prefer to use a more expensive yarn. You will certainly have a much better range of colors to choose from in any selection of needlepoint yarns. The only way to test the suitability of a yarn is to try it out on the canvas, and with the stitch you are going to use. The important point to watch for in Bargello work is that the yarn covers the canvas well. If you can see any canvas between the upright strands of the stitches, the yarn is too fine. On the other hand, if the yarn appears to be distorting the meshes, it is probably too thick.

In addition to canvas and yarn you will need a pair of embroidery scissors with fine, sharp points for cutting threads and ripping out any mistakes. The needles used for Bargello are blunt-ended with a large eye for ease in threading the relatively thick yarns needed to cover the canvas well. A size-18 tapestry needle is the correct one for working on 10-mesh-to-1-inch canvas. The needle and yarn should glide easily through the canvas, and not distort the mesh in doing so.

If you are accustomed to working with a frame for your needlepoint, then by all means continue to use one for Bargello. However, it is quite possible to achieve good results without one. Since Bargello is worked up and down the lines of the canvas, and not diagonally into the weave, the distortion, which causes so much extra work in ordinary needlepoint, does not occur. It would be rather unusual if you had to block your work when finished.

Liberated from the necessity of working with a frame, you can carry your work around with you, and make use of any spare moment to do a few stitches. Remember to keep the canvas neatly rolled when not in use—*never folded.* A large, protective plastic bag should be used to keep your Bargello clean.

## Working Bargello

Working in Bargello involves a considerable amount of counting to begin with, but once you have established the "foundation row," it is generally a matter of following the same line, repeating it in different colors, and working one row on top of another. The basic Bargello stitch can be worked over any number of meshes, the most common multiples being four and six.

To begin work, use a 4-ply knitting yarn and a 10-mesh-to-1-inch canvas. Start by cutting a piece of yarn some 20 to 22 inches long. Thread your needle and make a knot at the end. With the right side of the canvas facing you, push your needle through from the right to the wrong side, a few meshes to the left of where you intend to begin your pattern. Now bring your needle back up through the canvas to the right side at your true starting point (see Fig. 9-2). This technique, sometimes called "the waste knot," is always used for starting a Bargello stitch. As you work from right to left, your stitches will cover the end of the yarn lying at the back of the work. As you reach the knot, clip it away. This will prevent the ends of the yarn from working loose.

Now, to make the first stitch, ignore the mesh through which your yarn now passes and begin counting the first mesh directly above it (see Fig. 9-2). Go down into the fourth mesh you count and draw your yarn gently through to the back. Now count down two mesh in the row of holes to the left of the stitch you have just made (as shown in Fig. 9-3). Come up through the second mesh you count. This stitch is called "4-2 step" because you count up four and down two to create a staggered effect, like a series of steps. When you count up six and down three, you are working 6-3 step. Figure 9-4 shows how a series of stitches is

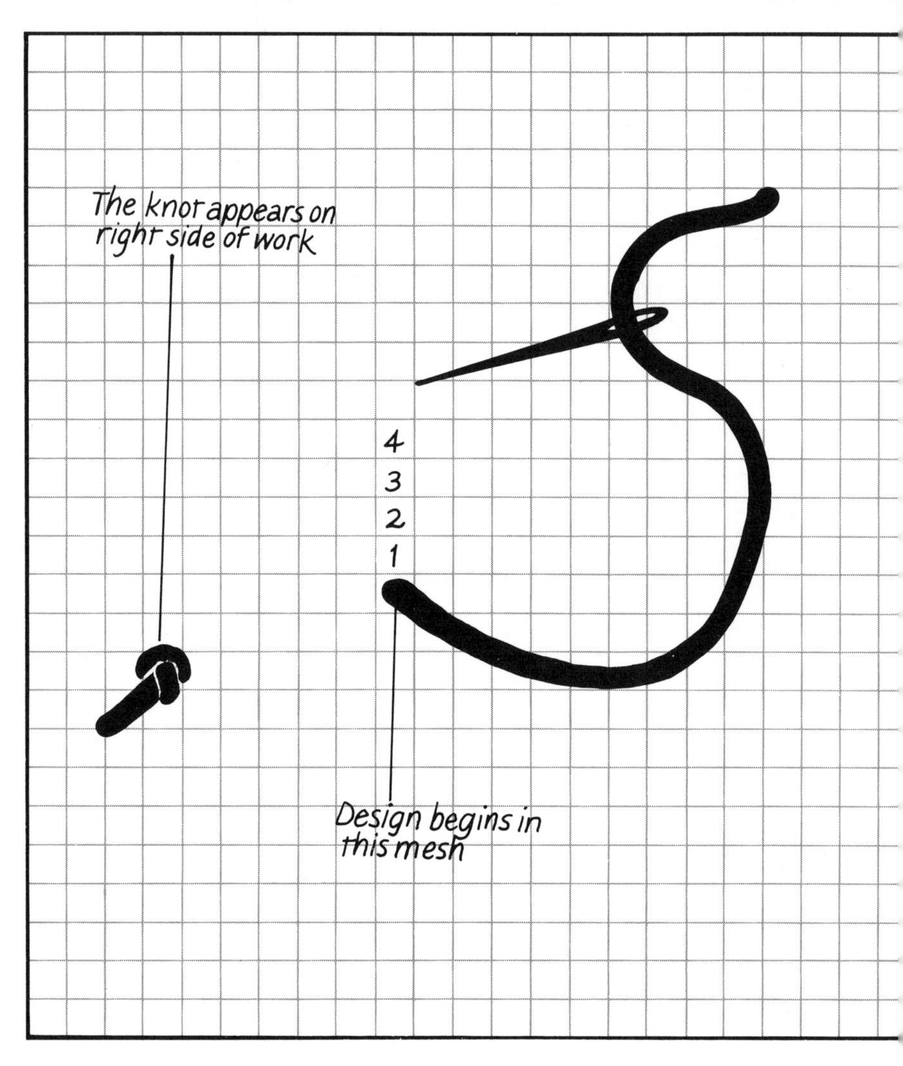


Fig. 9-2 *The "Waste Knot"*

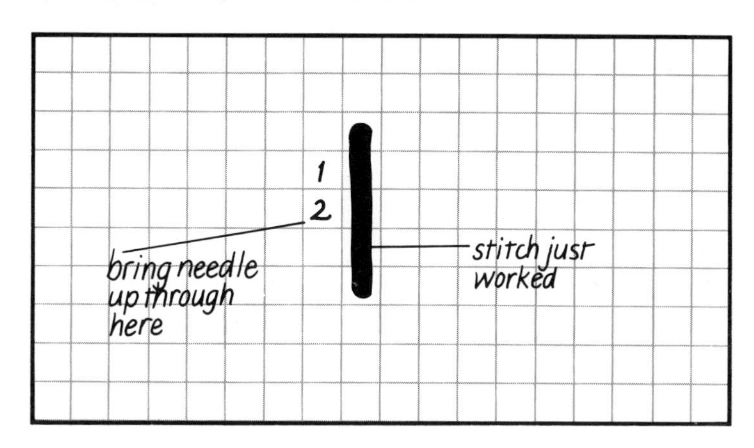


Fig. 9-3 *4-2 step*

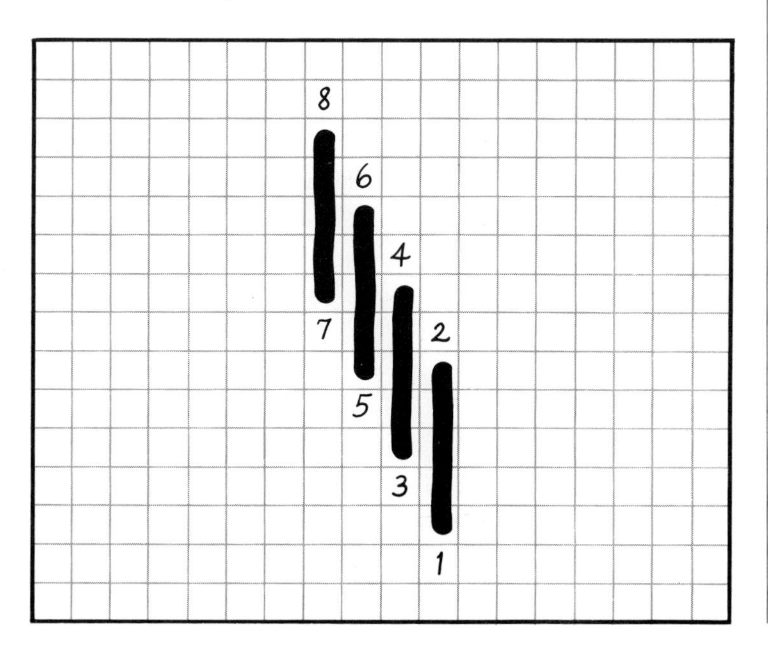


worked in this way, the numbers in the illustration being the order in which the stitches were taken.

As you work any Bargello pattern, you should take great care not to pull the stitches too tight. Pull the yarn slowly and gently the last few inches through the canvas. Do not tug it strongly or you will distort the weave of the canvas and leave ugly gaps between the rows of stitches and from the bottom of one stitch to the top of the next. The idea is to have the stitches lying flat, without excess yarn bulging on the right side—taut, that is, but not tight. You will get the feel of it after working for a while. A little extra care at the beginning will save a lot of trouble later. Once distorted, the weave of the canvas may never return to its original position, even after the offending stitches are ripped out.

Assuming that you have been working along smoothly and not pulling the stitches too tight, you now find yourself at the end of the thread. To finish the ends off neatly, bring your needle to the back of the work and weave the remaining yarn through the back of several

Fig. 9-4 *A series of Bargello stitches*

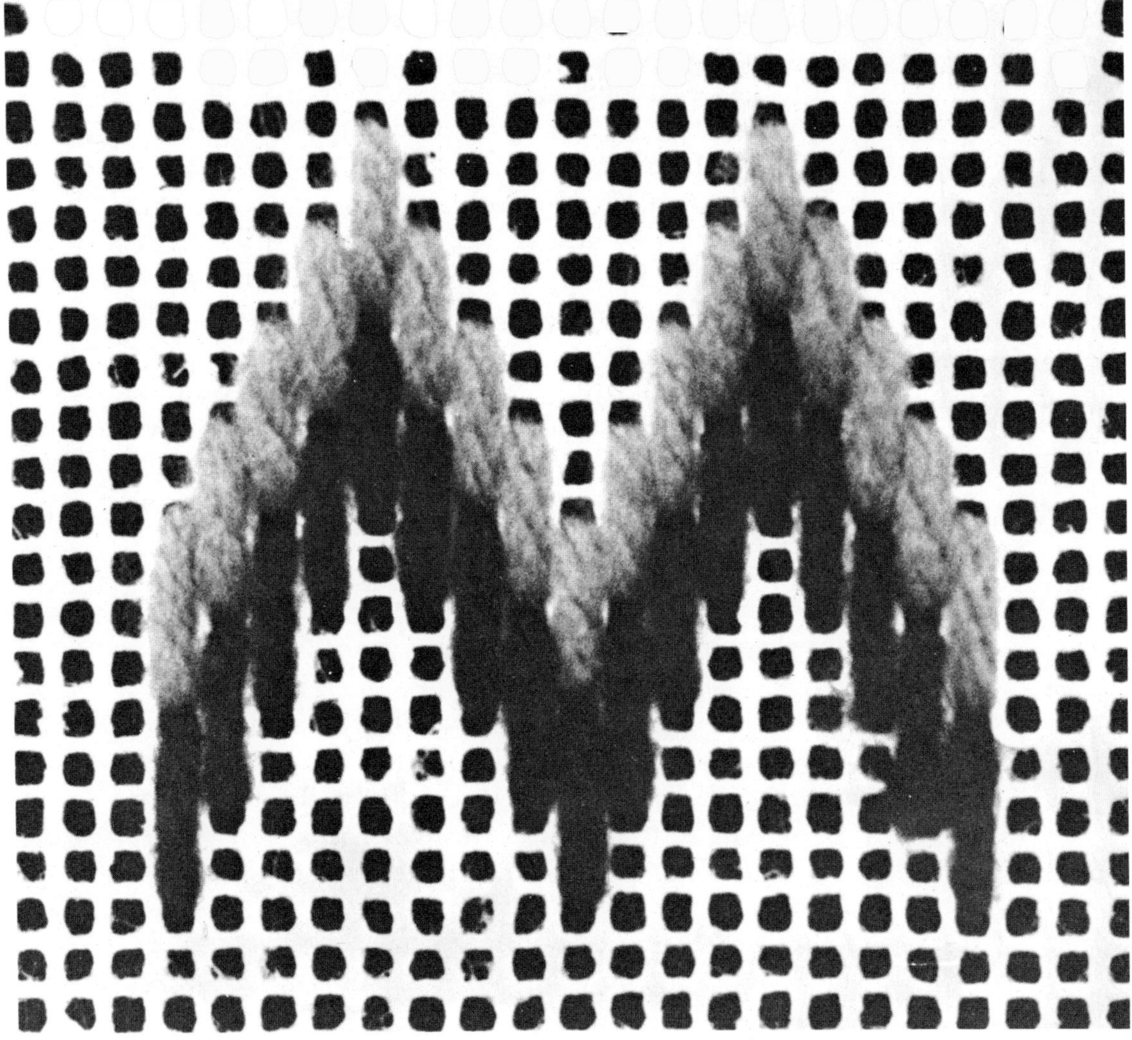

Fig. 9-5 *Working the second row*

stitches. This will keep the ends from springing loose—a point which is particularly important for any item likely to undergo hard wear, such as a cushion.

To work another row on top of the first, or foundation, row, return to the right-hand side of the work, and bring the needle up in the same hole in which the first stitch of the row below finishes. The second and all subsequent rows are worked following the pattern established in the first. You always bring your needle up into the same hole in which the stitch below finishes (Fig. 9-5). In this way one can avoid gaps between from the top of one stitch to the bottom of the one above it, and the canvas will be entirely covered over by the yarn.

Because of the very regular nature of Bargello achieved by counting meshes, mistakes usually become obvious very quickly, and should be ripped out before continuing. It is always hard to undo any hand work, but, because of the geometric patterns which predominate in Bargello, it is particularly important to correct any errors before they cause complete chaos! There is no way of covering up or working around a mistake in counted work.

There is, however, one comforting note to add here. Should you need to rip anything out, you will find it very easy to do. With the right side of the work facing you, simply insert one point of your embroidery scissors under the stitches to be taken out, and clip. Then, with the help of your needle, gently remove the ends of yarn from the other side of the work, taking care not to stretch the weave of the canvas out of shape in so doing. Care should also be taken not to clip the canvas itself by accident. Should you have that misfortune, pull off a strand of canvas from one of the edges, and work it across the hole, following the weave for a few meshes on either side. Trim off the excess from the ends of the woven-in strand. You can now work across this repair in the normal way.

You will find that, as you repeat row upon row of your Bargello pattern to fill the desired size of canvas, you are left with awkward, empty shapes at the edges. In order to fill these in, you will have to shorten some stitches to keep a straight line along the edge, at the same time following the sequence of stitches established in the foundation row. The design charts in the next two project chapters show clearly how stitches and patterns become modified to fit into the straight lines at the edges of a patch.

## Patchwork Bargello

Bargello, as one solid piece of fabric, merely creates the illusion of patchwork. In most traditional patchwork designs, one needs to create clearly defined edges, and there are two other stitches that are extremely useful in this respect for patchwork Bargello.

The first is called 4-1 (or 6-1) step and is shown in Figure 9-6. Worked straight up and down, like other Bargello stitches, you begin each new stitch by bringing your needle up through the canvas just one mesh above and to the left of the point at which the previous stitch was started. This gives a sloping edge which is very useful for making diamond-shaped or triangular patches. Figure 9-6 also shows how the stitches at each side are modified, from working over four mesh, down to one, to finish the triangle correctly. Follow the same method for working down from six to one.

The next stitch, the Gobelin stitch, is so useful in patchwork that I have devoted an entire chapter to projects using it. The Gobelin (Fig. 9-7) is basically the same vertical stitch used in all Bargello work, the difference being that here stitches are worked side by side across a straight horizontal line, instead of being

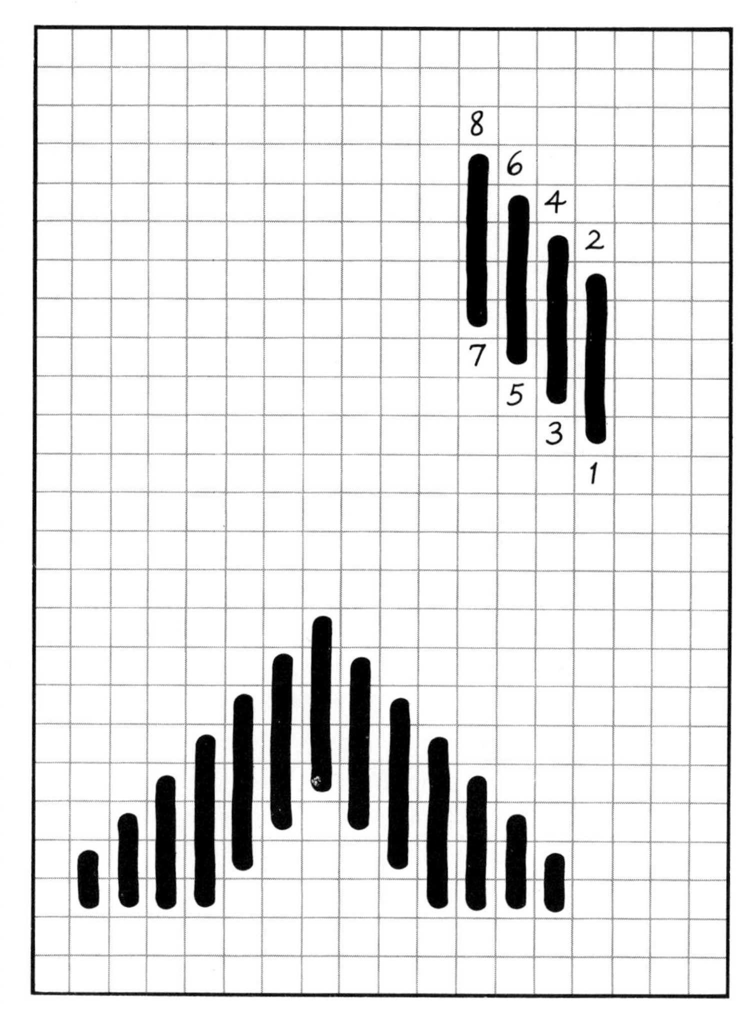


Fig. 9-6 *4-1 step*

staggered. Gobelin can be worked over any number of meshes, the most frequently used being four and six.

When applying this stitch to patchwork design, one can create neat square or rectangular frames for other stitches to be worked inside. First work a line of Gobelin stitches in the normal manner, that is, in a horizontal line, for four (or six) stitches. Then make groups of four (or six) stitches above that one until you reach the point where you want the corner of the frame. To miter the corner, simply work down from four (or six) stitches on the right, to one, at the inside corner of the frame (see Fig. 9-8). Then turn the work and begin with a short stitch over one mesh, increasing back to four (or six). These stitches are worked from the same holes as their counterparts on the side just completed, thus leaving no gaps where canvas might show through.

One of the most obvious ways of dividing a canvas into "patches" is to draw an X on it. The method for doing this is shown in Fig. 9-9. When making any marks on canvas, always use permanent markers. Should you need to steam or block your work when finished, you could be faced with the disastrous running of ink into yarn if you use anything but a waterproof pen.

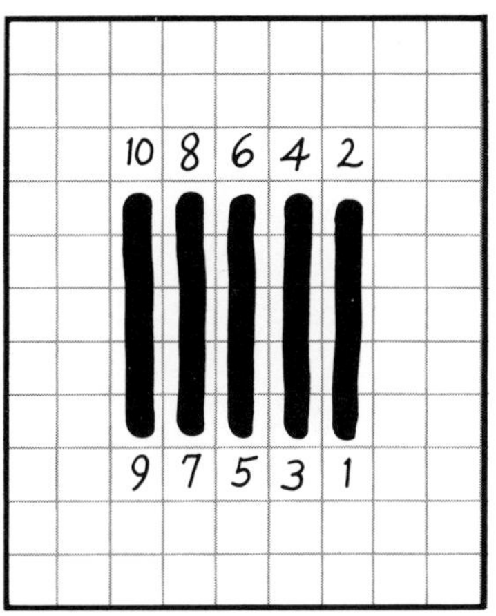

Fig. 9-7 *Gobelin stitch*

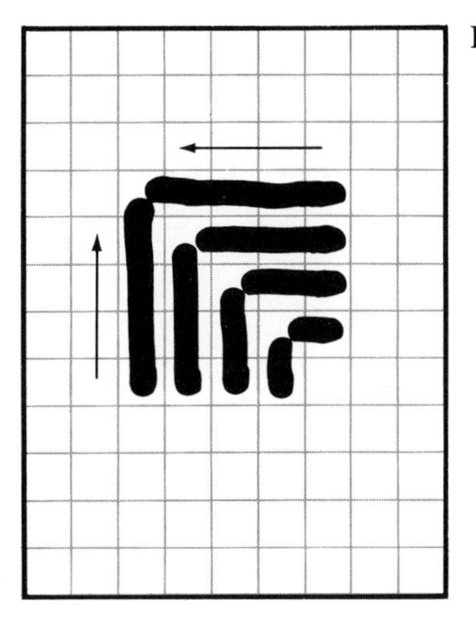
Fig. 9-8 *Mitered corner*

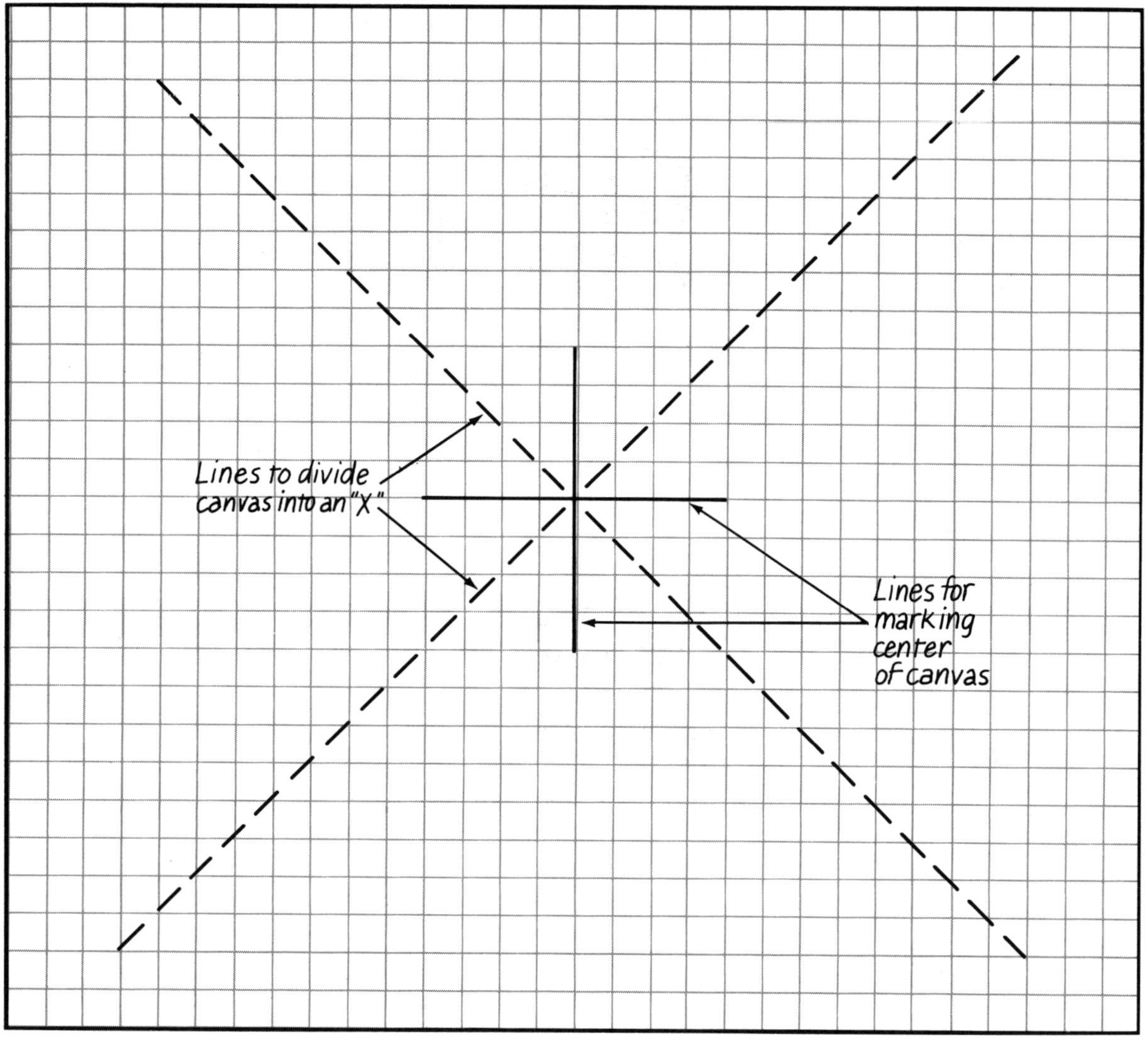

Lines to divide canvas into an "X"

Lines for marking center of canvas

Fig. 9-9 *Dividing a canvas*

Pencil is not satisfactory for marking canvas either, since particles of graphite tend to cling to the yarn, turning colors dirty, and white, gray.

Armed with a waterproof marker, fold the canvas in half lengthways. Mark the meshes that lie on the fold with a line about 2 inches long, as near the center of the canvas as your eye can judge. Now fold the canvas in half widthways. Mark the canvas as before. The mesh where both lines meet is the center of your canvas. Whenever instructions for a Bargello design require you to find the center of the canvas, this method should be used.

To make a diagonal X on the canvas, start at the center point and begin sketching in the arms of the cross, making certain to move diagonally across each mesh (Fig. 9-9). It is well worthwhile to take extra care to be accurate at this point. The lines you are drawing in are the boundaries between your patches, and give an invaluable guide to working the irregular stitches at the sides. If the lines are not precise, the results will be very unsatisfactory. Stitches from two adjacent patches will meet in the holes marked by these lines, in the same way that stitches meet each other in a mitered corner (Fig. 9-8).

## Finishing Bargello

If you have kept your work neatly rolled and clean, no blocking should be required. You may still feel, however, that the work lacks crispness and finish. In that case, you can steam your work by placing it right side down on a thick towel. Spray steam from the iron over the back of the canvas, allowing it to penetrate well. Do not press the iron onto the work itself. After the steam has had a chance to do its work, even out any distortions in the canvas by gently stretching it back into shape. The thick towel underneath will prevent the stitches from being flattened.

## Making a Cushion

You will need a piece of backing fabric in a color that will blend with and enhance your Bargello design. Trim your canvas so that you have a border of about ½ to ¾ of an inch on each side. Your backing fabric should be exactly the same size, which will allow for a ½- to ¾-inch seam.

If you are going to insert piping around the edges, you will need extra backing fabric to enable you to cut bias strips 1 inch wide. The strips, when joined, must be long enough to go around the entire outside edge of the cushion. Add an extra couple of inches for working around coners. You will also need a piece of heavy cord of the same length. Fold the bias strip in half lengthways to cover the cord, with the right side of the fabric on the outside. Using a sewing machine, stitch the folded fabric together as close to the cord as you can get.

With the right side of the Bargello facing you, stitch the piping in place, putting the raw edges of the bias strip together with the raw edges of the canvas. Work the line of stitching into the last mesh worked in Bargello along the edges.

Place the right side of the backing fabric down onto the right side of the Bargello. Begin stitching about 2 inches from the bottom corner. Work to the corner, around it, then around the next three sides and corners, and 2 inches past the other bottom corner, leaving a generous opening for putting the pad or filling through. Keep your stitches in the last Bargello mesh worked. To make it easier to follow a straight line, and to stitch into the correct line of mesh, work with the Bargello on top of the backing fabric.

It may be necessary to clip the canvas and backing fabric at the corners before turning the cushion right side out. Take great care not to cut into the machine stitching as that is now all that will hold the mesh in place at the corners. Now stuff the cushion pad or fiber filling through the opening. Stitch the open section of the bottom seam together by hand.

You may like to add tassels as a finishing touch. You will need about 50 yards of extra yarn to make four 4-inch tassels. Cut a strip of cardboard about 8 inches wide and fold it in half, so that it is now 4 inches wide, with the folded edge at the bottom. Snip off a piece of yarn about 20 inches long and place it doubled inside the fold, making sure that it extends beyond the outside edges of the cardboard. Wind yarn around the folded card about 50 times and cut the end. Now bring the doubled yarn, from inside the cardboard, to the top edge and tie it very firmly around the yarn which you have just wound on. Slide the yarn off the cardboard, and tie another piece of yarn around the tassel about ½ inch from the top. Cut and trim the loops at the bottom of the tassel. Apply the tassels to your cushion at the same time as the piping.

If you want to frame any of your Bargello, it is definitely best to have it done professionally. The canvas must first be mounted on stretchers and then framed.

## Designing Your Own Bargello Projects

Figure 9-10 illustrates a patchwork Bargello bag designed and executed by Angela Reuben. Because geometric motifs and counted stitches are used, you will find it relatively easy to plan a patchwork Bargello project for yourself. Use graph paper to plot your design, beginning with a general layout of the patches. This gives you a clear visual image of the shape your design will take. Have a look at the layouts and charts in the next two chapters to see how the design is elaborated on, section by section, from the overall layout.

You can use any Bargello stitches you like to fill in the patch shapes you chose, mixing 4-2 and 6-3 steps in the same design wherever it seems appropriate. If you are familiar with several Bargello stitches already, perhaps your first project should be to divide the canvas up into basic squares and work a different stitch in each. You can make all the squares in the same group of colors, in which case attention will be focused on the subtle differences in the stitch patterns, or you can use different color combinations in each square, creating a vibrant mixture of color and stitch variation. Try using a mitered corner frame (as shown in Fig. 9-8) to enclose each stitch, or, if you prefer, simply

Fig. 9-10 *Patchwork bag, designed and worked by Angela Reuben*

mark the squares with a waterproof pen on the canvas, and work each stitch right up to the dividing lines. If you experiment with both those methods, you will be able to judge which is better for your particular design.

Another type of design, not shown in the project sections but which anyone with a basic knowledge of a few Bargello stitches can create, is a "crazy patch" pattern. Find an example of a crazy patchwork quilt that appeals to you. There are plenty to choose from in the extensive range of books available on antique American quilts. You are going to use the outlines from a section of the quilt to create interesting shapes to fill in with Bargello stitching. It is best to choose a relatively simple area of design, or modify some of the shapes, to prevent your patches from becoming too small or awkward.

Having found a suitable pattern, take a piece of graph paper that is larger than you want your finished item to be. Use a heavy, permanent marker to draw the outside edges of the design to the size you want. You now have a square or rectangular frame for the design. Following the quilt you have chosen, sketch in the "crazy" outline in pencil, so that you can make modifications and correct mistakes if need be. When you are satisfied that you have the outlines you want, go over the pencil lines with your heavy marker.

It is a simple job to transfer this drawing to the canvas. Using a waterproof marker, and allowing a 2-inch border all around, mark the frame of your design on the canvas. Scotch-tape your drawing on a table, and place the canvas on top, making sure to have the outline of the frame directly over the corresponding lines on the drawing. Scotch-tape the canvas firmly into position. You will easily be able to see the heavy lines of your drawing through the canvas. Trace them onto the canvas with your marker, making certain that the canvas and drawing remain in place throughout. Your canvas is now ready to be filled in with whatever stitches you feel inclined to work. This design, although rather more venturesome than sitting down to work everything out on charts before you begin, will present a challenge which you can meet creatively and colorfully.

For those who like their charts done for them, there are plenty of designs to choose from in the next two chapters. Beginners are asked to look for the designs marked*, which are more suited to their abilities.

The previous chapter contains all the basic techniques required for making the projects that now follow. Any arrows on the charts show the direction in which each block of stitches is worked. When finished, the designs can be made into cushions or framed to hang on the wall. You can, of course, use the patches to make designs of your own, combining them in whatever way suits your purpose.

Projects marked* are considered suitable for beginners.

**Crazy Chess Board** (Fig. 10-1)

FINISHED SIZE: APPROX. 16″ × 16″

YOU NEED: 4-ply worsted-weight wool (approx. 280 yds. in a 4-oz. pull skein).

Black (Shade A) 1 skein or approx. 90 yds.
White (Shade B) 1 skein or approx. 88 yds.
A piece of 10-mesh-to-1-inch mono canvas measuring 20″ × 20″
A #18 tapestry needle

Method

1. This design is worked over six holes of the canvas, except where otherwise shown in the charts.
2. Mark the center of the canvas as shown in Fig. 9-9 and explained in the accompanying text.
3. Study the overall layout of the design in Fig. 10-2, and the charts of the individual patches in Figs. 10-3 to 10-8. Start working at the center of Patch #5 (Fig. 10-7). Complete this patch, including the border, taking care to miter the corners as shown in Fig. 9-8 and explained in the accompanying text.
4. Work Patch #1, following Fig. 10-3.
5. Work Patch #2 above and below Patch #5, following Fig. 10-4 and the layout (Fig. 10-2).
6. Work Patch #3 following Fig. 10-5.
7. Work Patch #4 following Fig. 10-6.
8. Work Patch #6 following Fig. 10-8.

**Razzle Dazzle** (Fig. 10-9)

Finished Size: Approx. 16″ × 16″

You Need: 4-ply worsted-weight wool (approx. 280 yds. in a 4-oz. pull skein).

Black (Shade A) 1 skein or approx. 98 yds.
White (Shade B) 1 skein or approx. 74 yds.
A piece of 10-mesh-to-1-inch mono canvas measuring 20″ × 20″
A#18 tapestry needle

Fig. 10-1 *"Crazy Chess Board"*

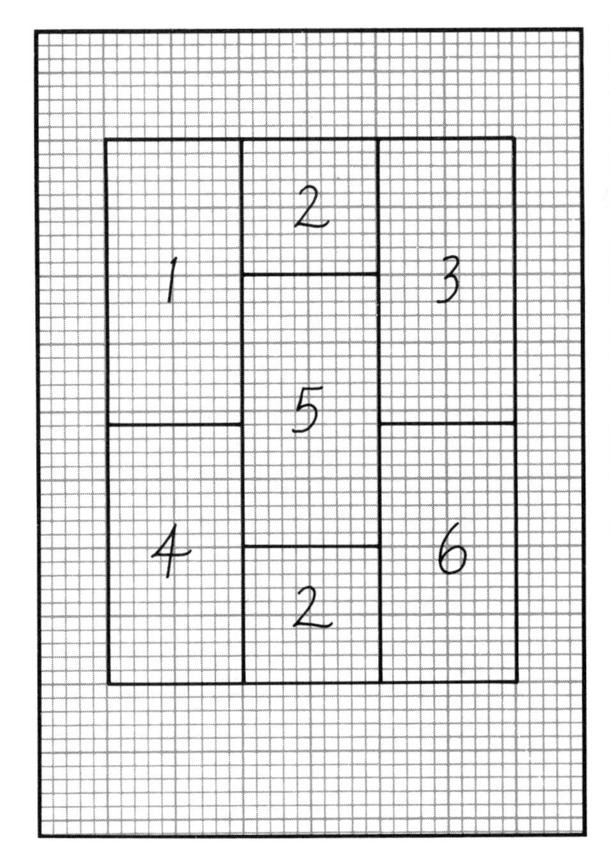


Fig. 10-2 *Layout for "Crazy Chess Board." (Not to scale.)*

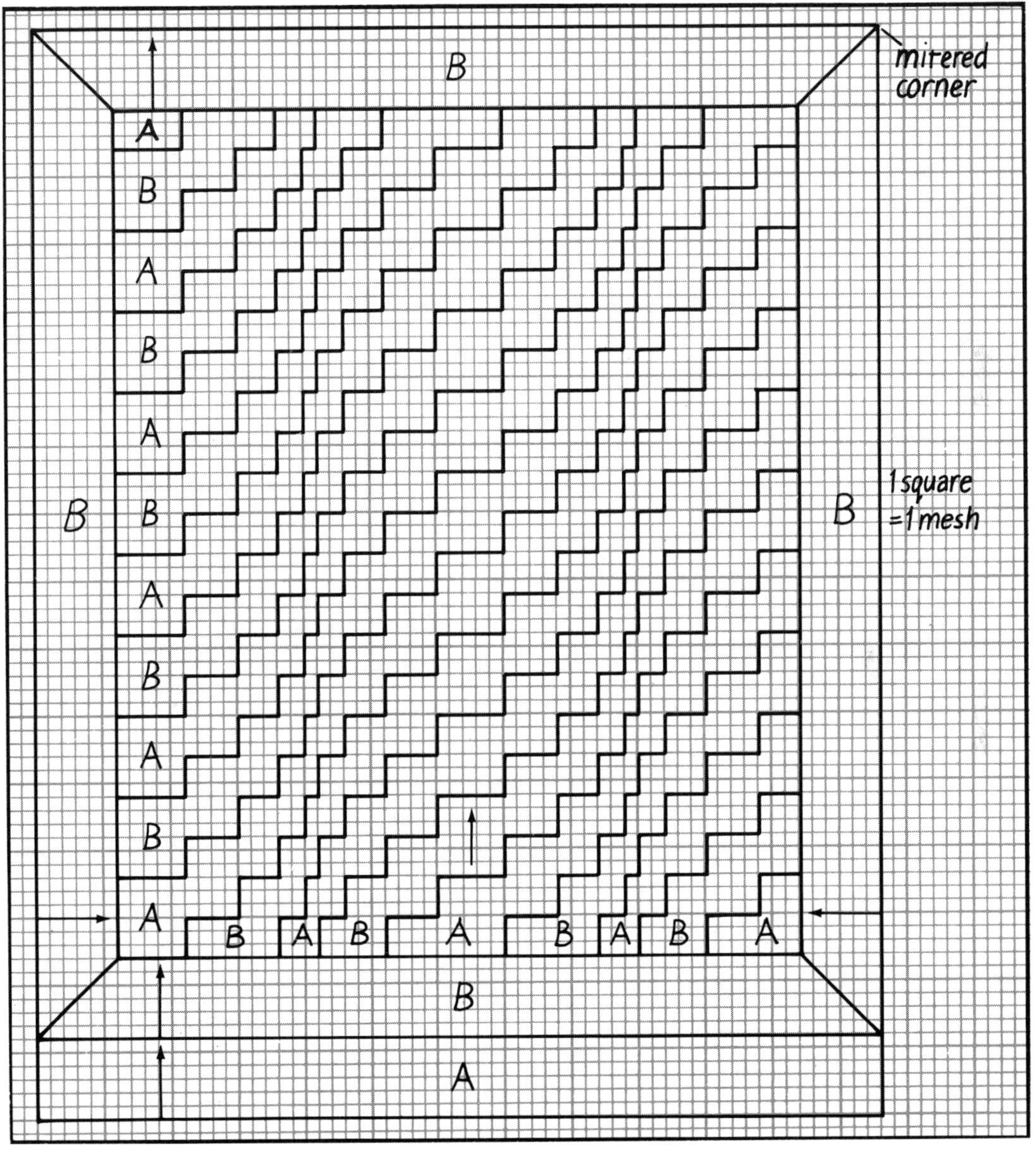


Fig. 10-3 *"Crazy Chess Board" patch #1*

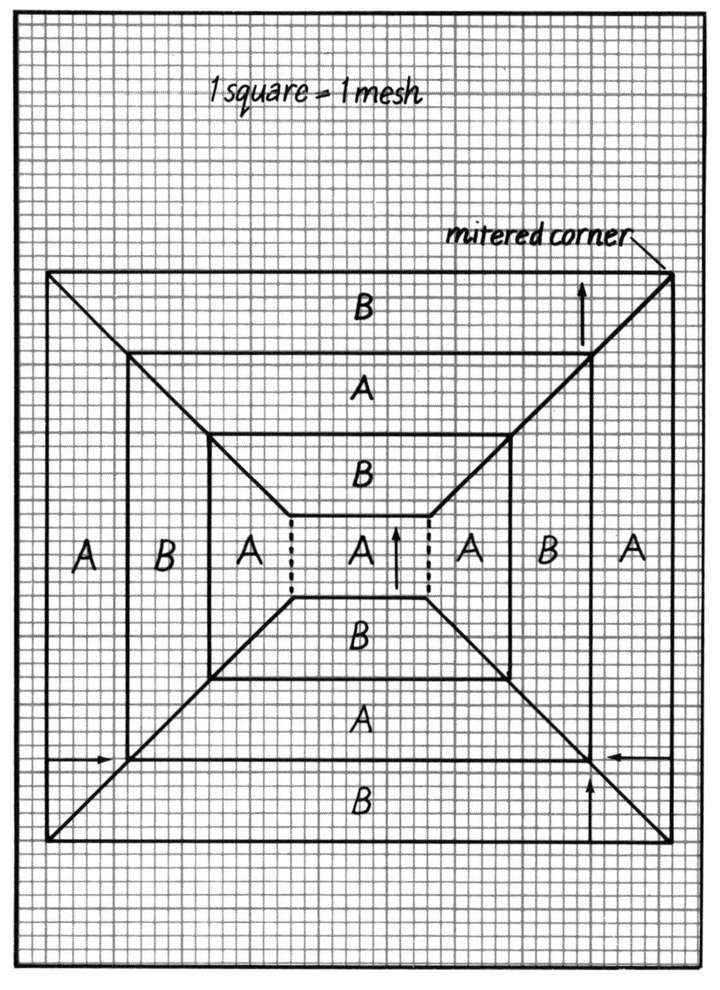


Fig. 10-4 *"Crazy Chess Board" patch #2*

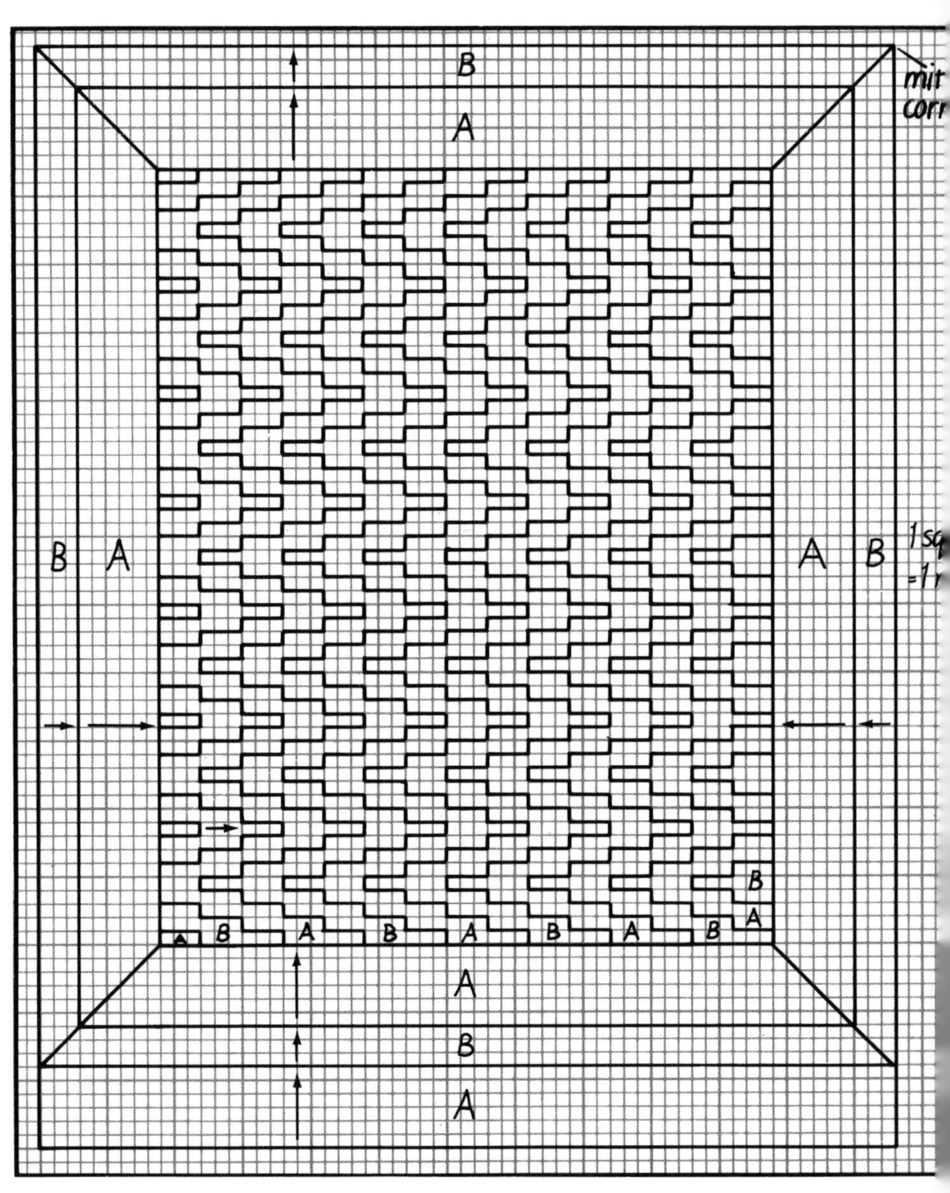


Fig. 10-5 *"Crazy Chess Board" patch #3*

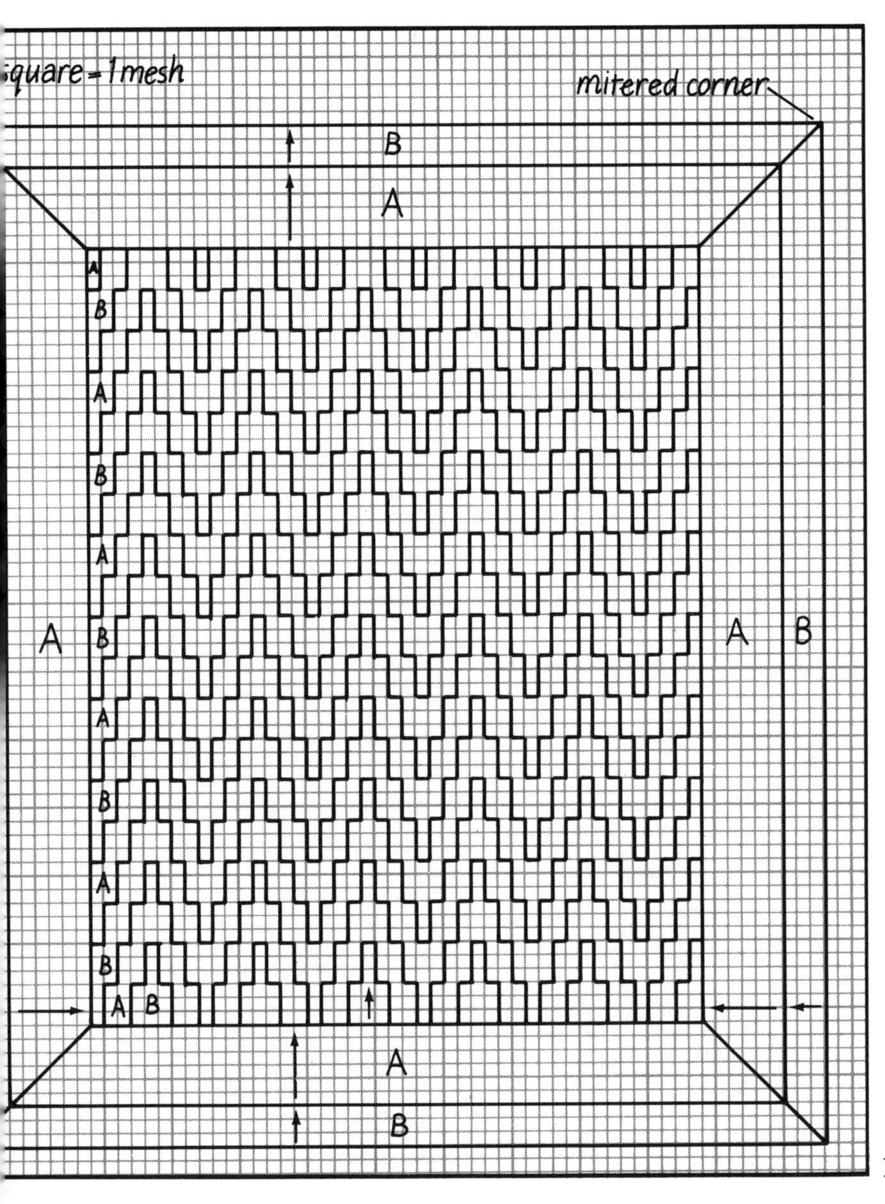


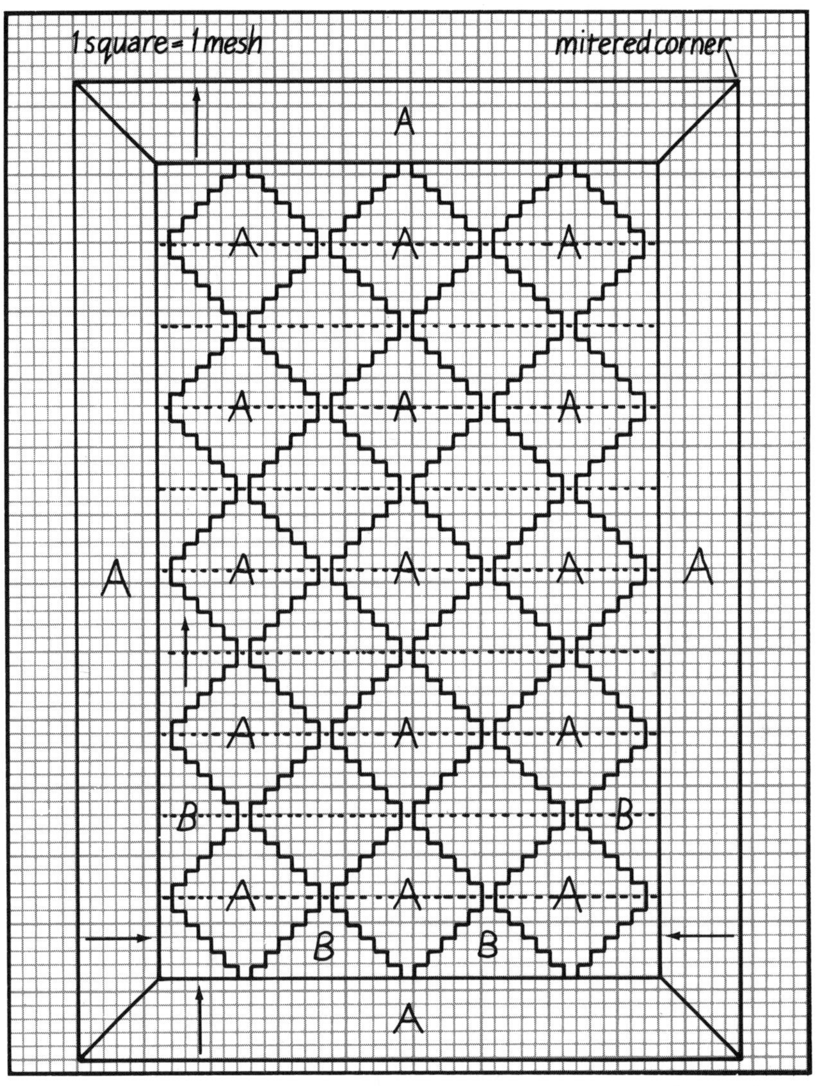


Fig. 10-7 *"Crazy Chess Board" patch #5*

Fig. 10-6 *"Crazy Chess Board" patch #4*

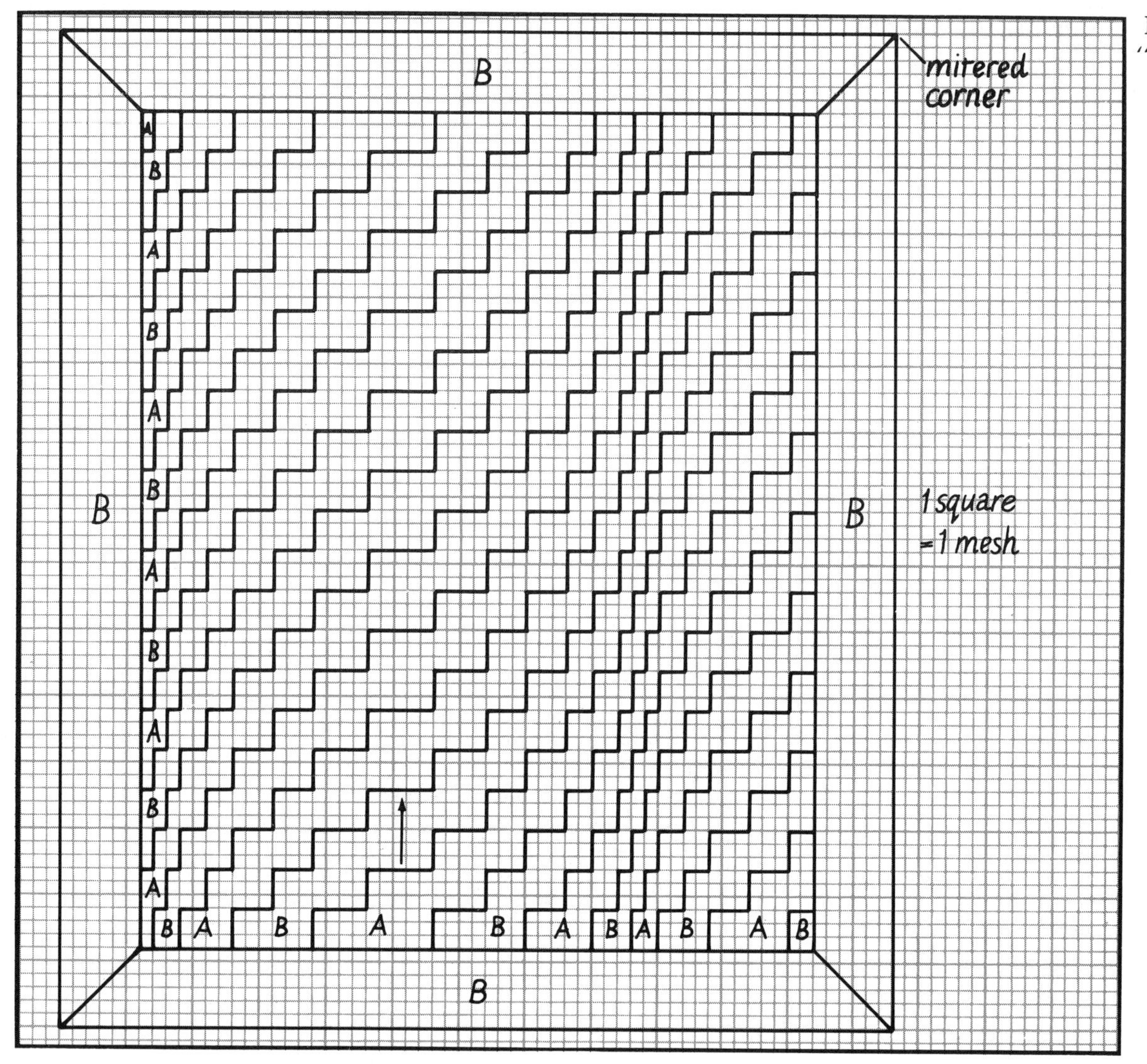


Fig. 10-8
*"Crazy Chess Board" patch #6*

Fig. 10-9 *"Razzle Dazzle"*

METHOD

1. The design is based on 6-3 step. The overall design is shown in Fig. 10-10; the individual patches, all variations of 6-3 step, appear in Figs. 10-11 through 10-15.
2. Start in the upper left-hand corner, at a point 2 inches down from the top and in from the side edge (1 inch if you are using interlocking canvas).
3. Work the patches in the following sequence: 1—2—3—4—3—5—1—6, as shown in Fig. 10-10.

**Waves** (Fig. 10-16)

This design is recommended only to those who have considerable experience in Bargello.

FINISHED SIZE: APPROX. 14″ × 14″

YOU NEED: 4-ply worsted-weight wool (approx. 280 yds. in a 4-oz. pull skein):

| | |
|---|---|
| Light tan (Shade A) | 1 skein or approx. 35 yards. |
| Dark tan (Shade B) | 1 skein or approx. 25 yds. |
| Copper (Shade C) | 1 skein or approx. 30 yds. |
| Bright tangerine (Shade D) | 1 skein or approx. 27 yds. |
| Tangerine (Shade E) | 1 skein or approx. 27 yds. |
| Scarlet (Shade F) | 1 skein or approx. 25 yds. |

A piece of 10-mesh-to-1-inch mono canvas measuring 18″ × 18″

A #18 tapestry needle

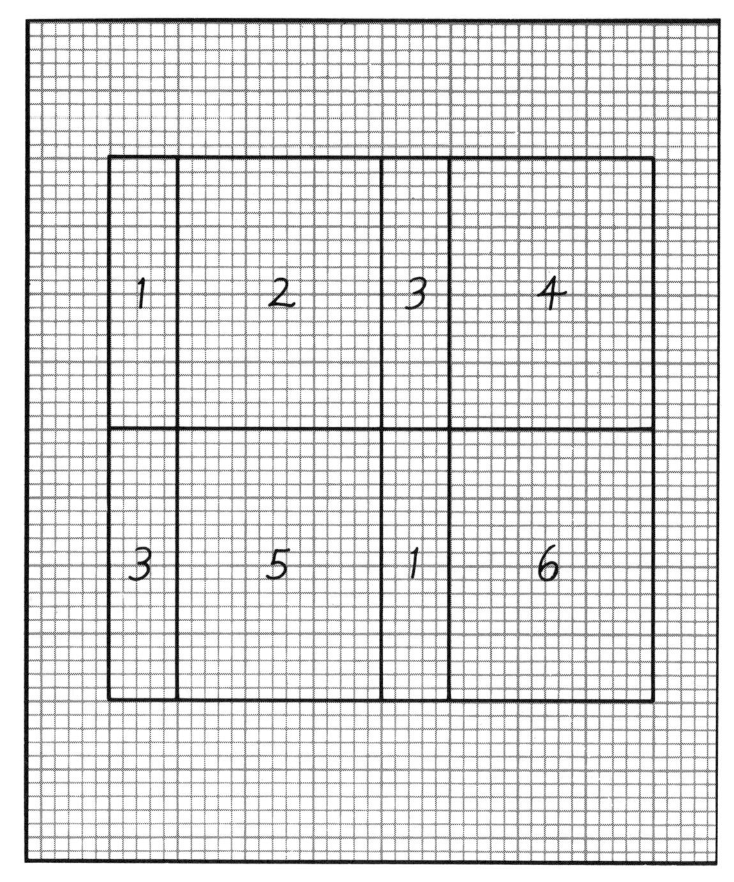


Fig. 10-10 *Layout for "Razzle Dazzle." (Not to scale.)*

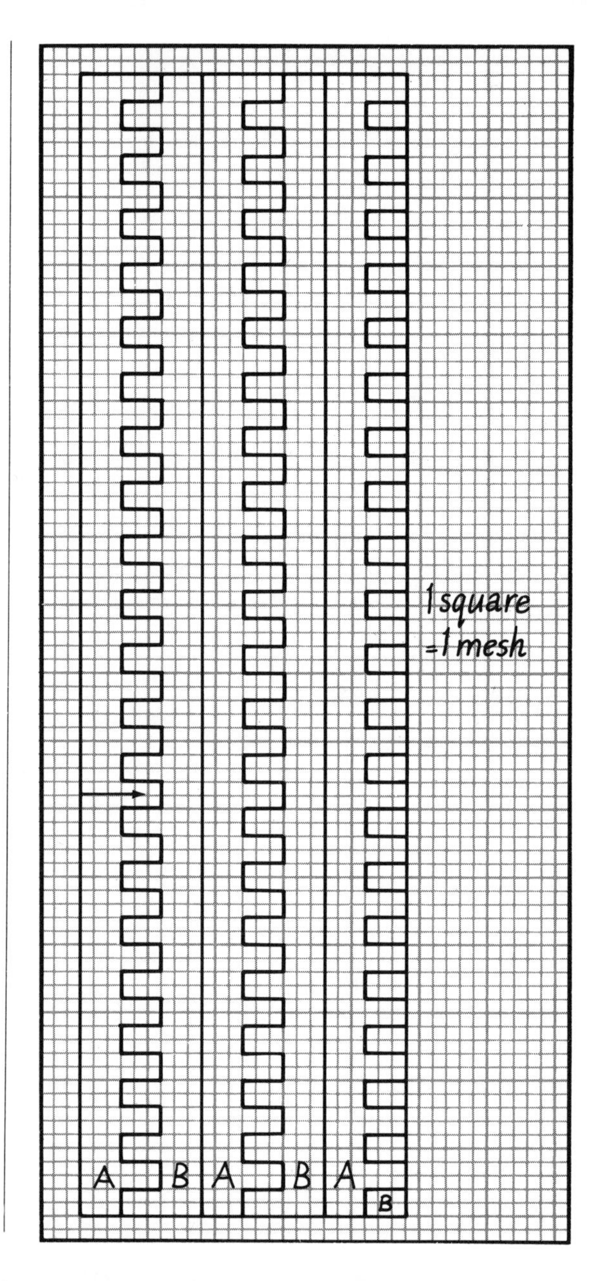


Fig. 10-11A *"Razzle Dazzle" patch #1*

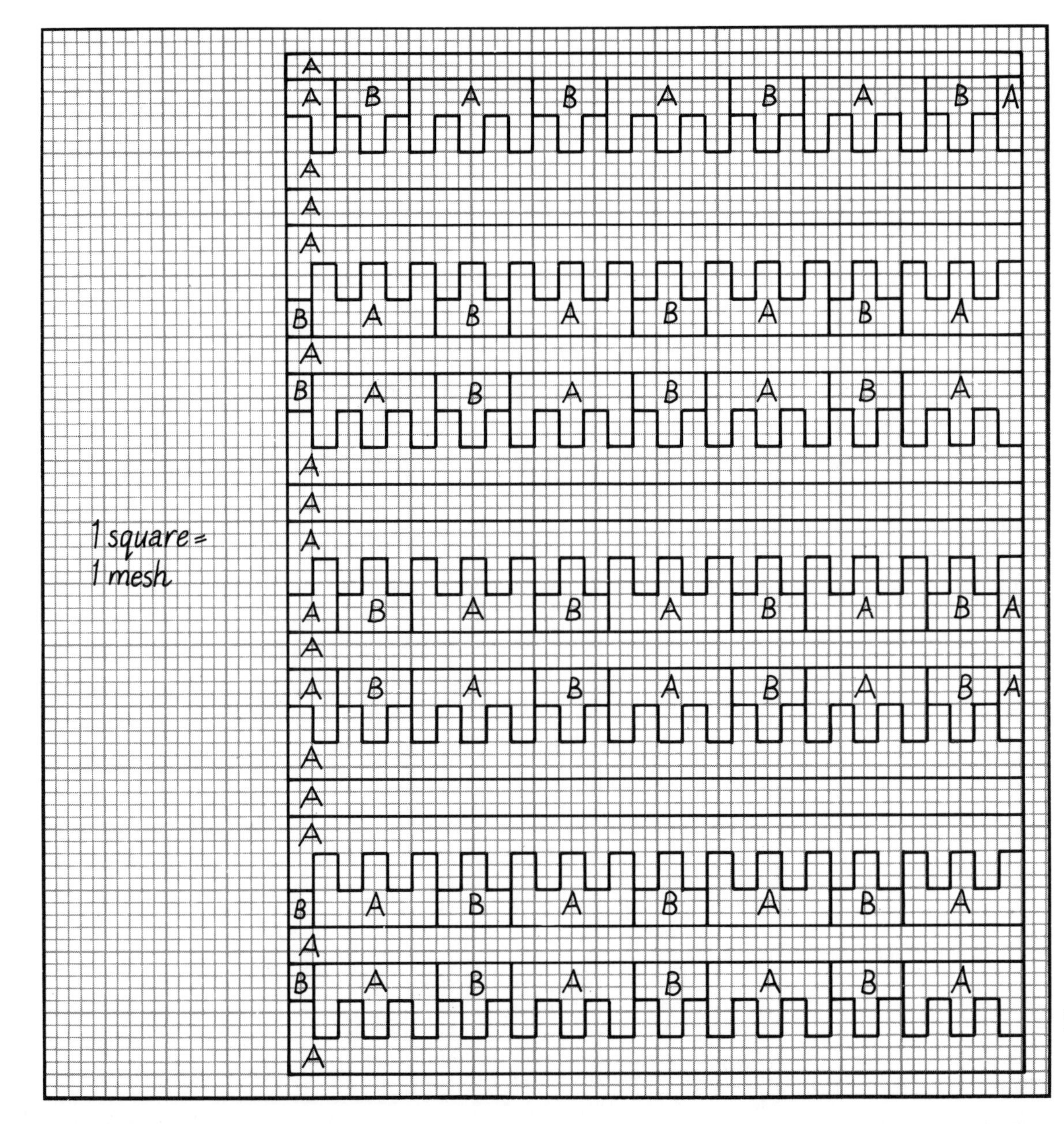


Fig. 10-11B *"Razzle Dazzle" patch #2*

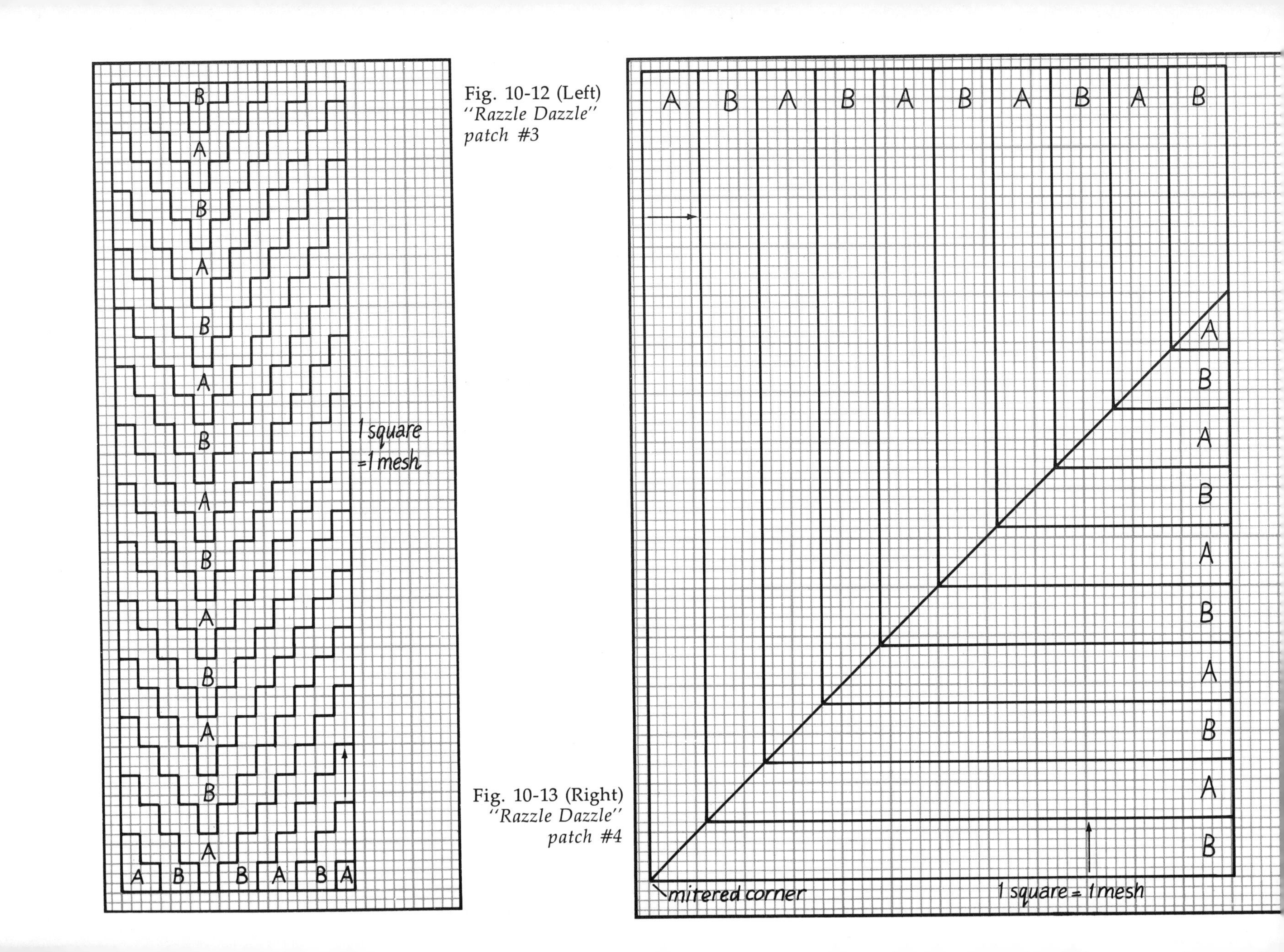


Fig. 10-12 (Left) *"Razzle Dazzle" patch #3*

Fig. 10-13 (Right) *"Razzle Dazzle" patch #4*

Fig. 10-14 *"Razzle Dazzle" patch #5*

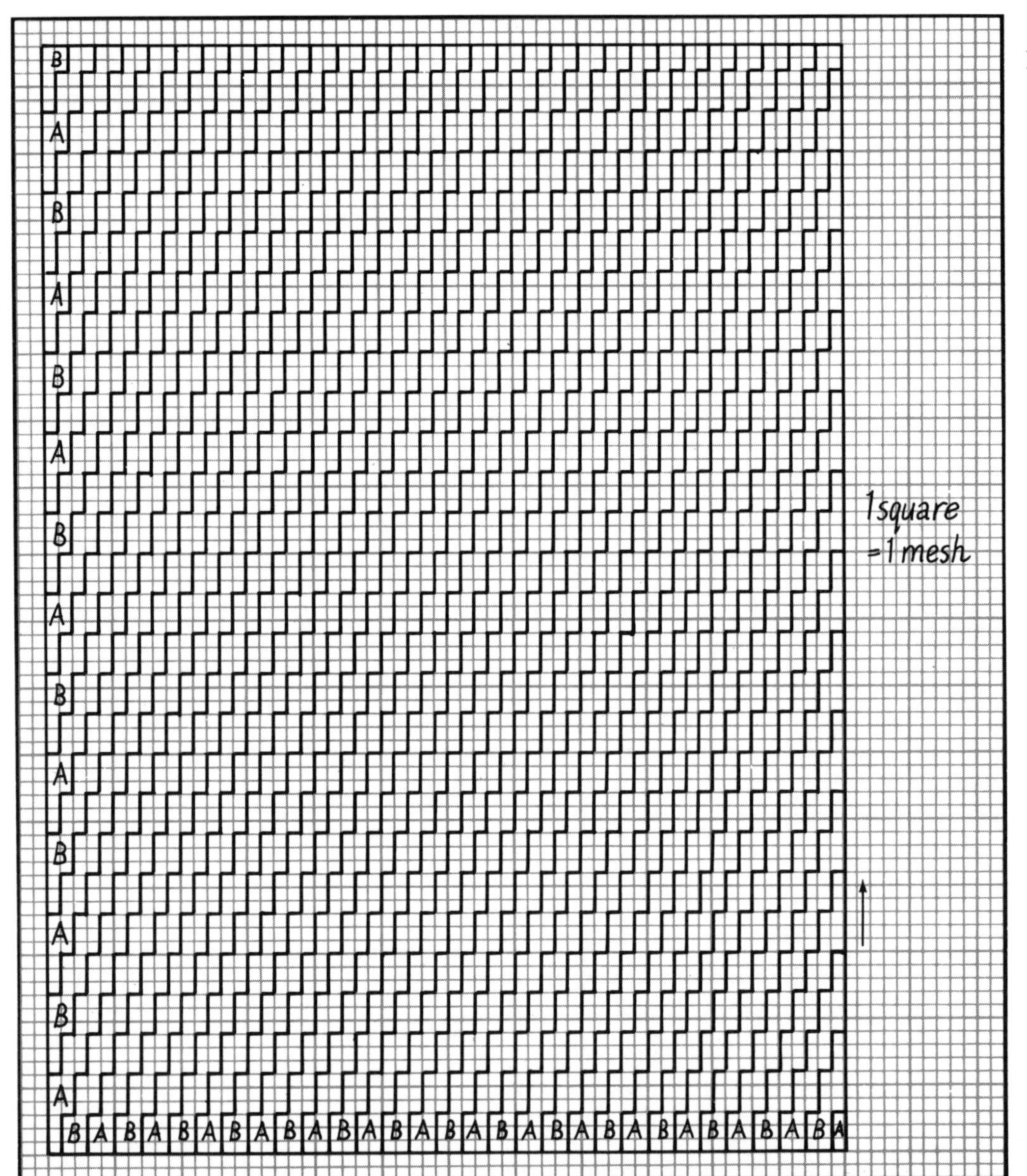


Fig. 10-15 *"Razzle Dazzle" patch #6*

Fig. 10-16 *"Waves"*

METHOD

1. Mark the center of the canvas as shown in Fig. 9-9.
2. This design is worked in 4-2 step except where otherwise shown on the charts.
3. Study the overall layout of the design (Fig. 10-17) and the charts of the individual patches (Figs 10-18 to 10-23). Begin working in the center of your canvas with the center stitch of Patch #7 (Fig. 10-23). The center stitch has been blocked in to help you locate the starting place.
4. When you have finished Patch #7, proceed to the other patches, working from #1 to #6 in numerical order.

**Blue Tile** (Fig. 10-24)

FINISHED SIZE: APPROX. 16″ × 16″
YOU NEED: 4-ply acrylic.

| | |
|---|---|
| Navy blue (Shade A) | 1 skein or approx. 70 yds. |
| Royal blue (Shade B) | 1 skein or approx. 30 yds. |
| Ombré blues (Shade C) | 1 skein or approx. 25 yds. |
| Sky blue (Shade D) | 1 skein or approx. 18 yds. |
| Medium blue (Shade E) | 1 skein or approx. 10 yds. |
| White (Shade F) | 1 skein or approx. 45 yds. |

A piece of 10-mesh-to-1-inch mono canvas measuring 20″ × 20″
A #18 tapestry needle

Fig. 10-17 *Layout for "Waves." (Not to scale.)*

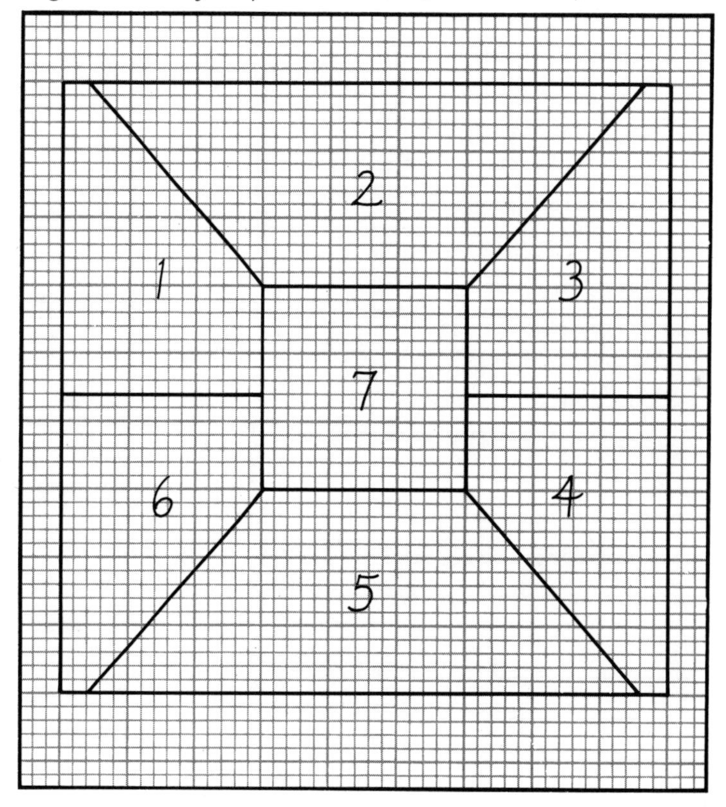

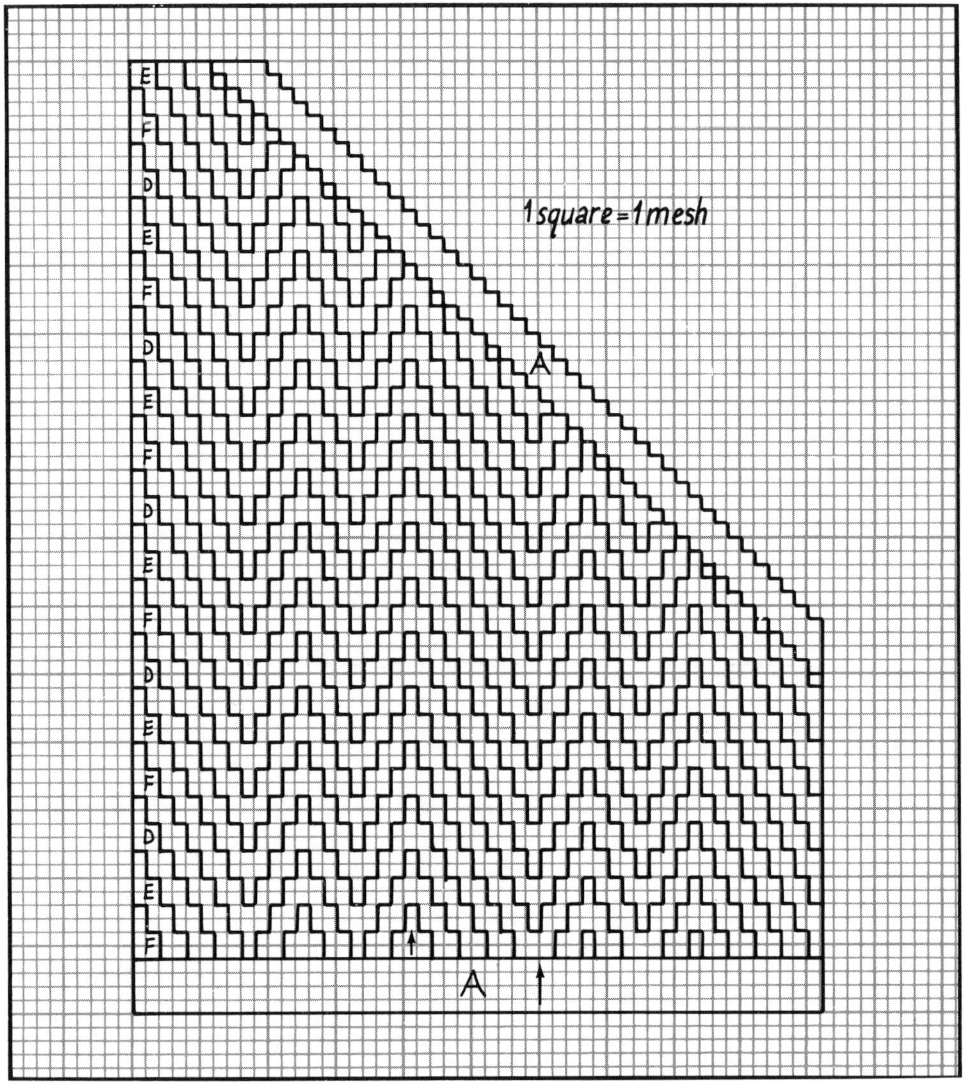

1 square = 1 mesh

E
F
D
E
F
D
E
F
D
E
F
D
E
F
D
E
F

A

A

Fig. 10-18 *"Waves" patch #1*

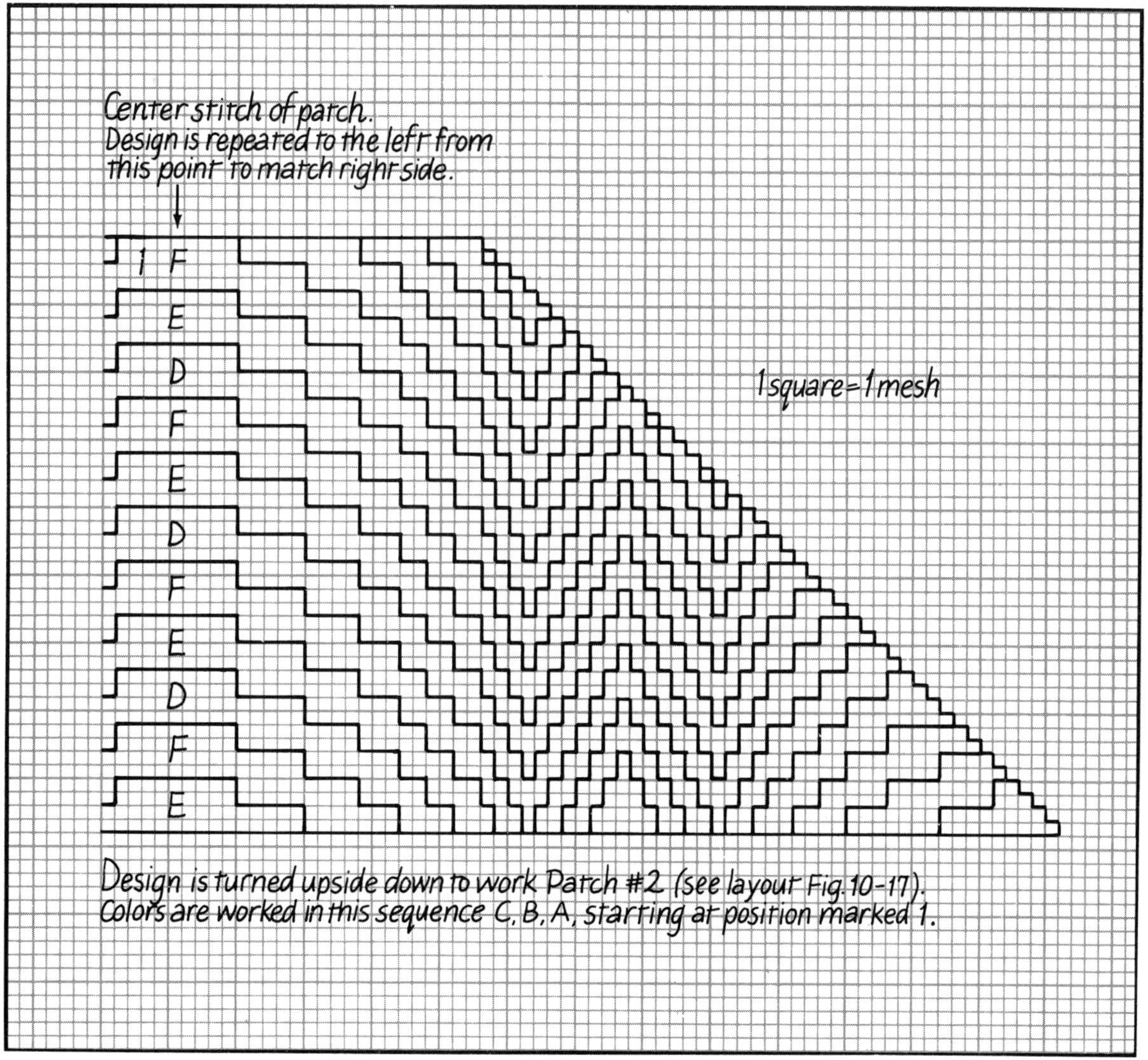
Center stitch of patch.
Design is repeated to the left from this point to match right side.
1
F
E
D
F
E
D
F
E
D
F
E
1 square=1 mesh
Design is turned upside down to work Patch #2 (see layout Fig. 10-17).
Colors are worked in this sequence C, B, A, starting at position marked 1.

Fig. 10-19 *Patch #5 for "Waves."*

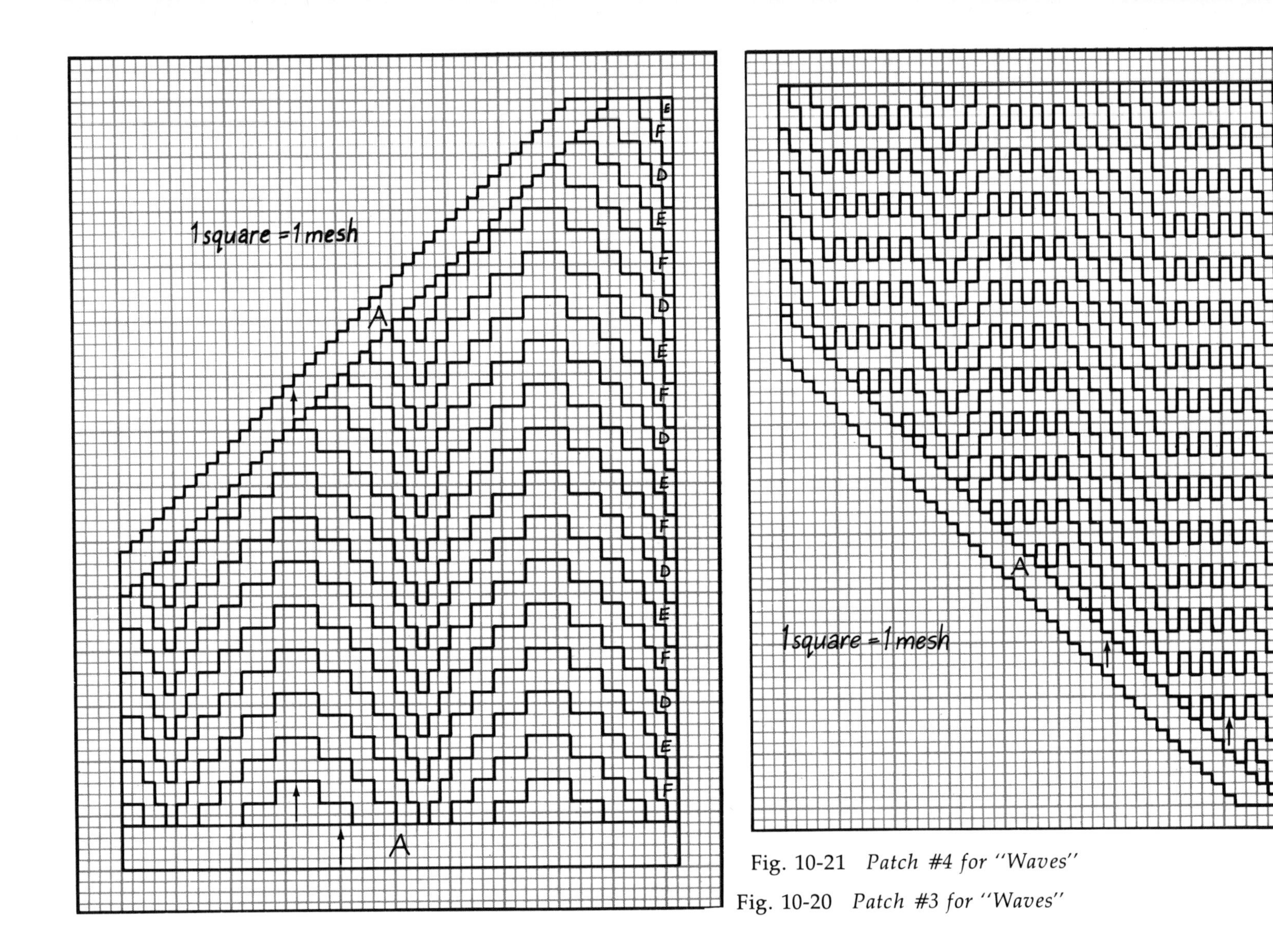


Fig. 10-21 *Patch #4 for "Waves"*

Fig. 10-20 *Patch #3 for "Waves"*

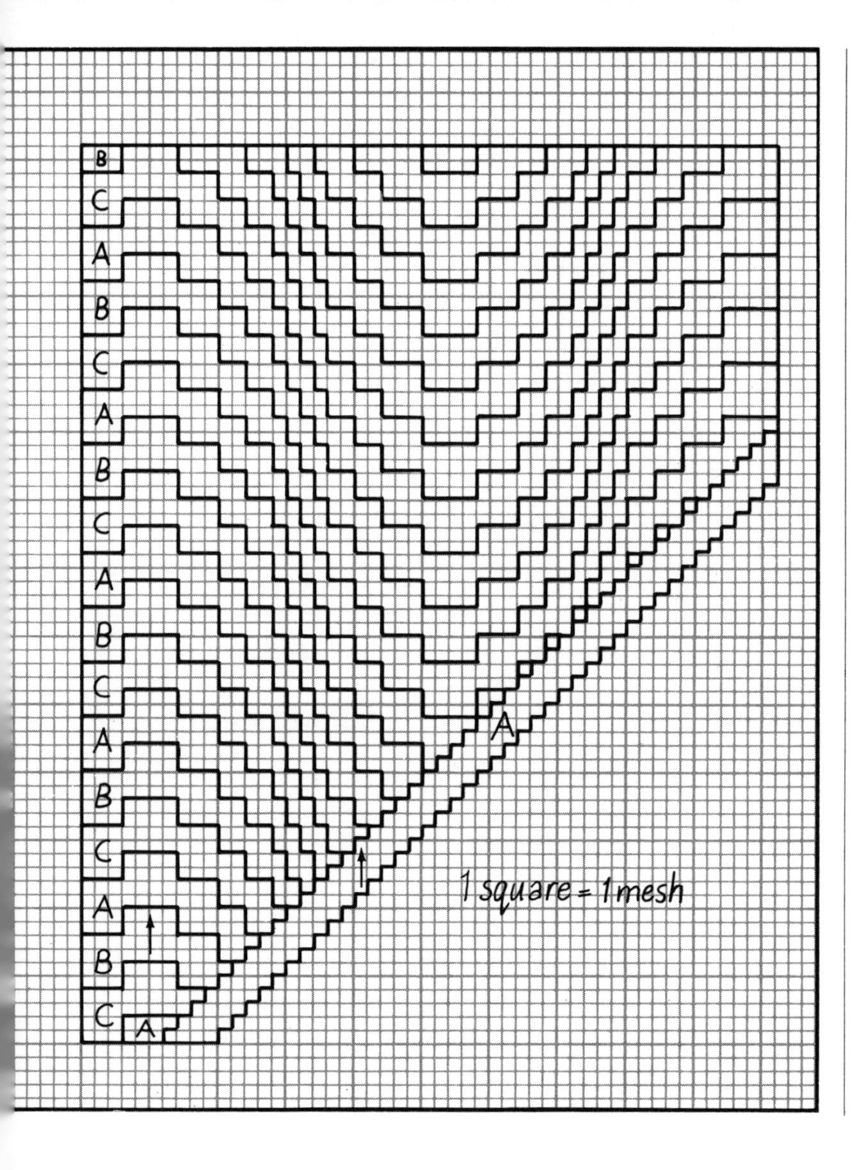


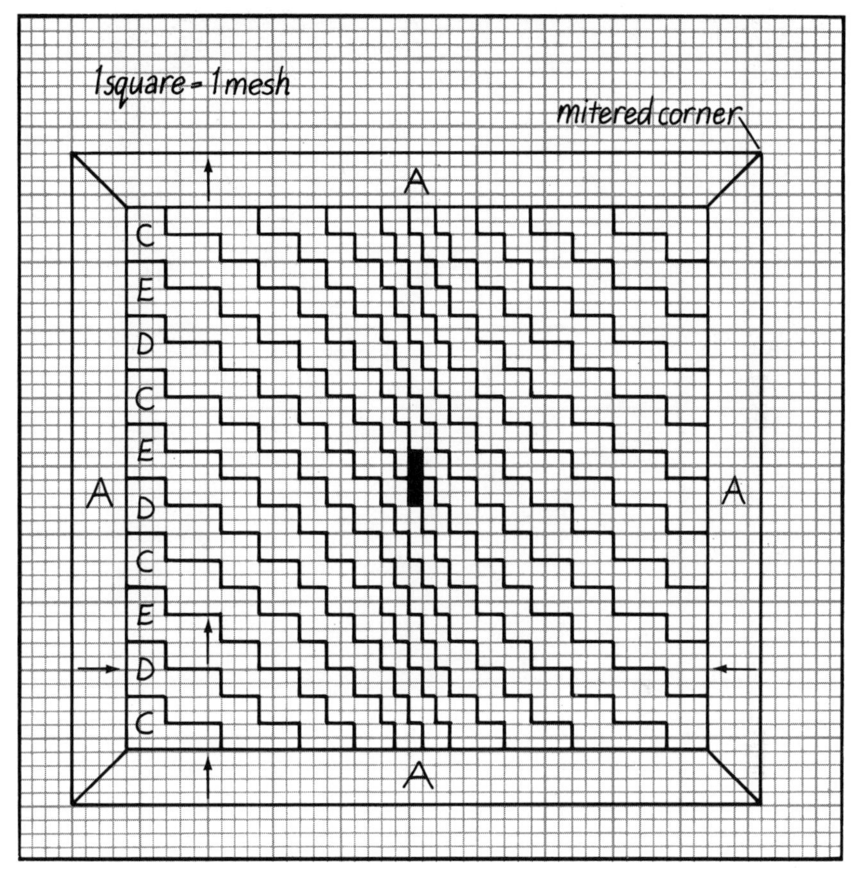


Fig. 10-23 *Patch #7 for "Waves"*

Fig. 10-22 *Patch #6 for "Waves"*

Fig. 10-24 *"Blue Tile"*

METHOD

1. The design is worked over 6 mesh of the canvas, and in 6-1 step unless otherwise shown on the chart.
2. Mark the center of the canvas (Fig. 9-9).
3. Fig. 10-25 shows one quarter of the finished design. Start where the center is marked, and repeat the pattern in all four quarters. Refer to the photograph, Fig. 10-24, for extra guidance.
4. The border should be worked last, and right around the completed canvas, following the stitch-direction arrows. For instructions on mitering the corners, refer to Fig. 9-8 and the accompanying text.

**Checkers** (Fig. 10-26)

FINISHED SIZE: APPROX. 16″ × 16″

YOU NEED: 4-ply acrylic (approx. 306 yds. in a 4-oz. pull skein).

| | |
|---|---|
| Copper (Shade A) | 1 skein or approx. 80 yds. |
| Dark tan (Shade B) | 1 skein or approx. 30 yds. |
| Beige (Shade C) | 1 skein or approx. 15 yds. |
| Tangerine (Shade D) | 1 skein or approx. 45 yds. |
| Coral (Shade E) | 1 skein or approx. 27 yds. |
| White (Shade F) | 1 skein or approx. 15 yds. |

Fig. 10-25 (Opposite) *Layout for "Blue Tile"*

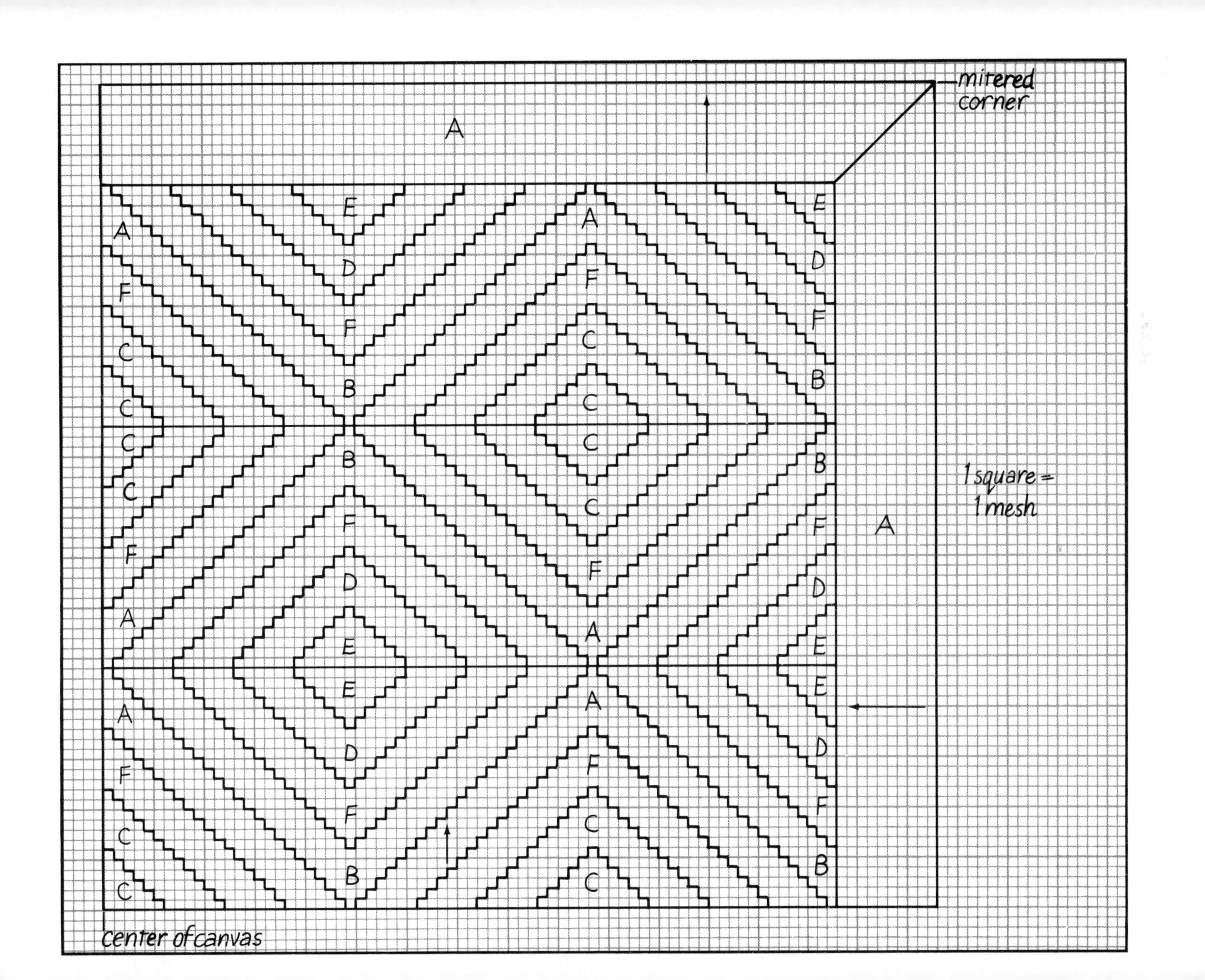
mitered corner
A
E
A
E
A
D
D
F
F
F
C
F
C
C
B
B
C
C
C
C
B
B
C
C
1 square = 1 mesh
F
F
A
F
D
D
A
A
E
E
E
E
A
A
D
D
F
F
F
C
F
C
B
B
C
C
center of canvas

Fig. 10-26 *"Checkers"*

A piece of 10-mesh-to-1-inch mono canvas measuring 20″ × 20″
A #18 tapestry needle

METHOD

Work exactly as for "Blue Tile," following Fig. 10-27 for details of the "Checkers" design and Fig. 10-26 for a clear picture of the finished work.

**Honeycomb** (Fig. 10-28)

FINISHED SIZE: APPROX. 16″ × 16″
YOU NEED: 4-ply worsted-weight wool (approx 280 yds. in a 4-oz. pull skein).

| | |
|---|---|
| Beige (Shade A) | 1 skein or approx. 40 yds. |
| Off-white (Shade B) | 1 skein or approx. 40 yds. |
| White (Shade C) | 1 skein or approx. 55 yds. |
| Canary (Shade D) | 1 skein or approx. 60 yds. |

A piece of 10-mesh-to-1-inch mono canvas measuring 20″ × 20″
A #18 tapestry needle

METHOD

1. The design is worked over 6 mesh of the canvas, and in 6-1 step unless otherwise shown on the chart.
2. First look at the layout given in Fig. 10-29 to see how the patches are fitted together.
3. Fold your canvas in half vertically, and mark the fold with a waterproof pen.
4. Lay the canvas flat on a table, and mark in the complete vertical center line from top to bottom.

Fig. 10-27 (Opposite) *Layout for "Checkers"*

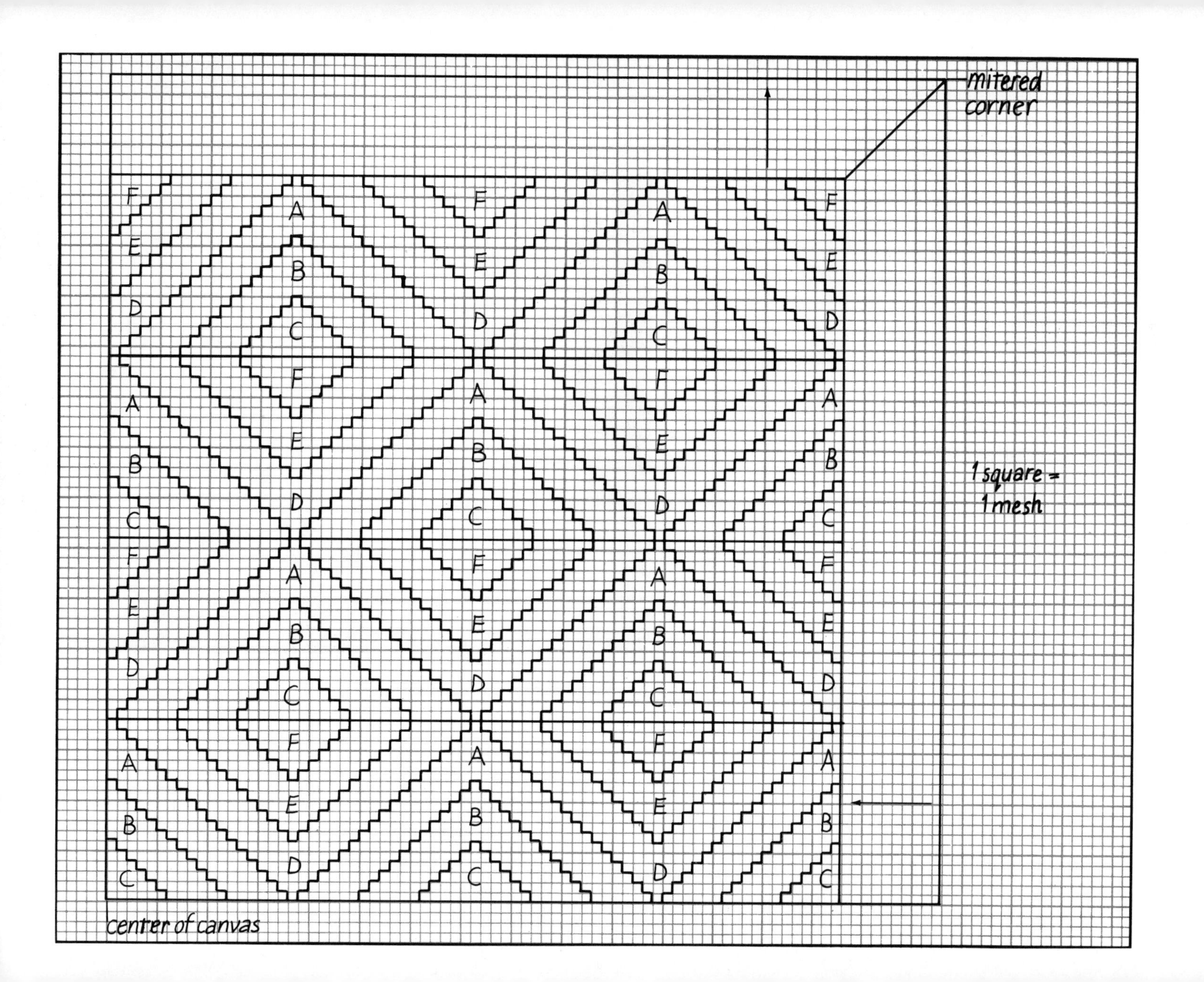

mitered corner
1 square = 1 mesh
center of canvas
F
E
D
A
B
C

5. Start working your first patch, detailed in Fig. 10-30, on this line about 2 inches up from the bottom of the canvas (1 inch up if you are using an interlocking canvas with smaller borders).
6. Follow Fig. 10-29 for the number of patches required.
7. Complete the canvas by working the borders as shown in Fig. 10-29. The borders are a continuation of the zig-zag lines of stitches established by the patches, and are worked in one color only—Shade D.

### Four-Way Bargello Designs

The designs that follow are recommended for those who have already attained some facility in working Bargello where the stitches are all in one direction. Instructions for dividing the canvas are given in Chapter 9 (Fig. 9-9). Work for each of the four triangular sections begins in the center mesh of the canvas, which marks the apex of the triangle, and proceeds—always in the same direction—to the outside edge, which is the base of the triangle. The charts and instructions that follow will give details of how to work each canvas.

Fig. 10-28 *"Honeycomb"*

Fig. 10-29 (Opposite)
*Layout for "Honeycomb." (Not to scale.)*

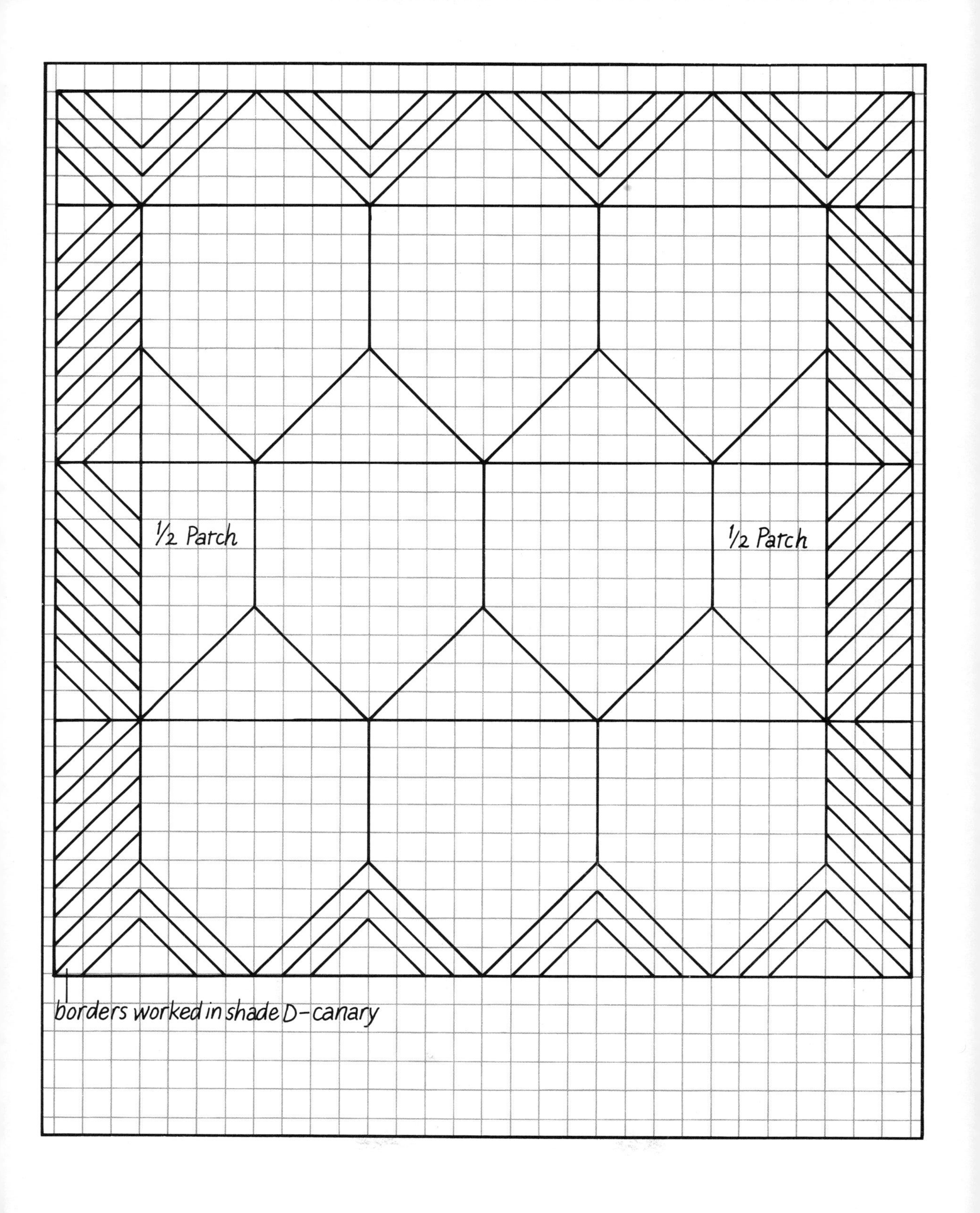
1/2 Patch
1/2 Patch
borders worked in shade D–canary

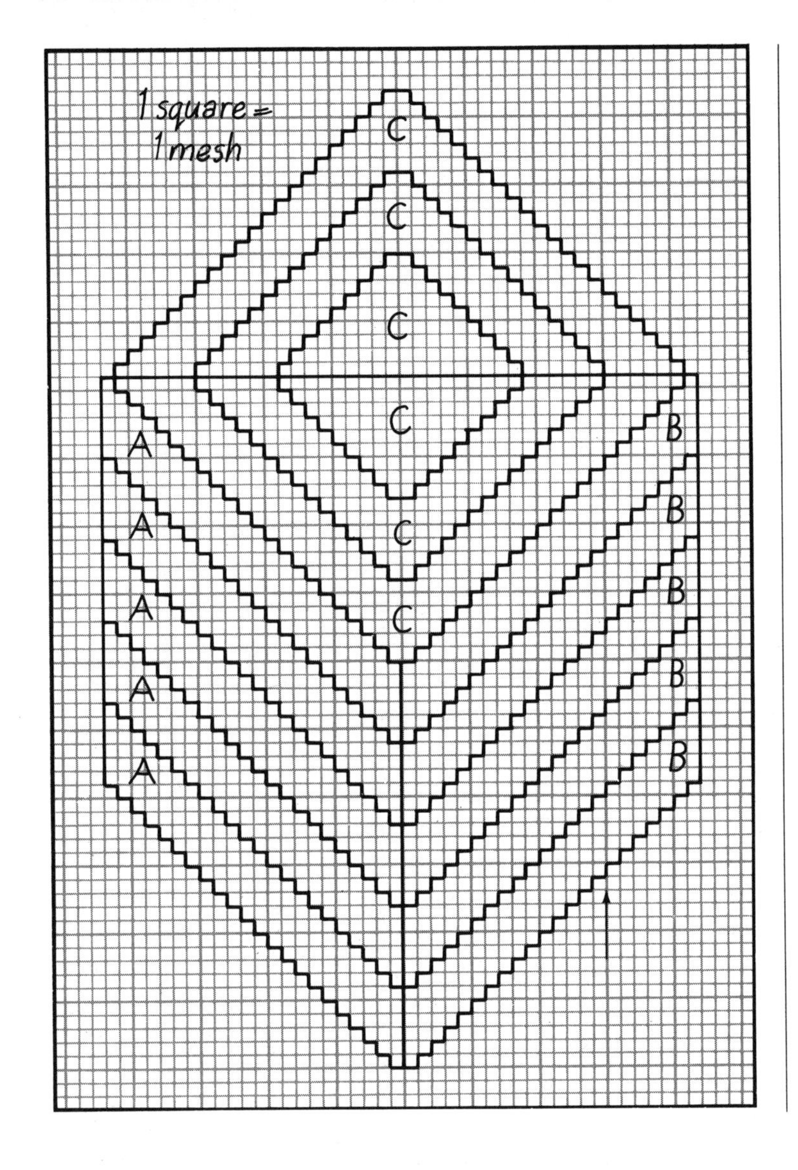


**Autumn Leaves** (Fig. 10-31)

FINISHED SIZE: APPROX. 14″ × 14″

YOU NEED: 4-ply worsted-weight wool (approx. 280 yds. in a 4-oz. pull skein).

Light Avocado (Shade A) 1 skein or approx. 10 yds.

Medium Avocado (Shade B) 1 skein or approx. 12 yds.

Dark Avocado (Shade C) 1 skein or approx. 20 yds.

Light tan (Shade D) 1 skein or approx. 36 yds.

Dark tan (Shade E) 1 skein or approx. 40 yds.

Copper (Shade F) 1 skein or approx. 45 yds.

A piece of 10-mesh-to-1-inch mono canvas measuring 18″ × 18″

A #18 tapestry needle

Fig. 10-30 *Detail of patch for "Honeycomb"*

Fig. 10-31 *"Autumn Leaves"*

METHOD

1. Divide the canvas into an X as shown in Fig. 9-9.
2. Also draw in the horizontal and vertical lines from the center to the outside edges of the canvas.
3. Start in the upper left-hand corner, at a point at the top 2 inches in from side edge (1 inch if you are using interlocking canvas).
4. Follow Fig. 10-32 for the first quarter of the design, also consulting the layout diagram.
5. Make the other three quarters in numerical sequence according to the layout diagram.

**Bullseye** (Fig. 10-36)

FINISHED SIZE: Approx. 16″ × 16″
YOU NEED: 4-ply worsted-weight wool (approx. 280 yds. in a 4-oz. pull skein).
Black (Shade A) 1 skein or approx. 100 yds.
White (Shade B) 1 skein or approx. 75 yds.
A piece of 10-mesh-to-1-inch mono canvas measuring 20″ × 20″
A #18 tapestry needle

METHOD

1. Divide the canvas into an X as shown in Fig. 9-9.
2. Fig. 10-37 shows one quarter of the complete design. Start work at the center mesh, and work each quarter as the one shown, following the direction of stitching as indicated by the arrows.

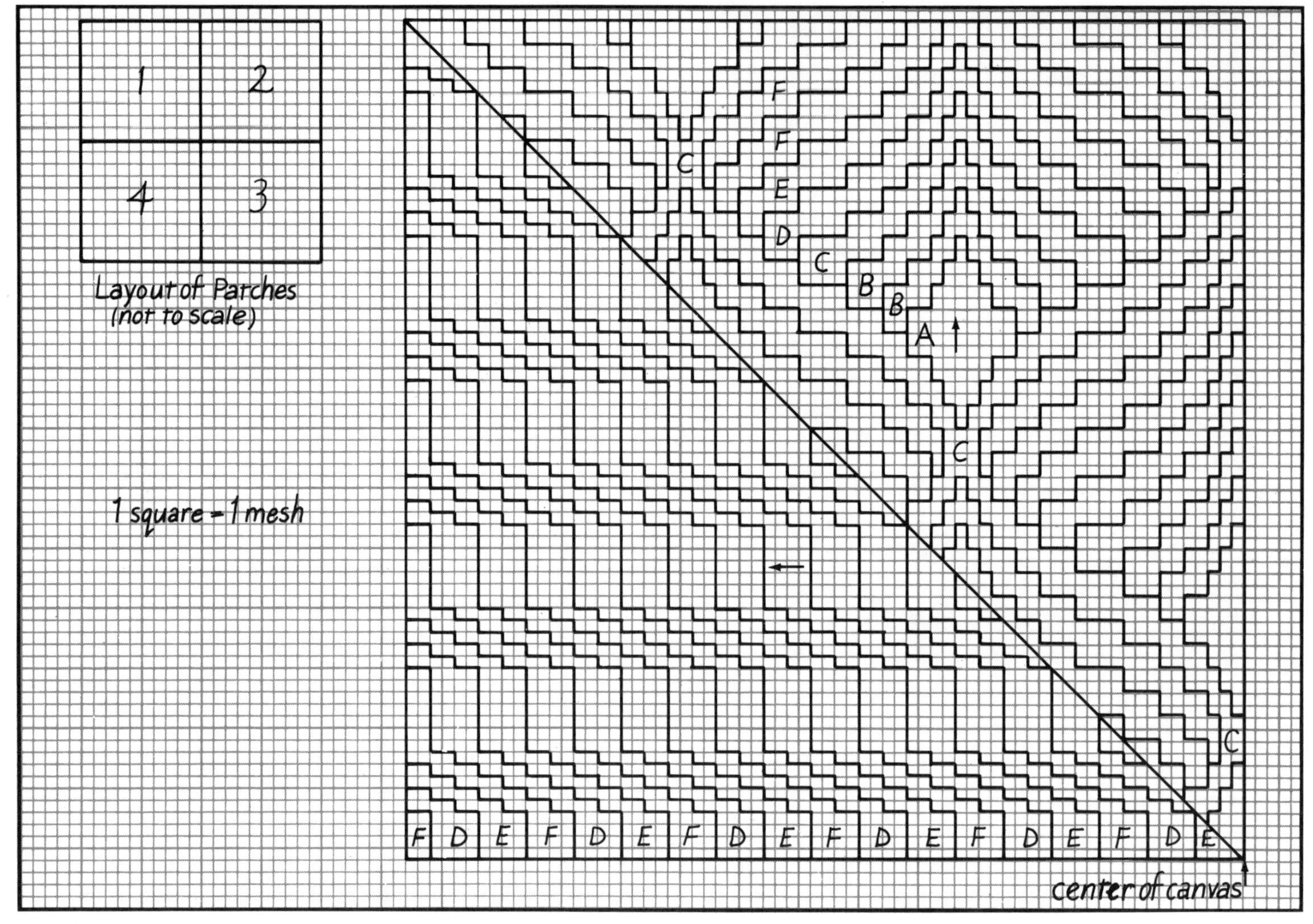


Fig. 10-32 *"Autumn Leaves" layout and patch #1*

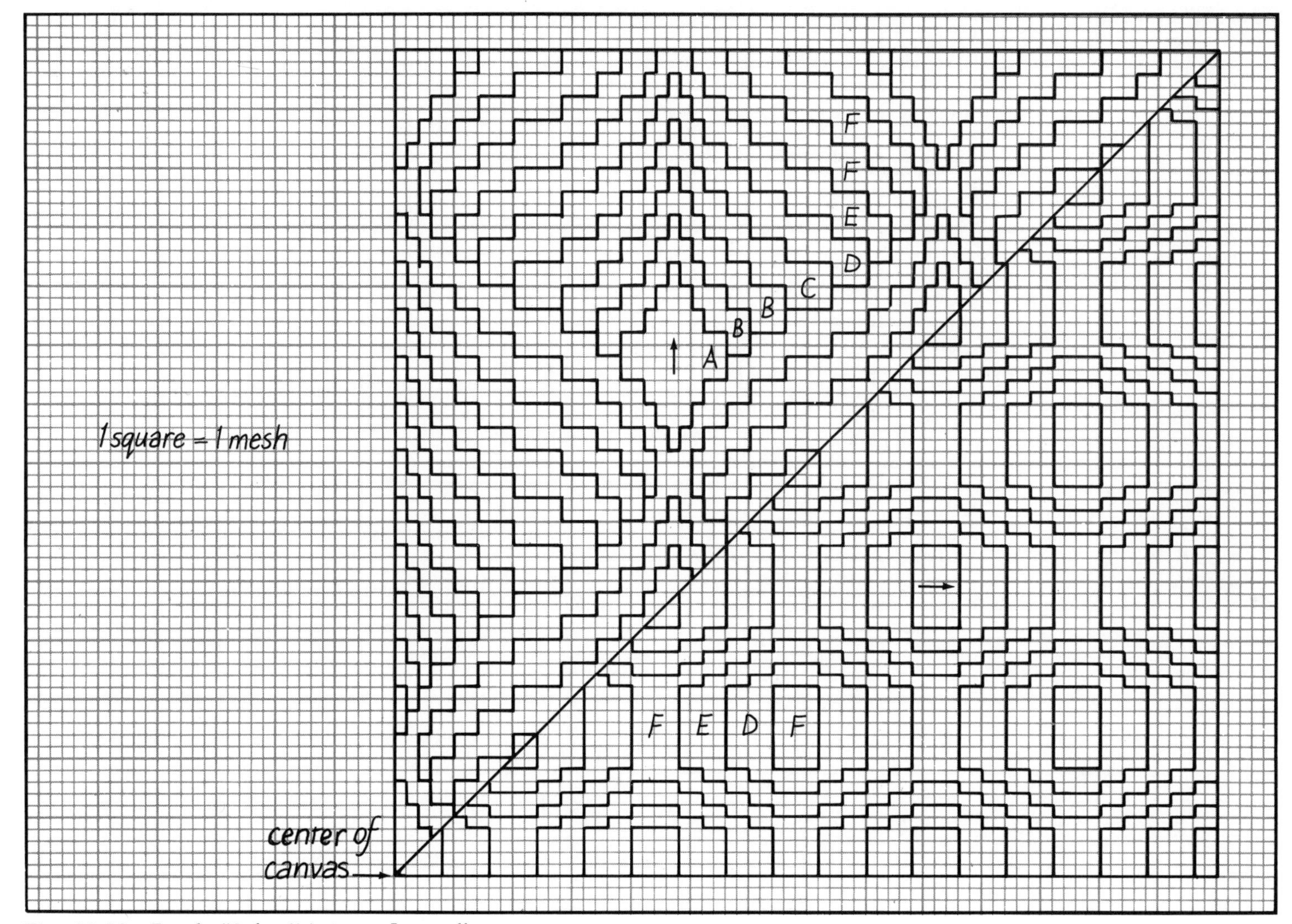


Fig. 10-33 *Patch #2 for "Autumn Leaves"*

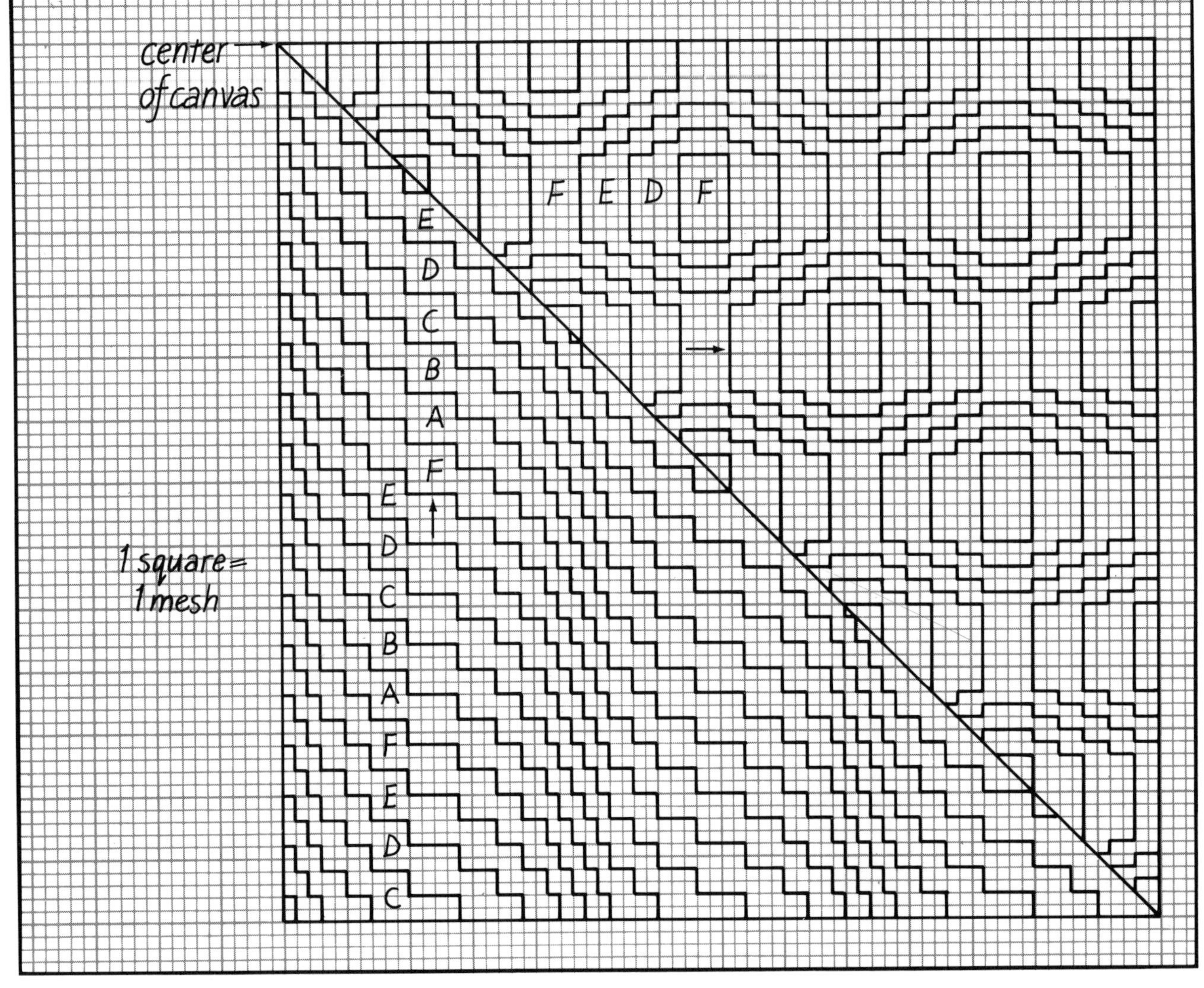


Fig. 10-34 *Patch #3 for "Autumn Leaves"*

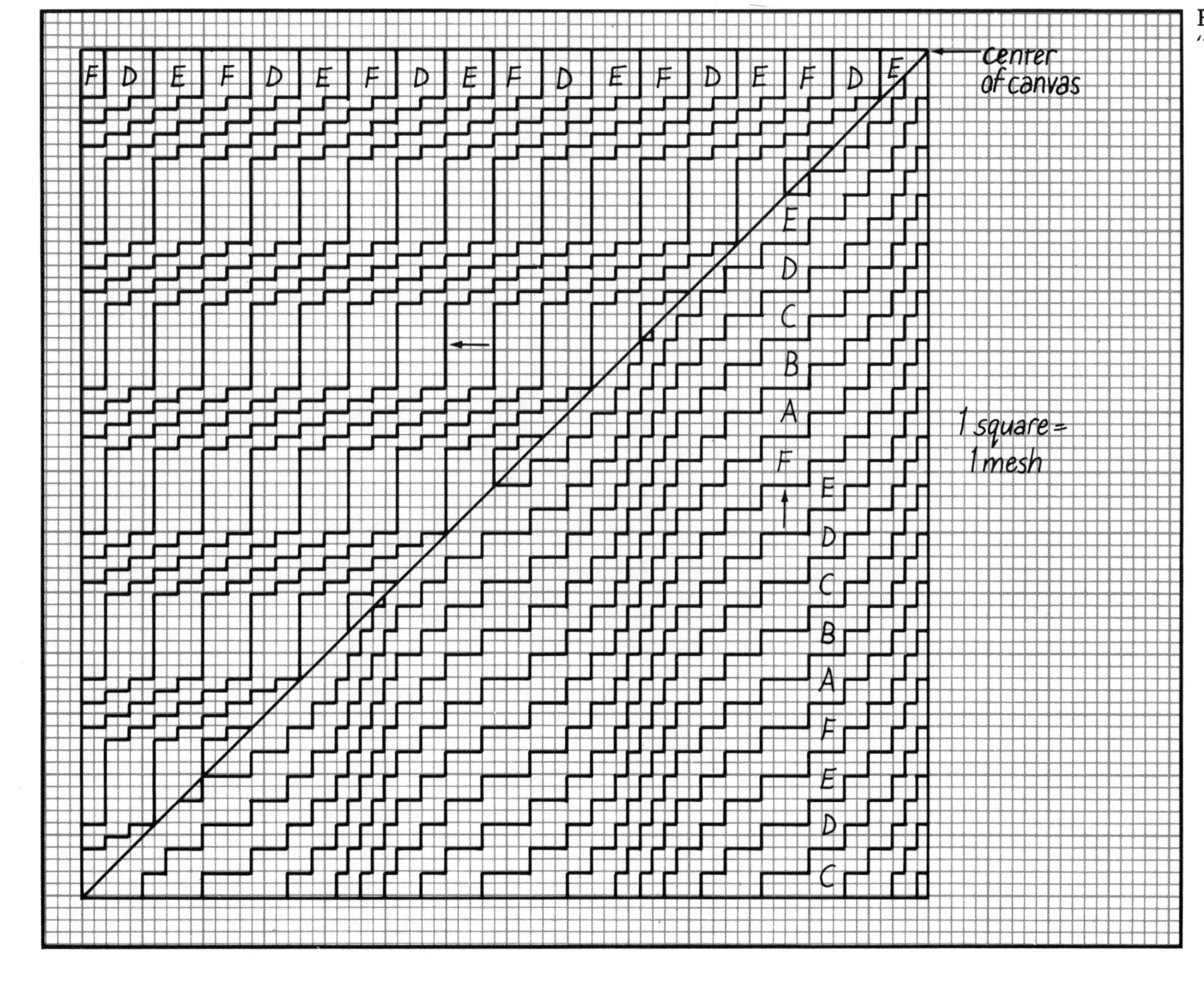


Fig. 10-35 *Patch #4 for "Autumn Leaves"*

**Compass** (Fig. 10-38)

FINISHED SIZE: APPROX. 16″ × 16″

YOU NEED: 4-ply worsted-weight wool (approx. 280 yds. in a 4-oz. pull skein).

| | |
|---|---|
| White (Shade A) | 1 skein or approx. 50 yds. |
| Beige (Shade B) | 1 skein or approx. 52 yds. |
| Natural (Shade C) | 1 skein or approx. 55 yds. |
| Dark tan (Shade D) | 1 skein or approx. 22 yds. |
| Tangerine (Shade E) | 1 skein or approx. 22 yds. |

A piece of 10-mesh-to-1-inch mono canvas measuring 20″ × 20″

A #18 tapestry needle

METHOD

1. Divide the canvas into an X as shown in Fig. 9-9.
2. Also draw in the horizontal and vertical lines from the center to the edges of the canvas.
3. Fig. 10-39 represents one quarter of the design. Each quarter is worked in exactly the same manner.
4. Start to work each quarter from the center of the canvas.

Fig. 10-36 *"Bullseye"*

Fig. 10-37 (Opposite) *Design for "Bullseye." One quarter of four-way symmetrical canvas.*

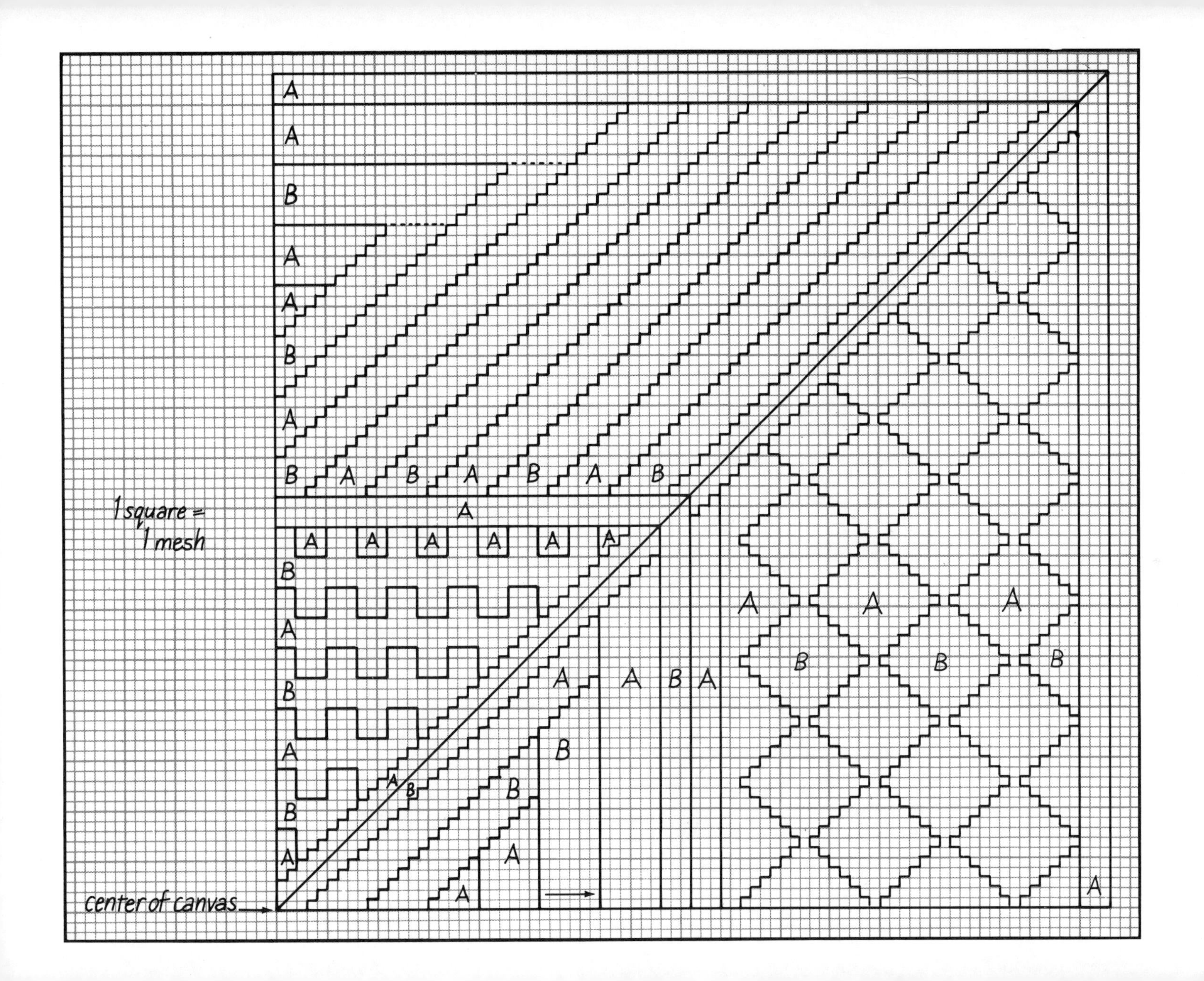

1 square = 1 mesh
center of canvas
A
B

Fig. 10-38 *"Compass"*

Fig. 10-39 (Opposite) *Design for "Compass." One quarter of four-way symmetrical canvas.*

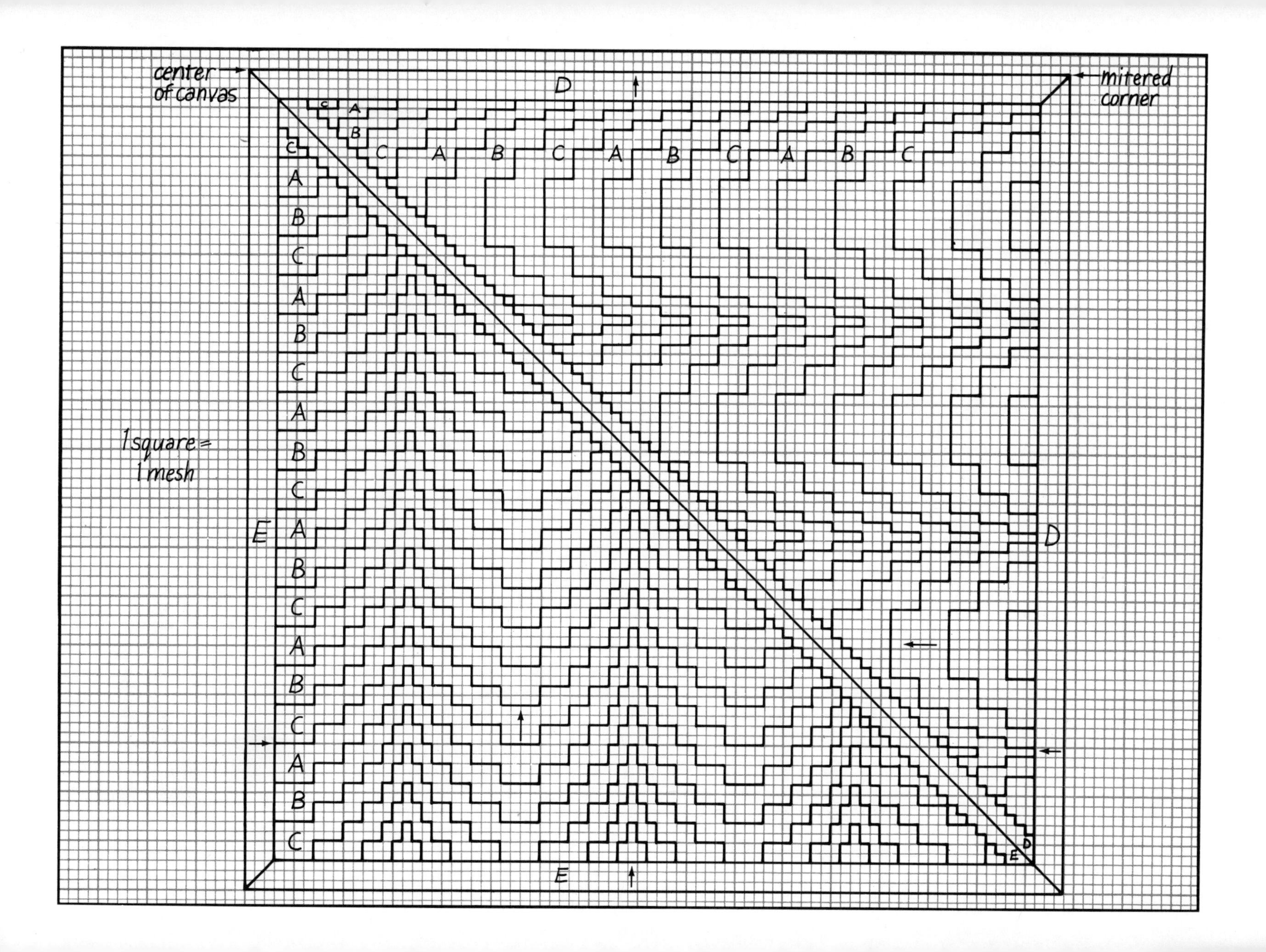
center of canvas
D
mitered corner
C
A
B
C
A
B
C
A
B
C
A
B
C
A
B
C
1 square = 1 mesh
E
D
E

# 11 Gobelin Projects

Before embarking on any of the following projects, the reader is advised to consult Chapter 9 for helpful information about canvas work in general, and Gobelin stitch in particular. The method of working Gobelin stitch is shown in Fig. 9-7.

Gobelin projects marked* are strongly recommended for beginners, who will find these even more straightforward than the starred Bargello items in the previous chapter.

**Patio*** (Fig. 11-1)

FINISHED SIZE: Approx. 16″ × 16″

YOU NEED: 4-ply worsted-weight wool (approx. 280 yds. in a 4-oz. pull skein).

| | |
|---|---|
| Black (Shade A) | 1 skein or approx. 40 yds. |
| White (Shade B) | 1 skein or approx. 30 yds. |
| Gold (Shade C) | 1 skein or approx. 35 yds. |
| Kelly green (Shade D) | 1 skein or approx. 45 yds. |
| Scarlet (Shade E) | 1 skein or approx. 35 yds. |
| Tangerine (Shade F) | 1 skein or approx. 27 yds. |

A piece of 10-mesh-to-1-inch mono canvas measuring 20″ × 20″

A #18 tapestry needle

METHOD

1. This design is worked entirely over six holes of the canvas.
2. Study Figs. 11-1 and 11-2 carefully for an overall picture of the design, and the placing of colors.
3. Start in the lower right-hand corner, at a point 2 inches up from the bottom edge and in from the side (1 inch if you are using an interlocking canvas).

Fig. 11-1 *"Patio"*

4. Follow the chart (Fig. 11-3) given for a single patch. The broken lines show where the stitches end, but the next row continues in the same color.
5. Refer back to Fig. 11-2 for the coloring of each patch as you work.
6. The patches worked entirely in one color are the same size as those using two. Simply work all seven rows of the patch straight across, ignoring the center square of a contrasting color.

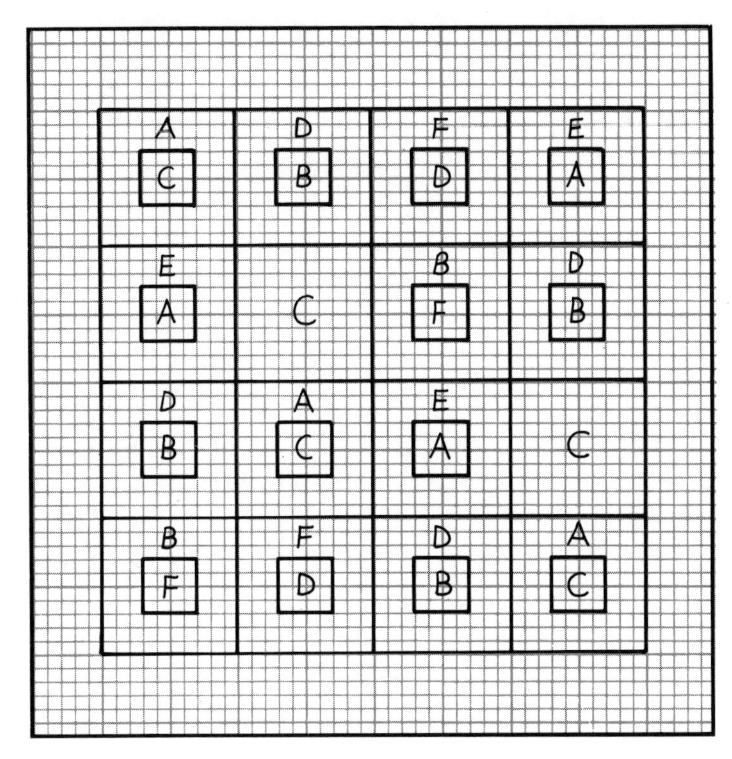


Fig. 11-2 *Layout for "Patio." (Not to scale.)*

7. It is suggested that you work the patches row by row across the canvas from right to left.

**Winter Spruces*** (Fig. 11-4)

FINISHED SIZE: APPROX. 16″ × 16″
YOU NEED: 4-ply worsted-weight wool (approx. 280 yds. in a 4-oz. pull skein).

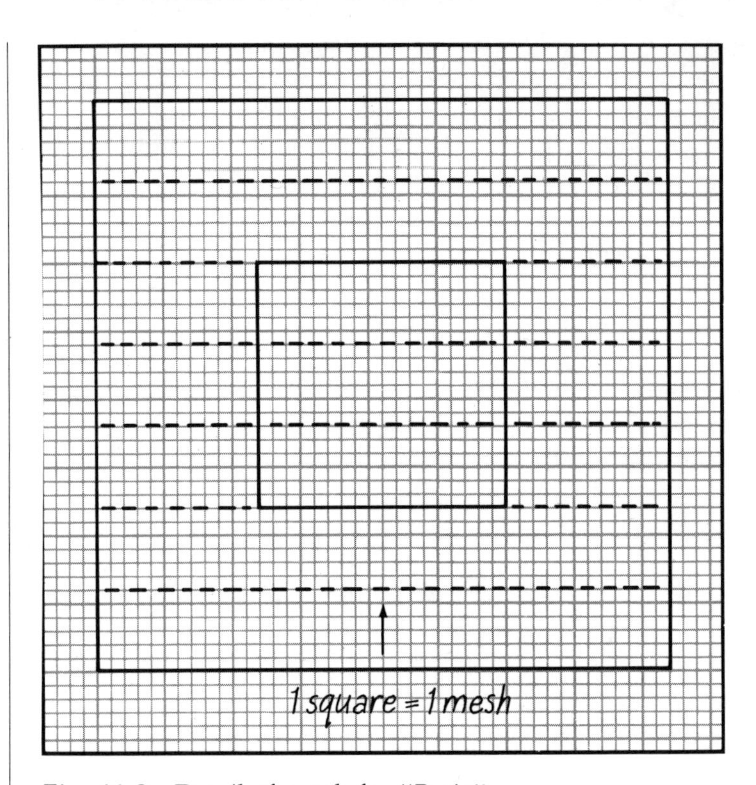


Fig. 11-3 *Detail of patch for "Patio"*

| | |
|---|---|
| Black (Shade A) | 1 skein or approx. 55 yds. |
| White (Shade B) | 1 skein or approx. 50 yds. |
| Kelly green (Shade C) | 1 skein or approx. 45 yds. |

Fig. 11-4 *"Winter Spruces"*

| | |
|---|---|
| Tangerine (Shade D) | 1 skein or approx. 45 yds. |

A piece of 10-mesh-to-1-inch mono canvas measuring 20″ × 20″

A #18 tapestry needle

METHOD

1. This design is worked entirely over six holes of the canvas.
2. Mark the center of the canvas as shown in Fig. 9-9.
3. Study Fig. 11-5 for the complete layout of the patches, the photograph (Fig. 11-4) for the position of colors, and the charts of individual patches (Fig. 11-6 through 11-8) for details.
5. Return to the center of the canvas and work Patch #3 (see Fig. 11-8) below Patch #2.
6. Using Fig. 11-5 as a guide, work Patch #1 (Fig. 11-6) four times on each side of the center panel created by Patch #2 and Patch #3.
7. The broken lines on the charts represent divisions between rows of stitches where the color does not change.

**Log Cabin*** (Fig. 11-9)

FINISHED SIZE: Approx. 16″ × 16″

YOU NEED: 4-ply worsted-weight wool (approx. 280 yds. in a 4-oz. pull skein).

| | |
|---|---|
| Copperglo (Shade A) | 1 skein or approx. 30 yds. |
| Dark tan (Shade B) | 1 skein or approx. 33 yds. |
| Light tan (Shade C) | 1 skein or approx. 36 yds. |

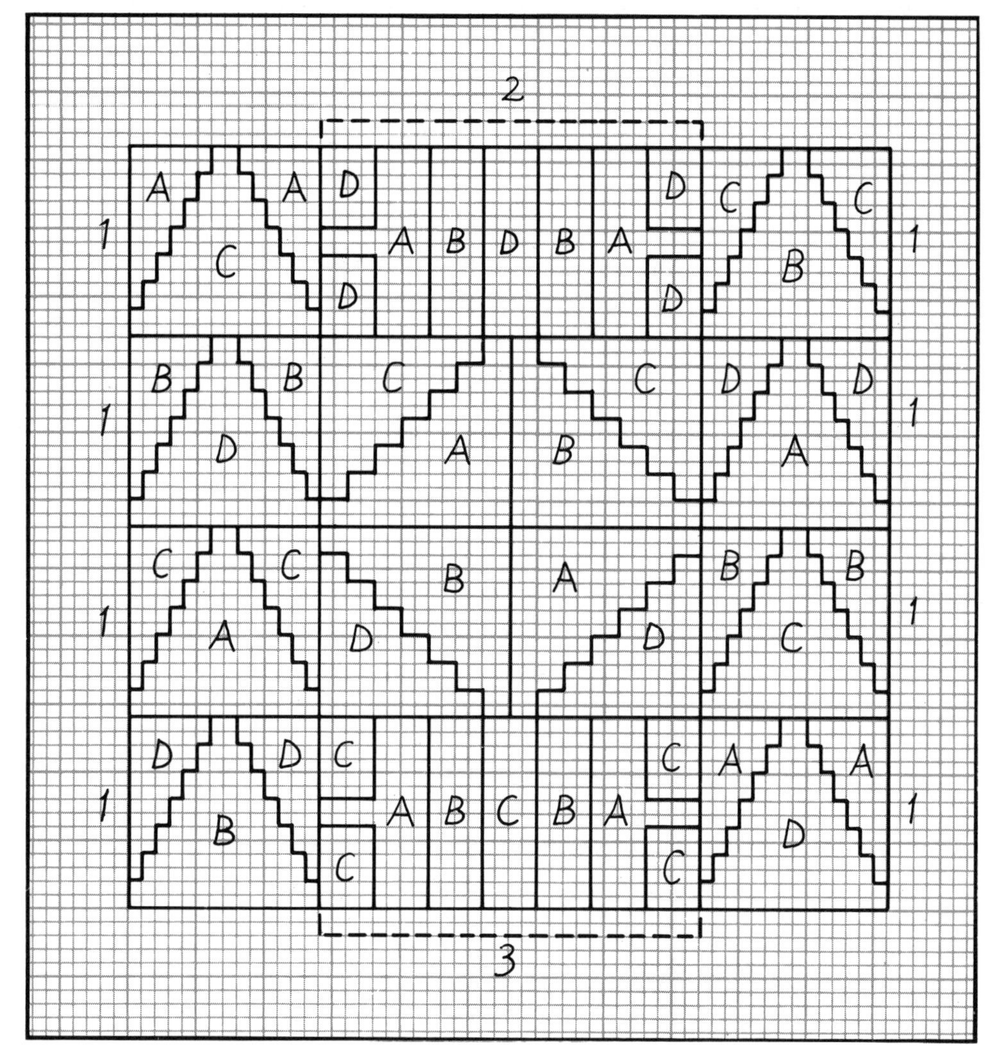


Fig. 11-5 *Layout for "Winter Spruces." (Not to scale.)*

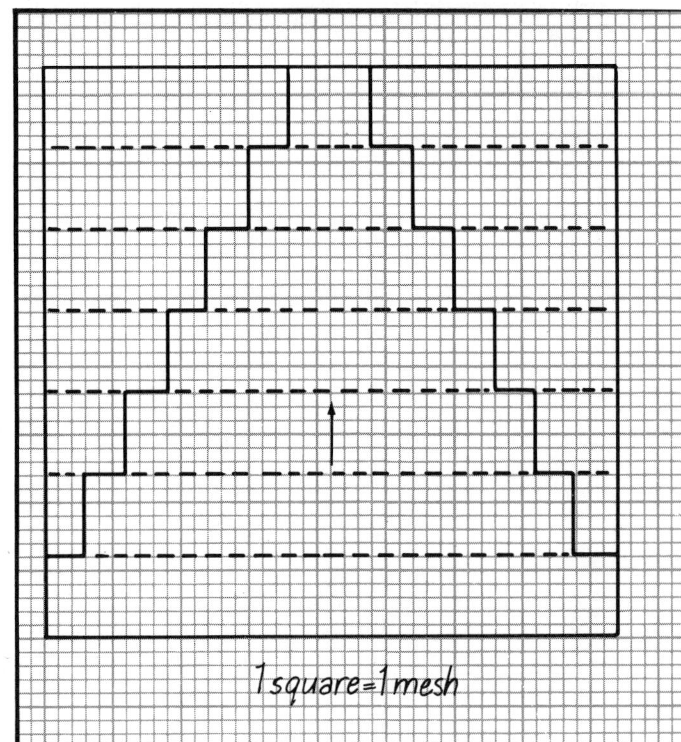


Fig. 11-6 *Patch #1 for "Winter Spruces"*

Fig. 11-7 (Opposite)
*Patch #2 for "Winter Spruces"*

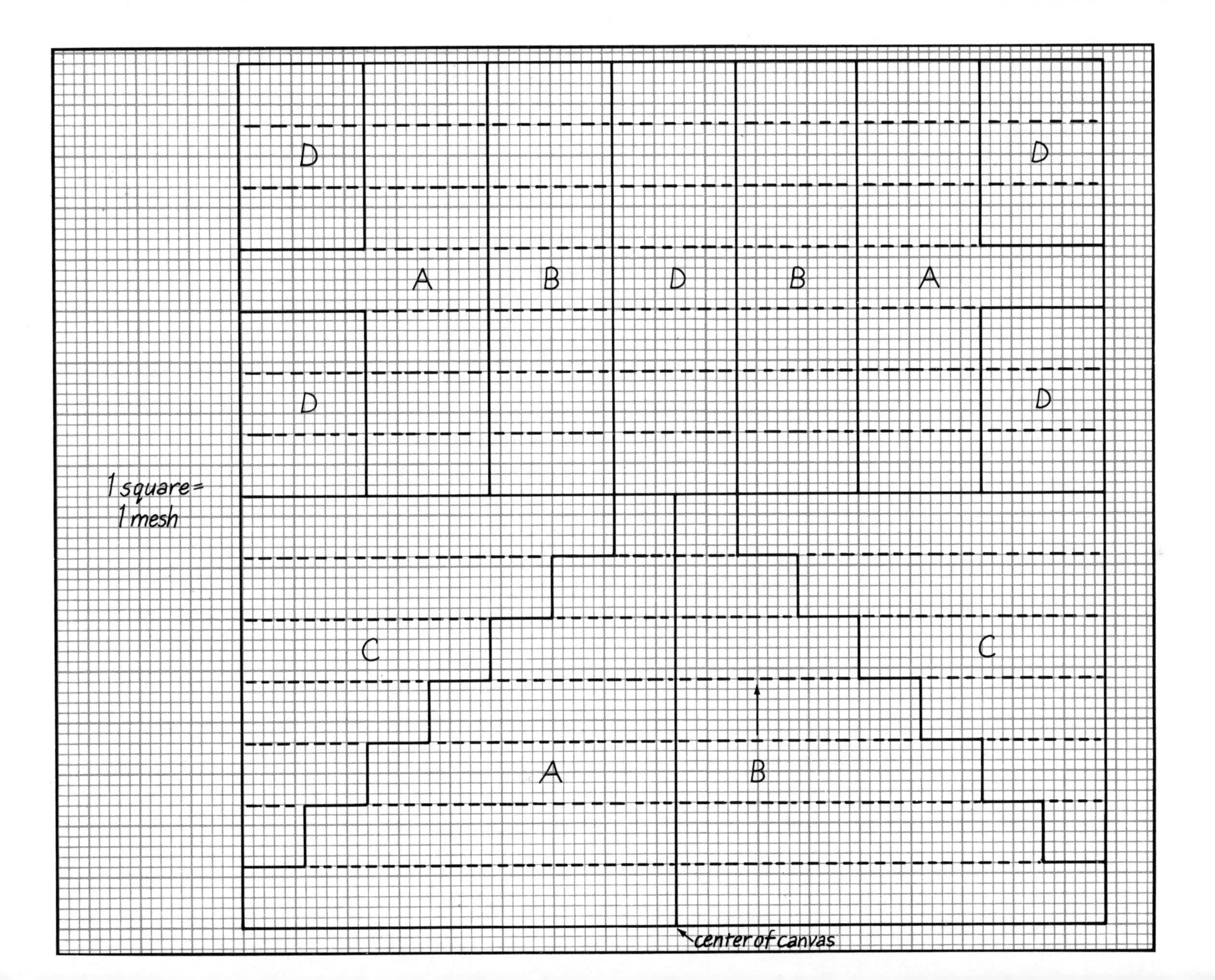
D
D
A
B
D
B
A
D
D
1 square=
1 mesh
C
C
A
B
center of canvas

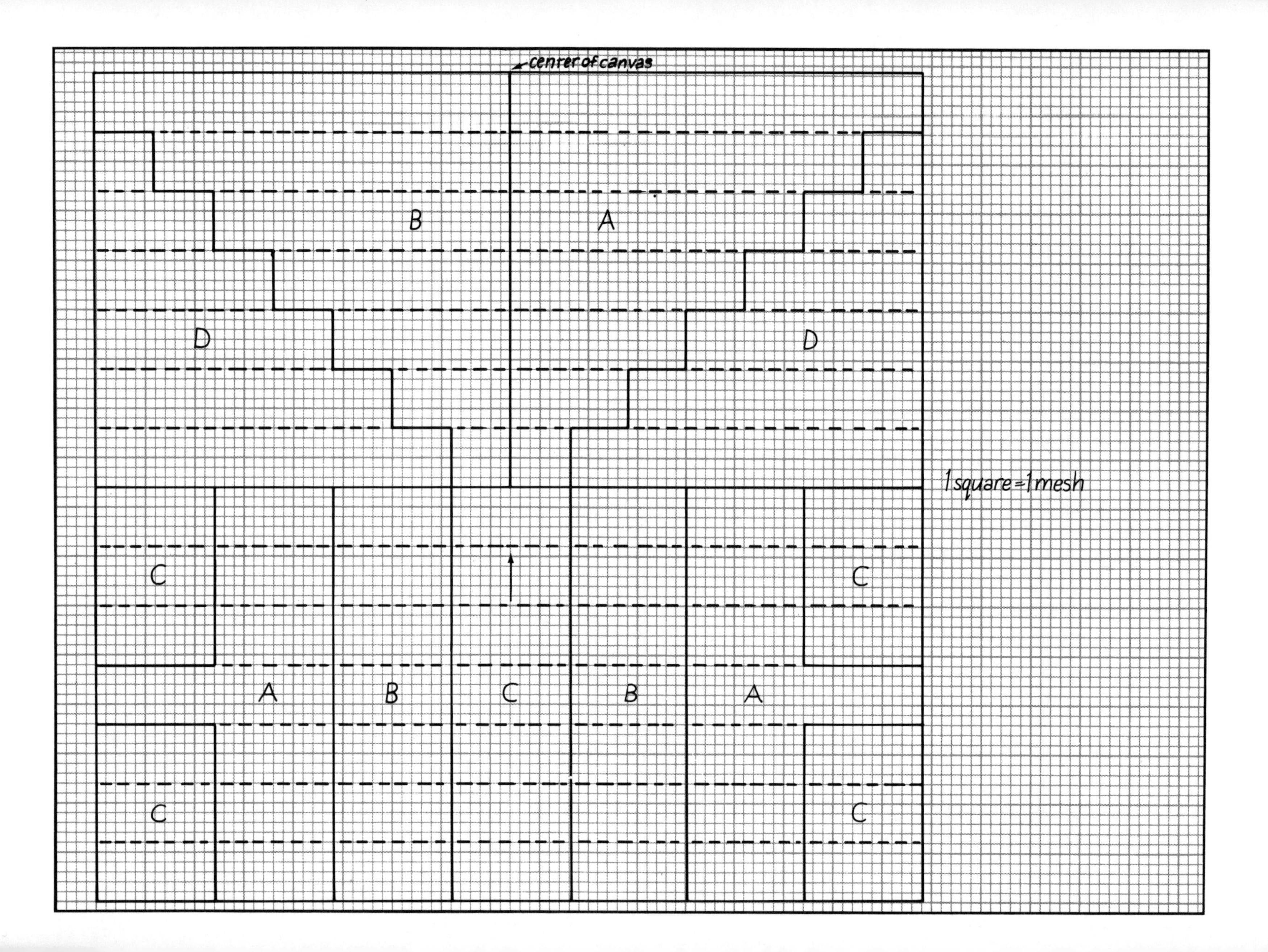

center of canvas
B
A
D
D
1 square = 1 mesh
C
C
A
B
C
B
A
C
C

Fig. 11-9 *"Log Cabin"*

Fig. 11-8 (Opposite) *Patch #3 for "Winter Spruces"*

| | |
|---|---|
| Off-white (Shade D) | 1 skein or approx. 36 yds. |
| Bright tangerine (Shade E) | 1 skein or approx. 35 yds. |
| Scarlet (Shade F) | 1 skein or approx. 35 yds. |

A piece of 10-mesh-to-1-inch mono canvas measuring 20″ × 20″
A #18 tapestry needle

METHOD

1. This design is worked entirely over six holes of the canvas.
2. Mark the center of the canvas as shown in Fig. 9-9.
3. Study Fig. 11-10 for a complete layout of the patches. You will see that the canvas is divided into four equal squares, and that the design for the "Log Cabin" patch is the same in each, except that the colors are slightly rearranged. Have a look at the photograph (Fig. 11-9) to get a clear idea of the positioning of the colors.
4. Start work at the center of the canvas and make Square 1, following Fig. 11-11 for details of the stitching, and Fig. 11-10 for the color-key. Broken lines on the chart show where a line of stitches ends and another begins above it in the same color.
5. Follow the Fig. 11-10 to complete the other three quarters of the canvas in the same way.

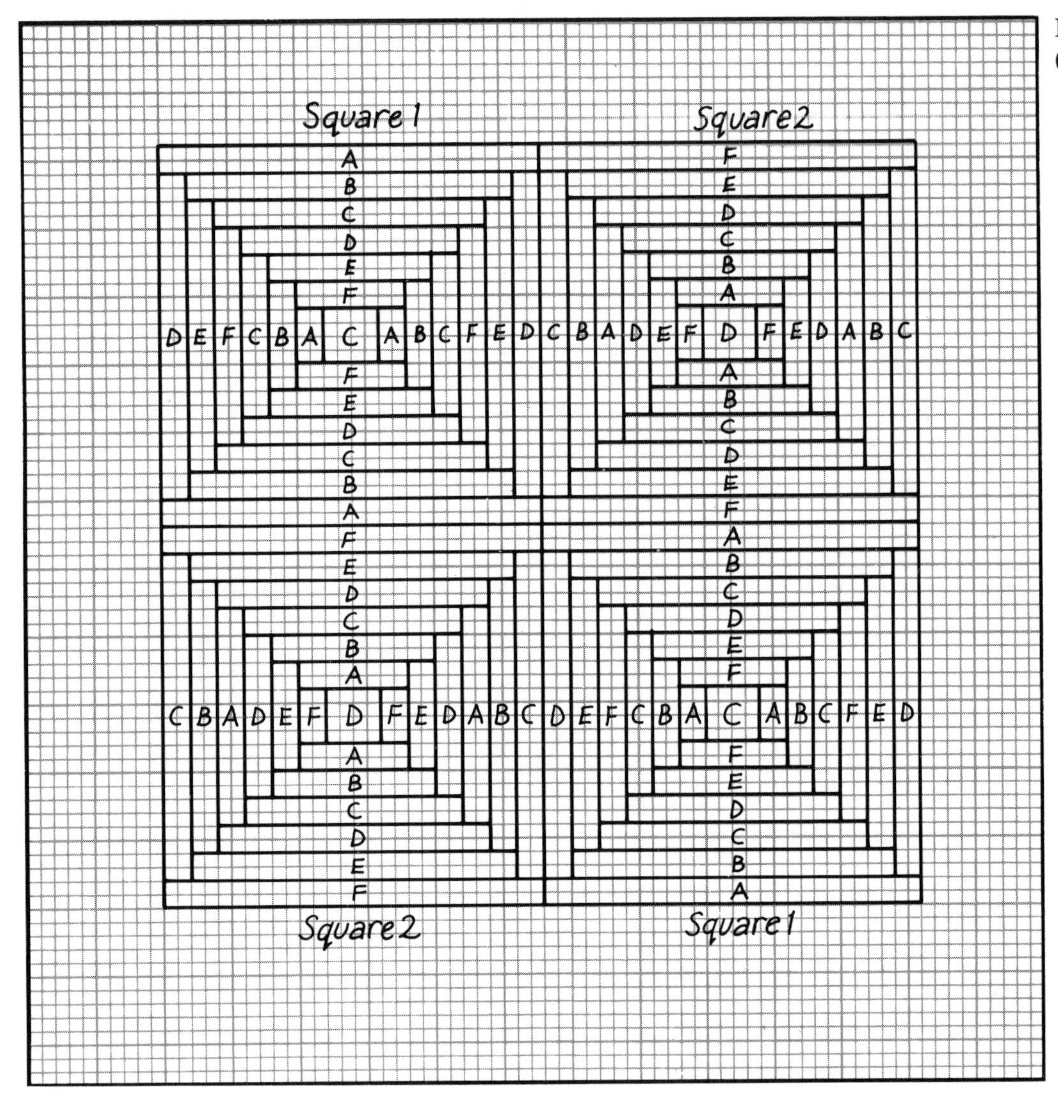


Fig. 11-10 *Layout for "Log Cabin." (Not to scale.)*

Fig. 11-11 (Opposite) *Design for all four patches for "Log Cabin." Follow Fig. 11-10 for different color design of each.*

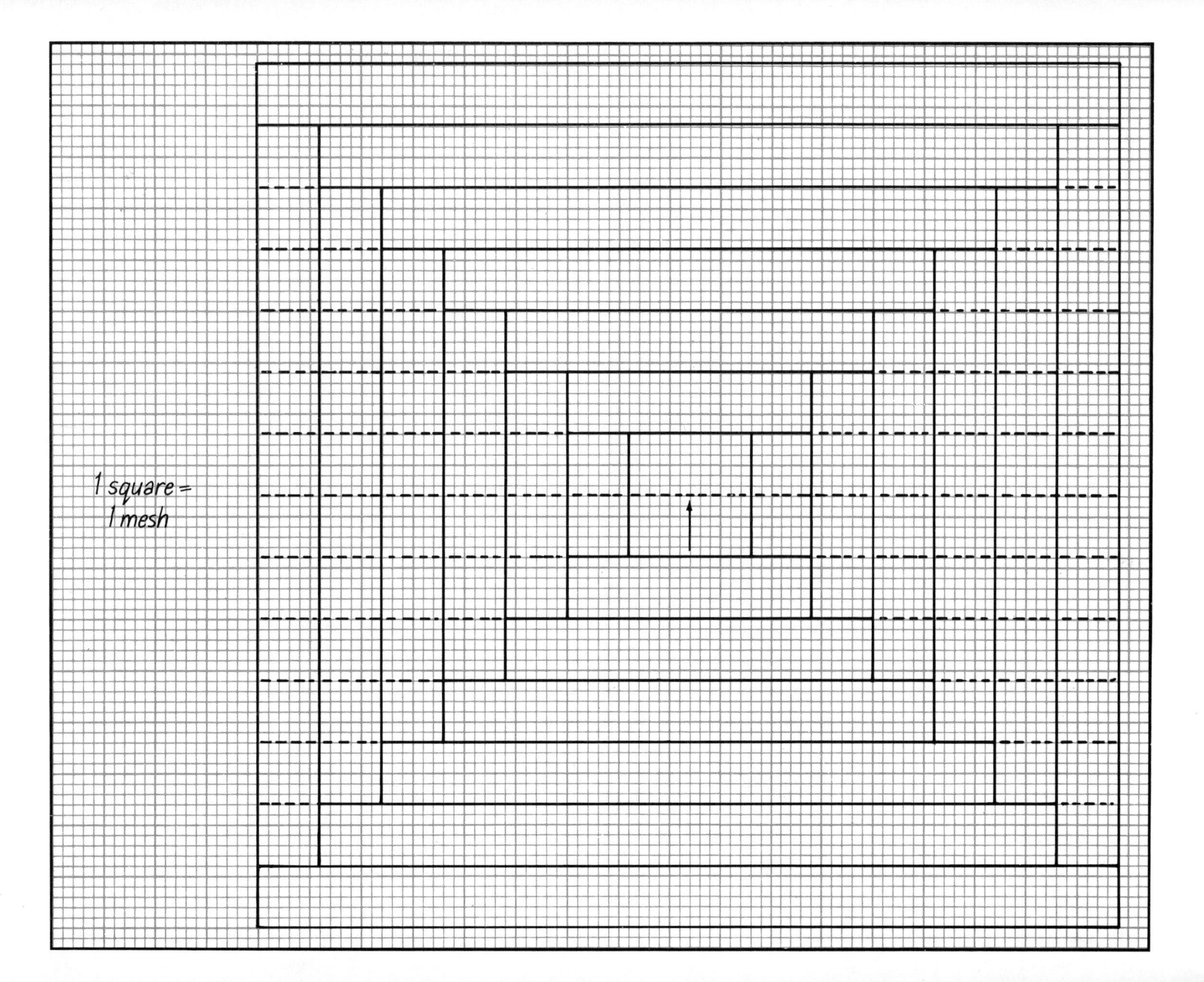
1 square =
1 mesh

**Magic Lantern** (Fig. 11-12)

FINISHED SIZE: Approx. 20″ × 20″

YOU NEED: 4-ply worsted-weight wool (approx. 280 yds. in a 4-oz. pull skein).

| | |
|---|---|
| Magenta (Shade A) | 1 skein or approx. 65 yds. |
| Dusty rose (Shade B) | 1 skein or approx. 80 yds. |
| Off-white (Shade C) | 1 skein or approx. 70 yds. |
| Beige (Shade D) | 1 skein or approx. 70 yds. |

A piece of 10-mesh-to-1-inch mono canvas measuring 24″ × 24″

A #18 tapestry needle

METHOD

1. The design is worked over six holes of the canvas, except where otherwise shown in the charts.
2. Mark the center of the canvas as shown in Fig. 9-9.
3. Study the layout diagram (Fig. 11-13) very carefully. It shows the position of patches by number and color. Also study the diagrams for the individual patches in Figs. 11-14 through 11-17. Note that Patches #6 and #4 appear on the design both as on the charts (Fig. 11-17 and Fig. 11-14) and inverted. Patch #5 appears as in the chart (Fig. 11-16) and laterally reversed, that is, turned over

Fig. 11-12 *"Magic Lantern"*

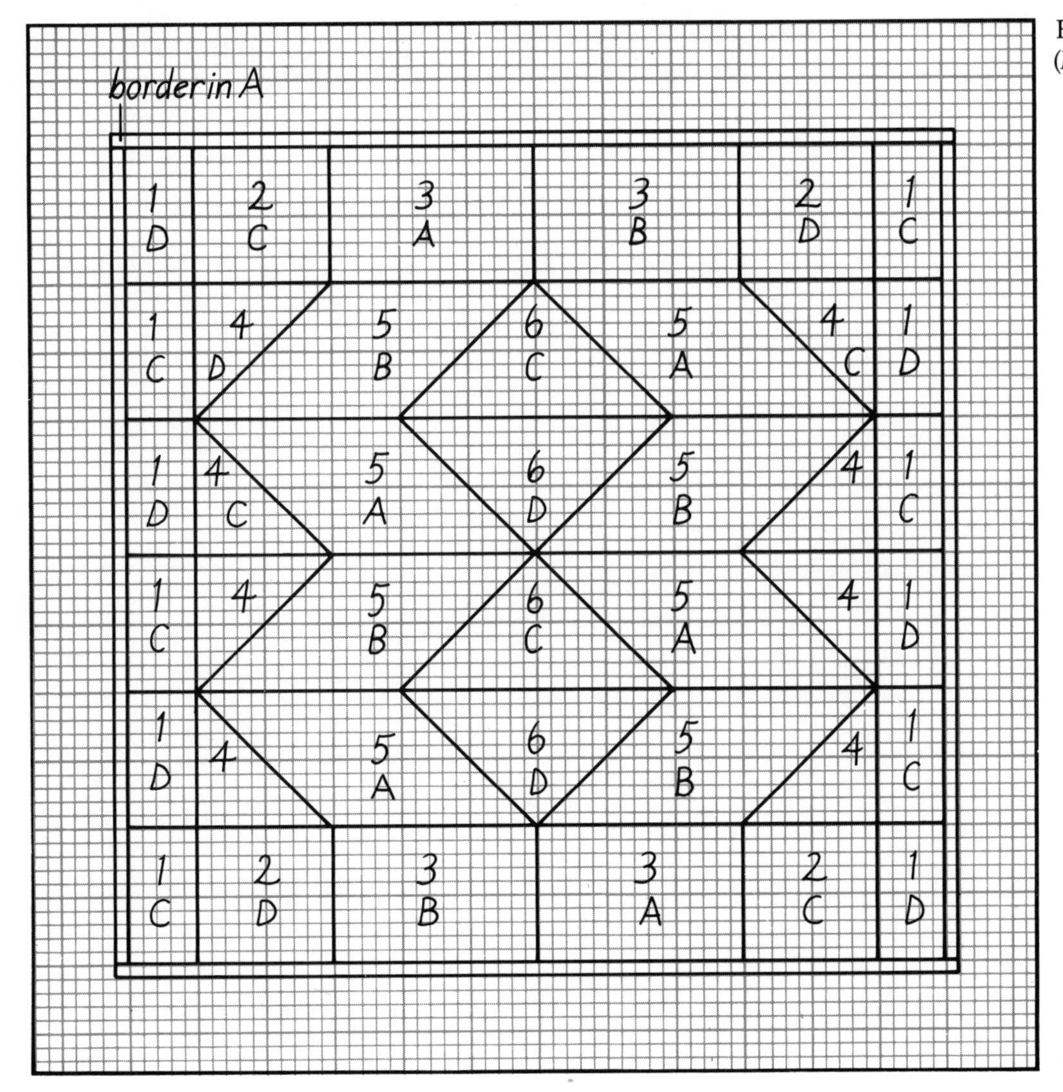


Fig. 11-13 *Layout for "Magic Lantern."* *(Not to scale.)*

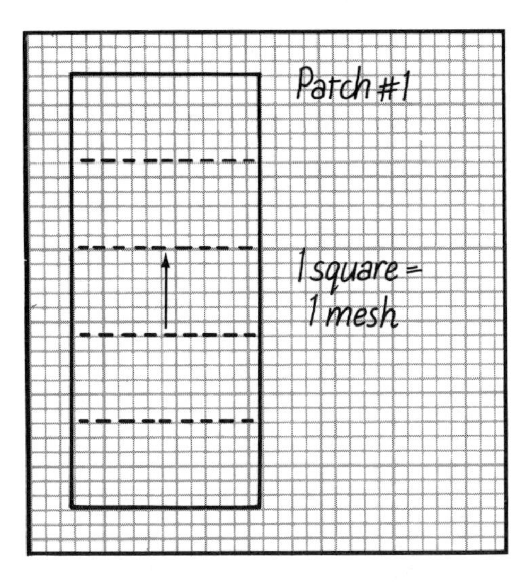


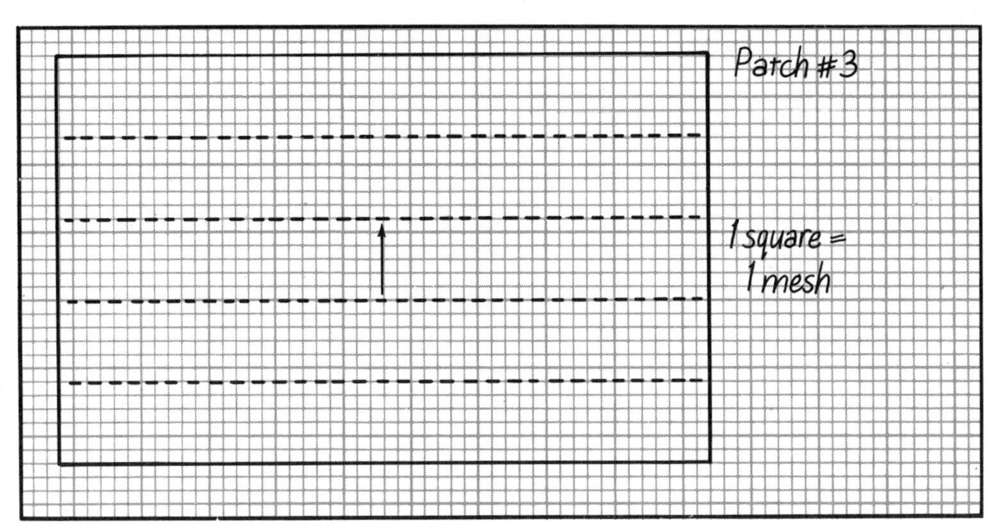


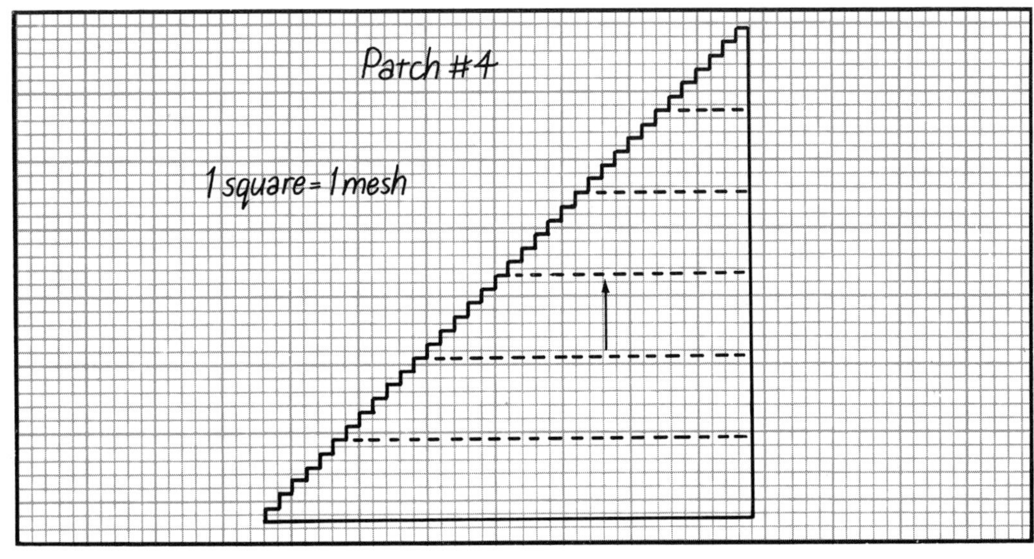


Fig. 11-14 *Some patches for "Magic Lantern"*

Fig. 11-15
*Patch #2 for "Magic Lantern"*

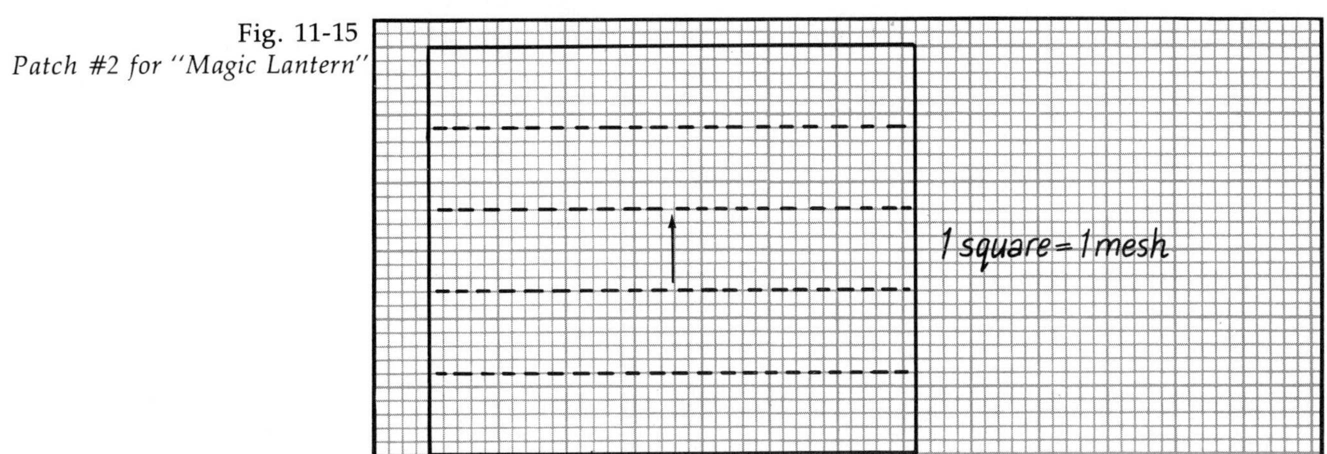


Fig. 11-16
*Patch #5 for "Magic Lantern"*

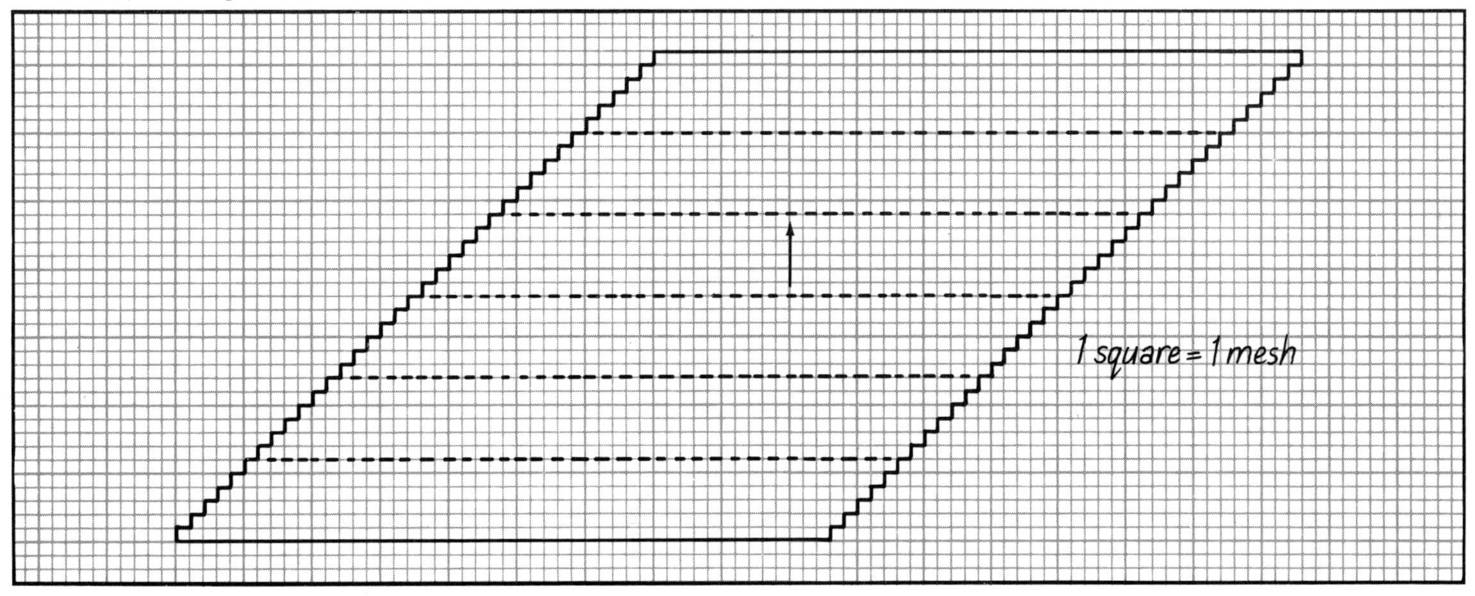

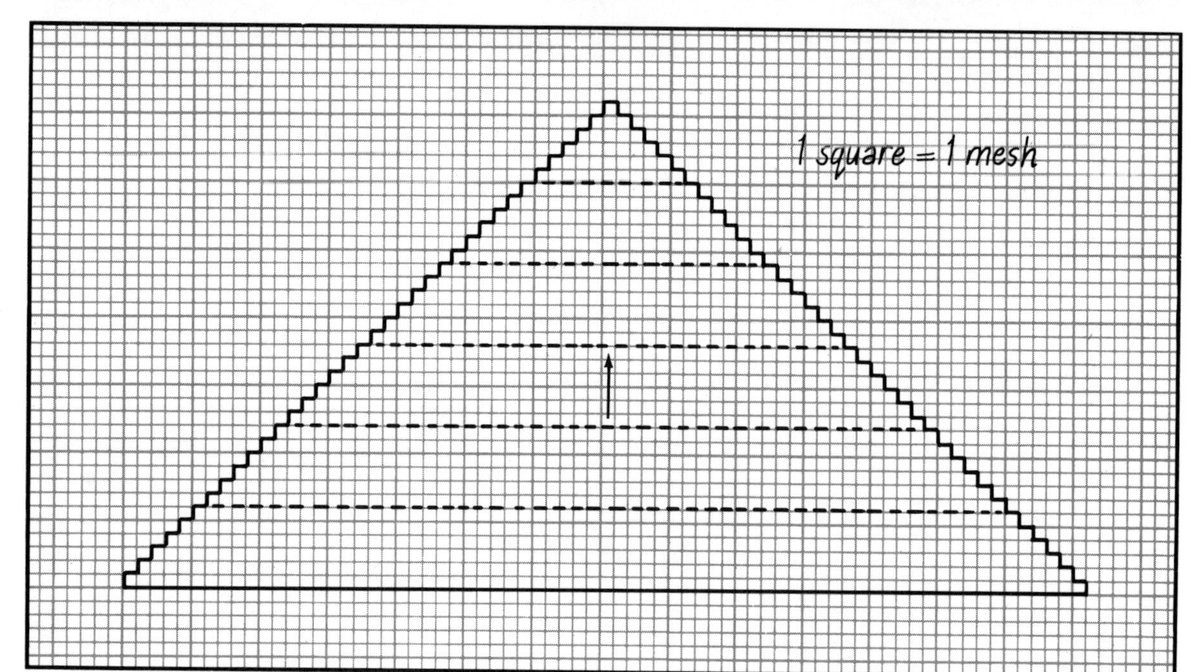


Fig. 11-17
*Patch #6 for "Magic Lantern"*

sideways. All these variations are shown on the layout (Fig. 11-13), and sound far more complicated than they actually are!

4. It is suggested that you start at the center hole of the canvas and work from there out, patch by patch, doing the Patch #6 above the center first.
5. When the entire design has been completed, add the border, in Shade A, which is worked over three mesh at top and bottom. At the sides, three stitches are made side by side, but they are worked over six mesh to coincide with the rows on the patches themselves.
6. Broken lines on the charts represent divisions between rows of stitches where the color does not change.

**Snow Crystal** (Fig. 11-18)

FINISHED SIZE: Approx. 16″ × 16″

YOU NEED: 4-ply acrylic (approx. 306 yds. in a 4-oz. pull skein).

| | |
|---|---|
| Black (Shade A) | 1 skein or approx. 35 yds. |
| Beige (Shade B) | 1 skein or approx. 36 yds. |
| Off-white (Shade C) | 1 skein or approx. 40 yds. |
| White (Shade D) | 1 skein or approx. 36 yds. |
| Gray (Shade E) | 1 skein or approx. 36 yds. |

A piece of 10-mesh-to-1-inch mono canvas measuring 20″ × 20″

A #18 tapestry needle

METHOD

1. The design is worked over six holes of the canvas, except where otherwise shown on the chart.
2. Mark the center of the canvas, and draw in the diagonal dividing lines as shown in Fig. 9-9.
3. This design is worked in four directions, and it is suggested that the reader refer to the section "Four-Way Bargello Designs" in Chapter 10.

Fig. 11-18 *"Snow Crystal"*

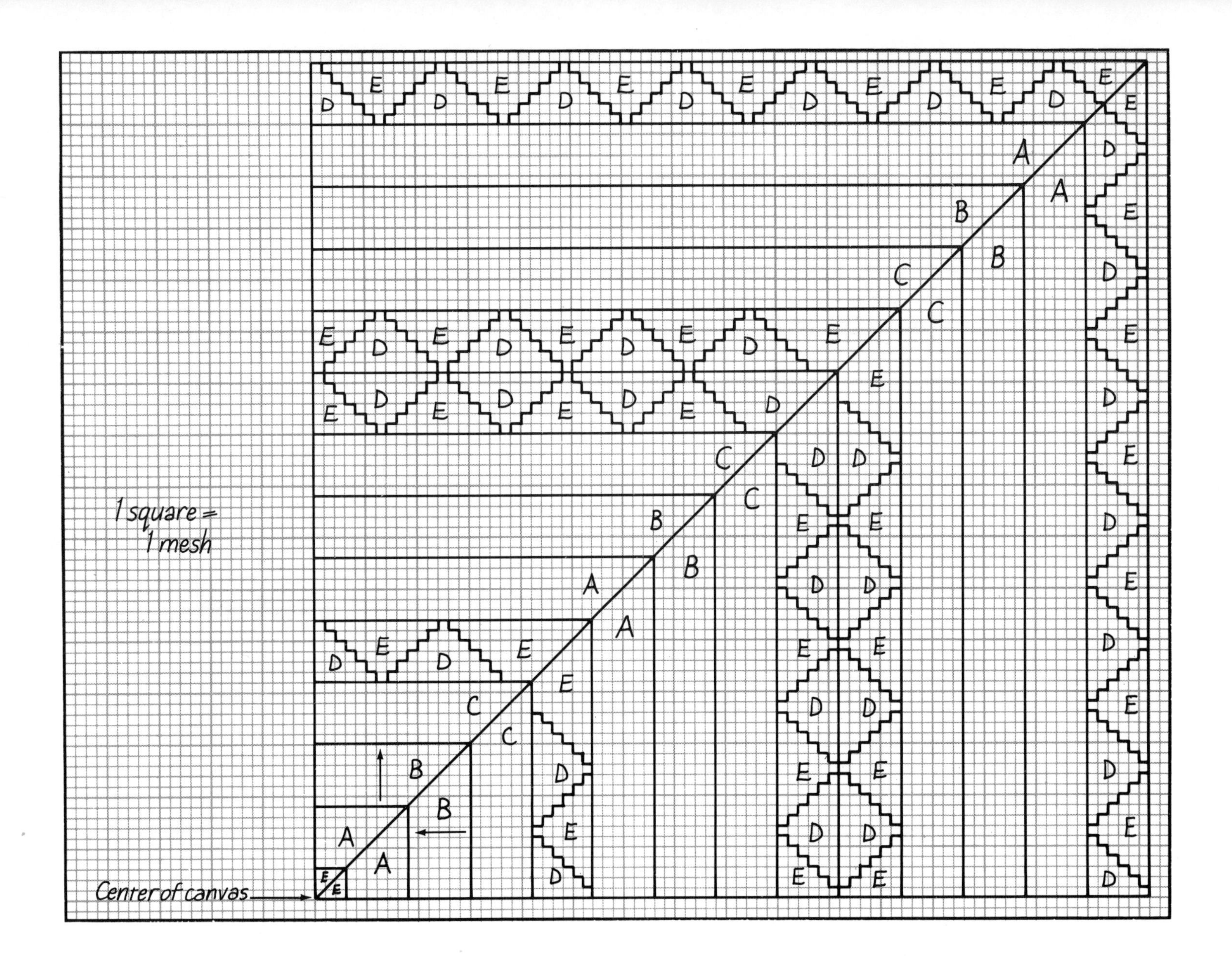
1 square = 1 mesh
Center of canvas

Fig. 11-20 *"Kaleidoscope"*

Fig. 11-19 (Opposite) *Layout for "Snow Crystal." One quarter of four-way symmetrical canvas.*

4. Fig. 11-19 shows one quarter of the design. Starting at the center mesh in each case, work the other three quarters of the design to match. The arrows on the chart show the direction of stitches.

**Kaleidoscope** (Fig. 11-20)

FINISHED SIZE: Approx. 16″ × 16″
YOU NEED: 4-ply worsted-weight wool (approx. 280 yds. in a 4-oz. pull skein).

| | |
|---|---|
| Black (Shade A) | 1 skein or approx. 45 yds. |
| White (Shade B) | 1 skein or approx. 15 yds. |
| Scarlet (Shade C) | 1 skein or approx. 22 yds. |
| Kelly green (Shade D) | 1 skein or approx. 30 yds. |
| Purple (Shade E) | 1 skein or approx. 25 yds. |
| Shocking pink (Shade F) | 1 skein or approx. 18 yds. |
| Tangerine (Shade G) | 1 skein or approx. 26 yds. |
| Bright tangerine (Shade H) | 1 skein or approx. 12 yds. |
| Royal blue (Shade J) | 1 skein or approx. 16 yds. |

A piece of 10-mesh-to-1-inch mono canvas measuring 20″ × 20″
A #18 tapestry needle

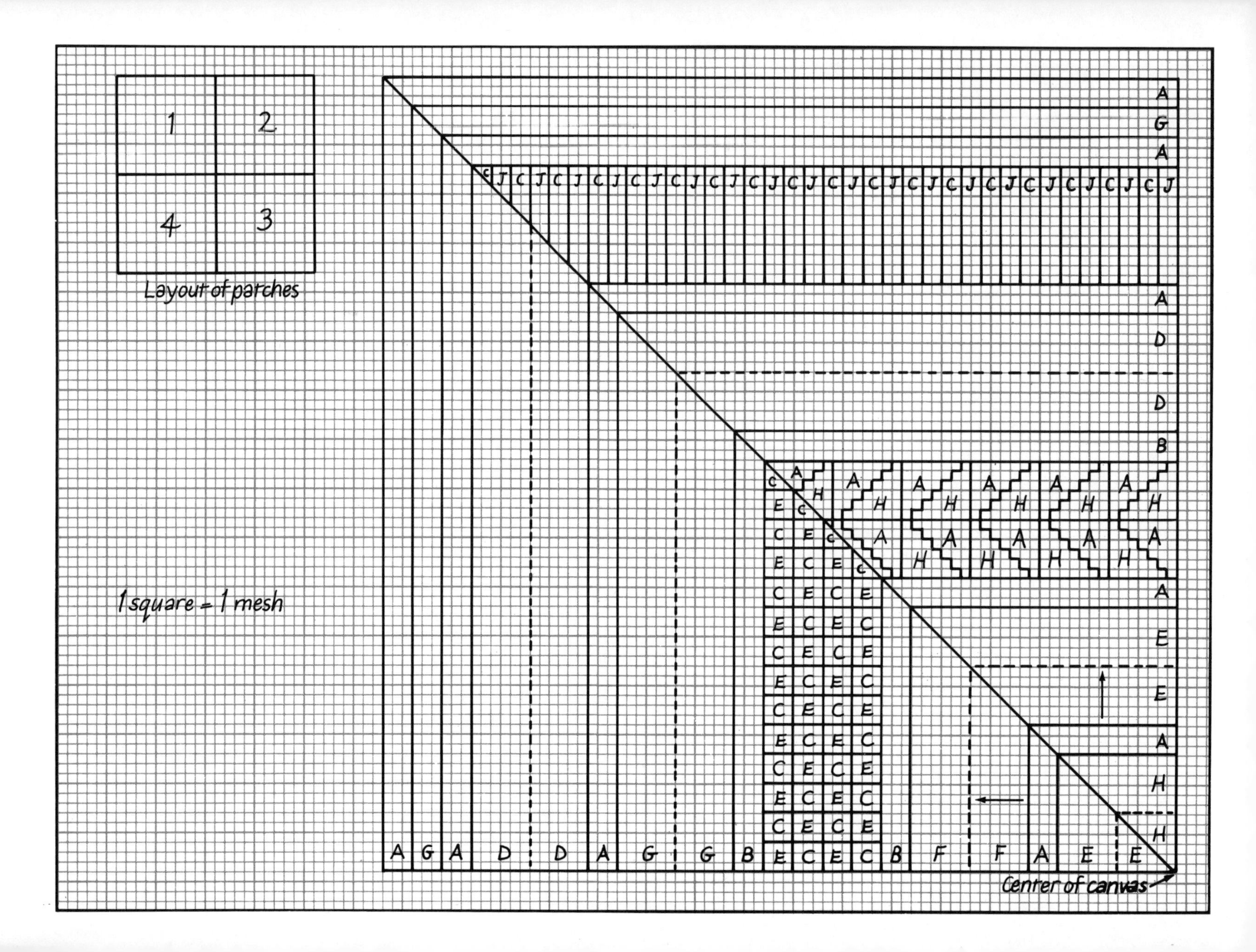

1
2
4
3
Layout of patches
1 square = 1 mesh
Center of canvas

Fig. 11-22
*Patch #2 for "Kaleidoscope"*

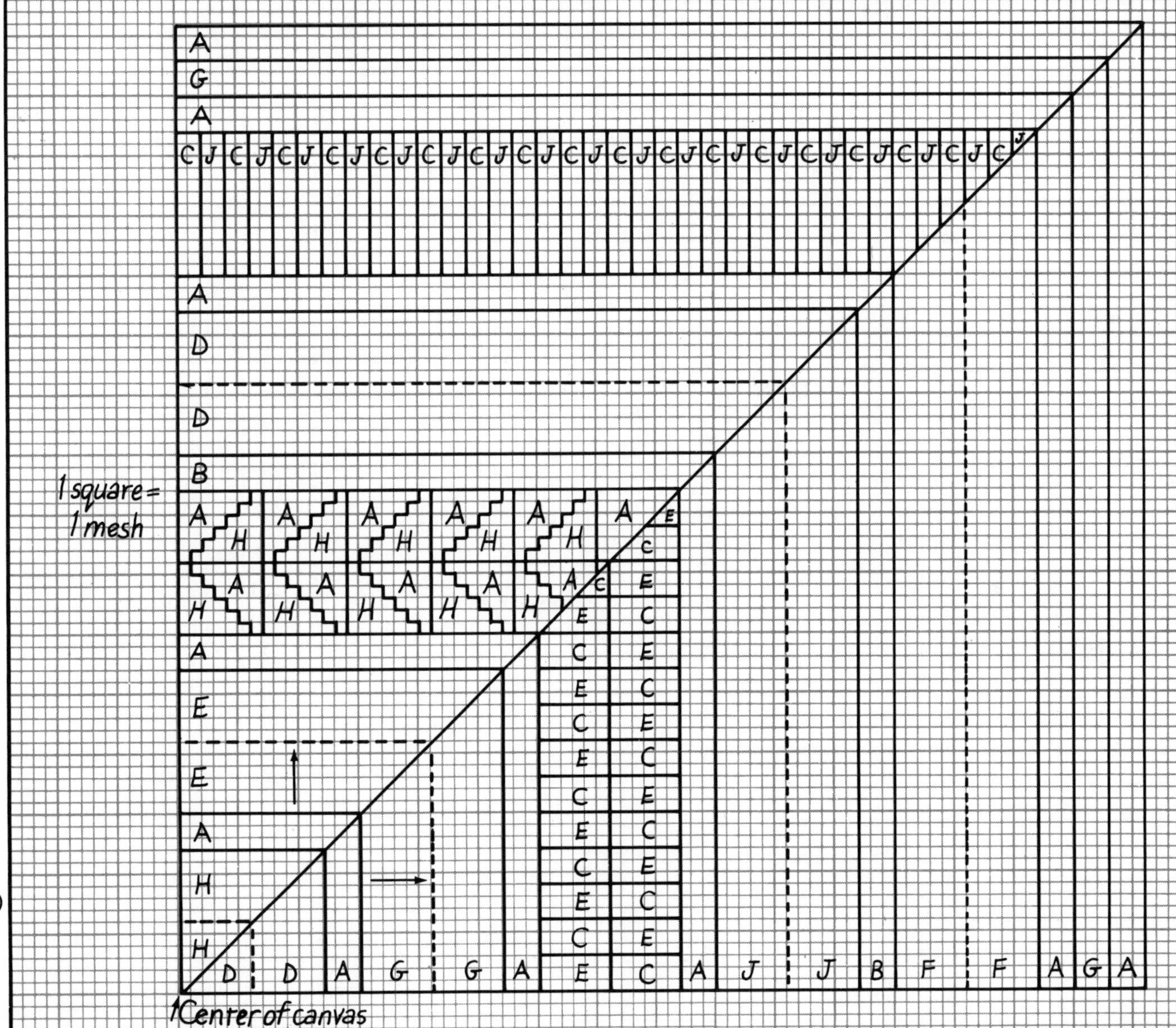


Fig. 11-21 (Opposite)
*"Kaleidoscope" layout and Patch #1*

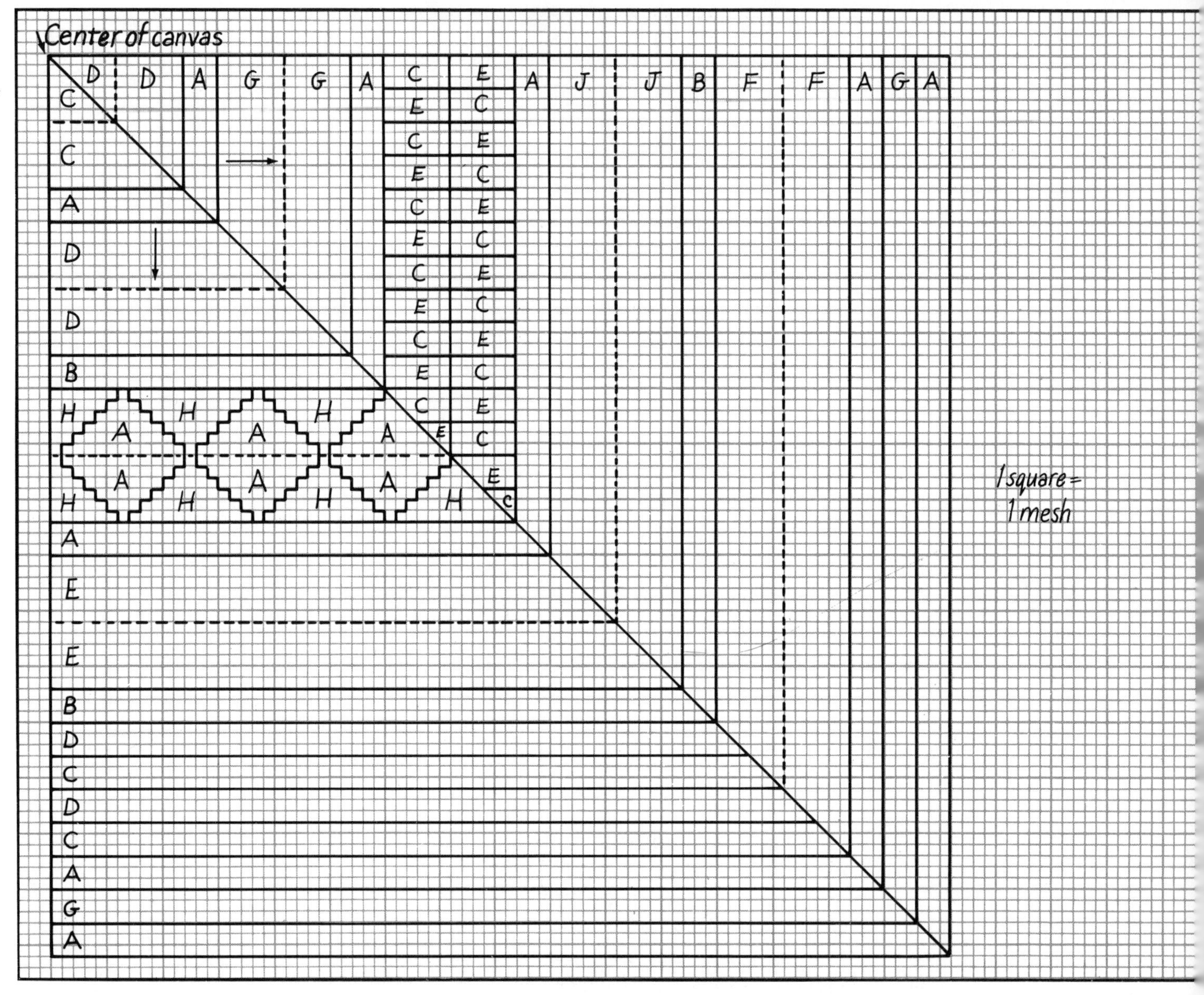


Fig. 11-23
*Patch #3 for "Kaleidoscope"*

Fig. 11-24
*Patch #4 for "Kaleidoscope"*

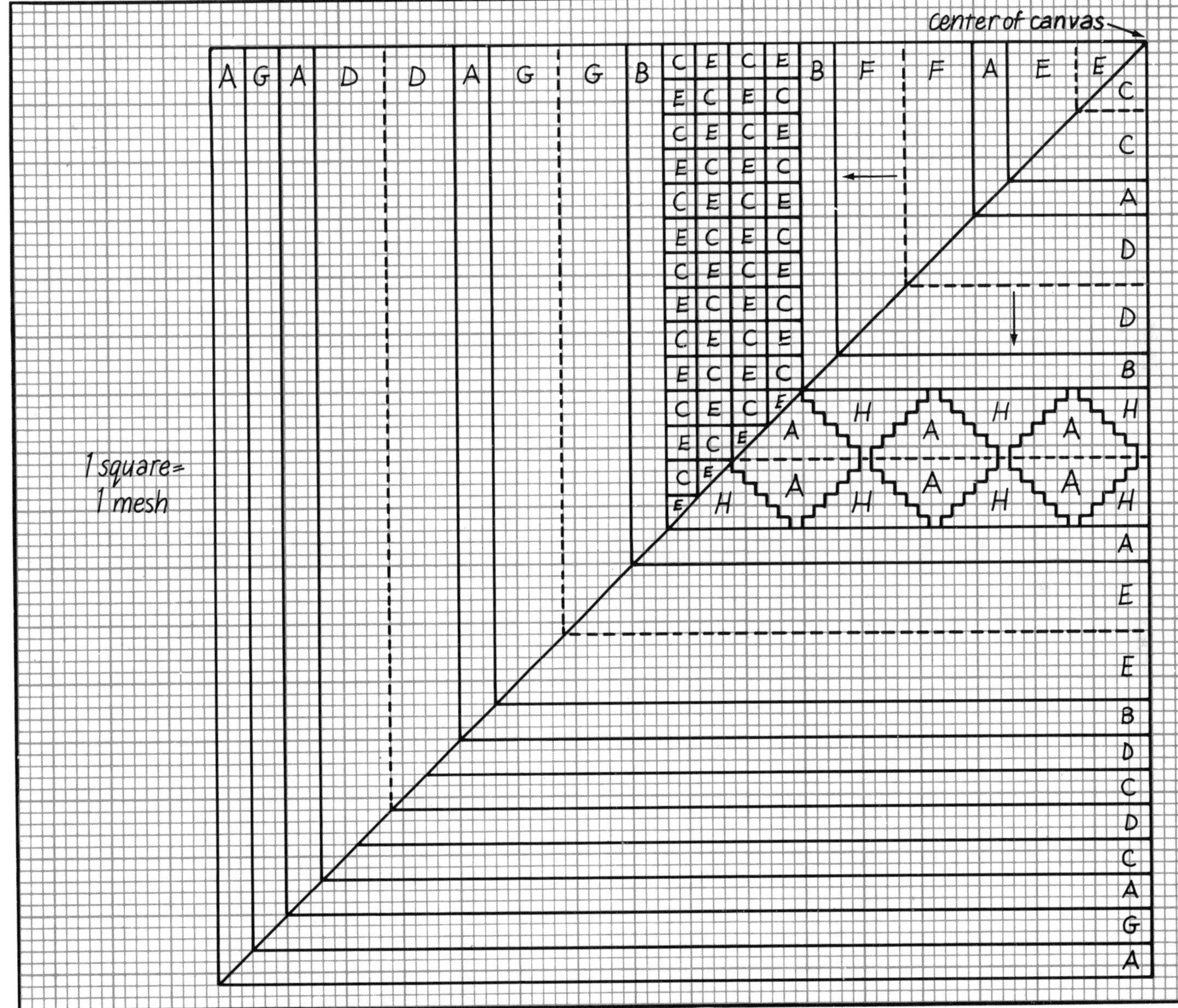

METHOD

1. This design is worked over six or three holes of the canvas, except where shown otherwise on the chart.
2. Mark the center of the canvas, and draw in the diagonal dividing lines as shown in Fig. 9-9.
3. Mark the vertical and horizontal dividing lines from the center out to the edges.
4. This canvas, like "Snow Crystal" (Project V), is worked in four directions, and the reader is referred back to the section in Chapter 10 called "Four-Way Bargello Designs," for helpful information on how to work this kind of project.
5. Following the four-way technique, start at the center of the canvas and make the first quarter of the design as shown in Fig. 11-21. That illustration also includes the layout for the complete design.
6. Now work the other three quarters in numerical sequence, following Figs. 11-22 through 11-24.

## Rugs in Gobelin Stitch

The canvas used for making rugs is not readily available in mono weave. Therefore, for the two rug projects that now follow, I have chosen a 7-mesh-to-1-inch duo canvas. As it is woven double, a smaller border can be left around the work—fraying being less of a problem than with a mono canvas. A border of 1½ inches will be ample.

When doing counted work such as Bargello or Gobelin stitch on a double weave canvas, it is important to count only the large holes, and not the smaller spaces between the double-woven threads. One soon adjusts to this difference. Another problem most of us face when handling a piece of canvas the size of a rug is keeping such a cumbersome bundle under control. The simplest way of dealing with this is to roll up the canvas to the point at which you are working. You can secure the roll in position with safety pins or use one of the more elaborate gadgets created for this purpose, which are available in most needlework departments. Rolling up your work in this manner has the added advantage of helping to prevent the surface from being rubbed up, so that the yarn looks used before the piece is even finished!

**Variations in Blue and Green*** (Fig. 11-25)

FINISHED SIZE: APPROX. 24½" × 35"
YOU NEED: Bulky acrylic (approx. 75 yds. in a 2-oz. pull skein).

| | |
|---|---|
| Heather (Shade A) | 3 skeins or approx. 180 yds. |
| Sky blue (Shade B) | 1 skein or approx. 50 yds. |
| Turquoise (Shade C) | 1 skein or approx. 45 yds. |
| Bright avocado (Shade D) | 1 skein or approx. 60 yds. |
| Light avocado (Shade E) | 1 skein or approx. 48 yds. |
| White (Shade F) | 1 skein or approx. 25 yds. |

A piece of 7-mesh-to-1-inch rug canvas measuring 28" × 38"
A rug needle

METHOD

1. The entire design is worked over seven holes of the canvas.
2. Starting the design in the lower right-hand corner at a point 1½ inches in from the side edge and up from the bottom.
3. Follow Fig. 11-26 for details of working the design.

**Sun Squares** (Fig. 11-27)

FINISHED SIZE: APPROX. 24½" × 36½"
YOU NEED: Bulky acrylic (approx. 75 yds. in a 2-oz. pull skein).

| | |
|---|---|
| Burnt orange (Shade A) | 2 skeins or approx. 90 yds. |
| Orange (Shade B) | 1 skein or approx. 60 yds. |
| Yellow (Shade C) | 1 skein or approx. 70 yds. |
| Dark gold (Shade D) | 1 skein or approx. 55 yds. |

Fig. 11-25 *"Variations in Blue and Green"*

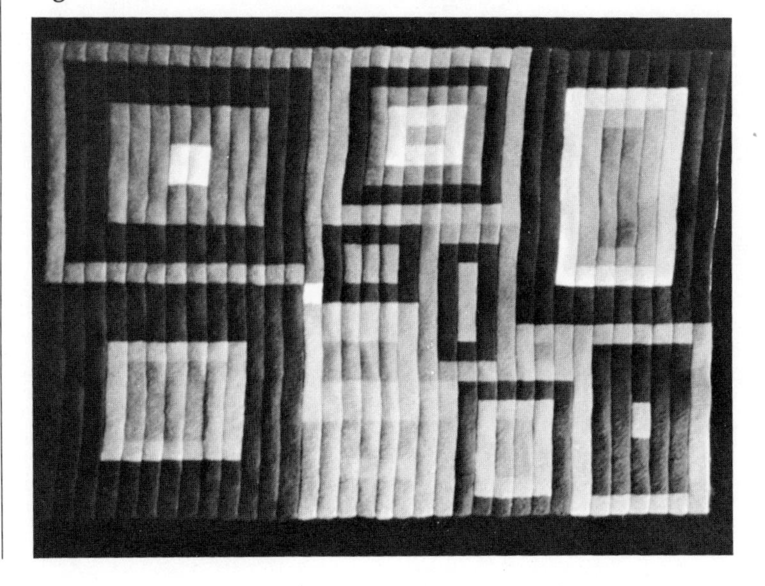

| | |
|---|---|
| Medium gold (Shade E) | 2 skeins or approx. 85 yds. |
| Pale yellow (Shade F) | 2 skeins or approx. 90 yds. |

A piece of 7-mesh-to-1-inch rug canvas measuring 28″ × 40″
A rug needle

METHOD

1. This design is worked over six holes of the canvas, except where otherwise indicated on the charts.
2. Study Fig. 11-28 which shows the complete layout of the design.
3. Start working at a point 1½ inches in from the bottom and side edges at the lower righthand corner.
4. Follow Fig. 11-29 for detailed working of a single square, referring back to Fig. 11-28 for layout and color key.

## Finishing the Rug

When the design is completed, you will need to back the canvas with a good-quality closely woven cotton. A piece of fabric 1 inch larger in width and length than the finished area of the design itself is required. This will give you a ½-inch seam allowance all around.

Begin by turning the raw edges of the canvas to the wrong side, folding neatly along the line of the last row of stitches. Miter each corner as you work around the rug. With strong thread, stitch down the turned-in edge of canvas. Place the backing fabric flat on the wrong side of the canvas, with the right side of the fabric facing up. Turn under the ½-inch seam allowance all around. Sew the backing to the canvas, making sure that your stitches do not show on the right side.

If you want to hang your rug on the wall, simply add a row of loops at the top and bottom of the backing fabric. Insert rods into these loops to keep the canvas in shape while hanging. The rod at the bottom of the work should be heavy enough to pull the canvas taut when it is hanging to avoid the unattractive curling and bulging.

Fig. 11-26 (Opposite)
*Layout for "Variations in Blue and Green"*

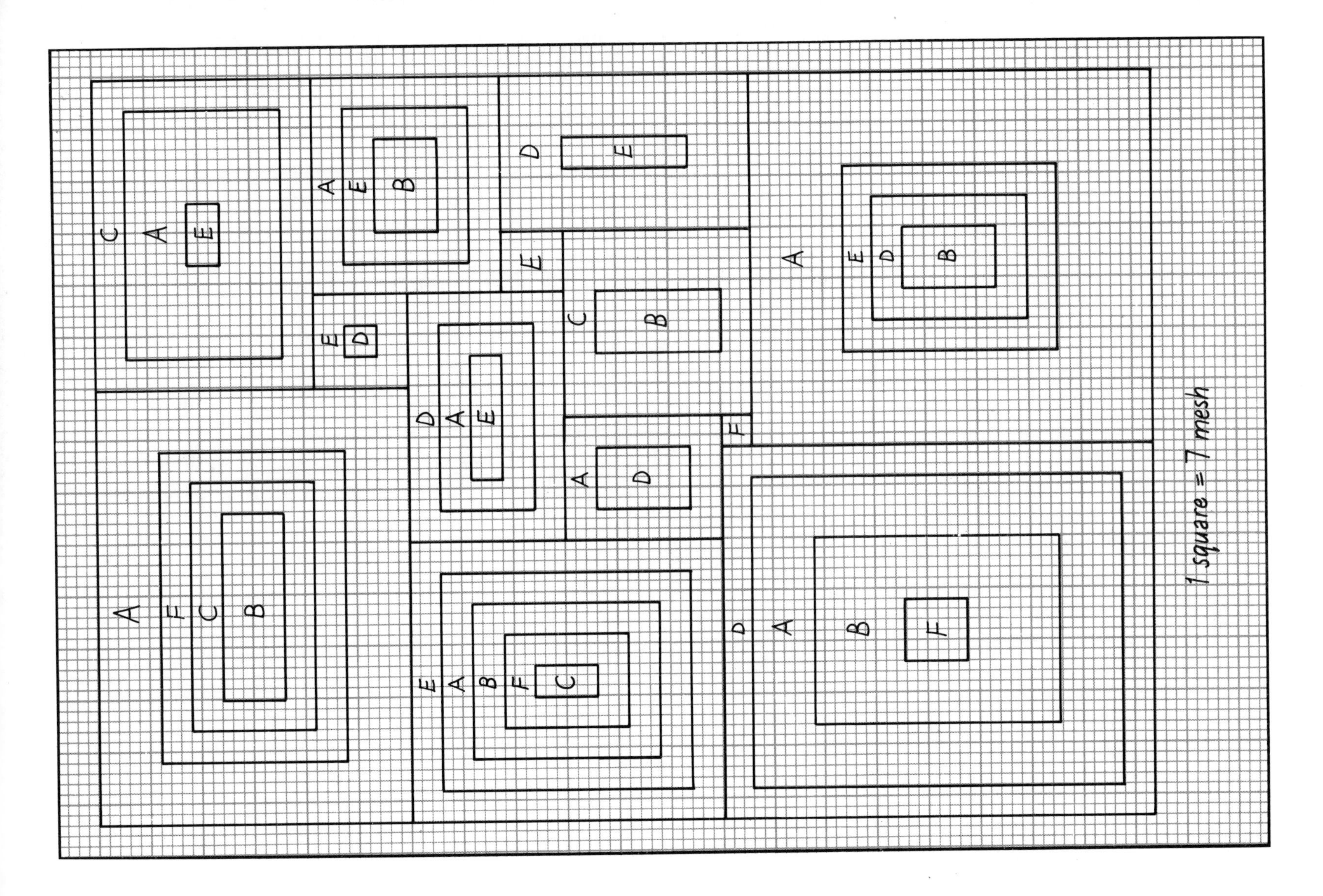
1 square = 7 mesh

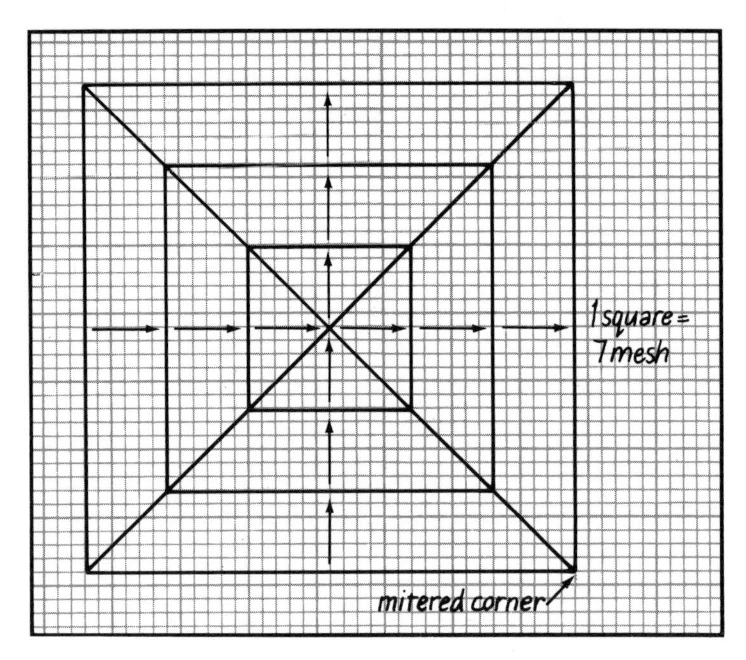


Fig. 11-27 *Detail of one square for "Sun Squares"*

Fig. 11-28 *"Sun Squares"*

Fig. 11-29 (Opposite) *Layout for "Sun Squares"*

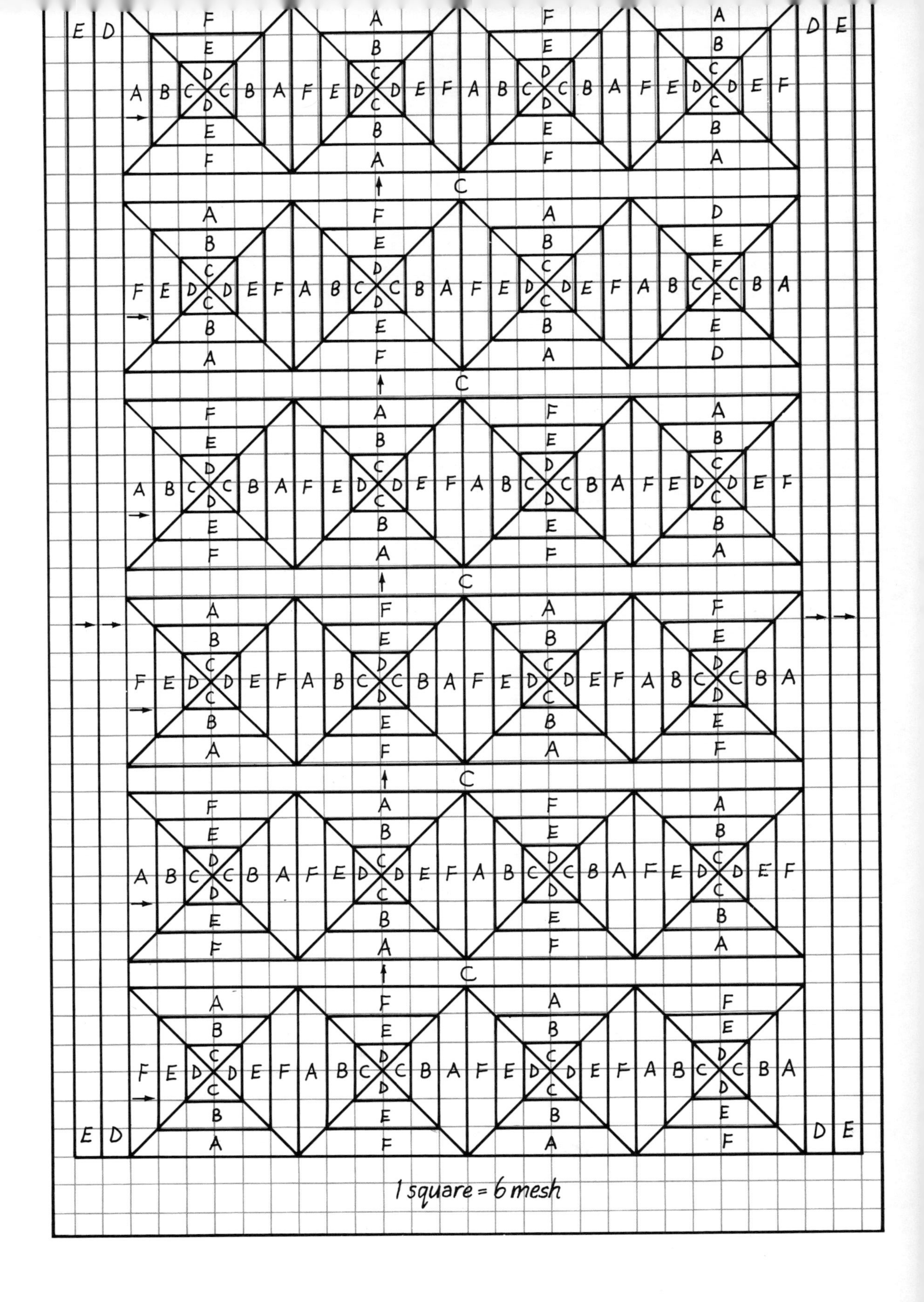
1 square = 6 mesh

ABOUT THE AUTHOR

**Pauline Chatterton** is the author of *Crochet: Fashions and Furnishings* (1973), *The Art of Crochet* (1973), and a forthcoming book on Scandinavian knitting designs. A British citizen, she holds an M.A. in Literature and Psychology from the University of Sussex, and makes her home in Brighton, England.